Bear Attacks II
Myth & Reality

by

JAMES GARY SHELTON

Canadian Cataloguing in Publication Data

Shelton, James Gary, 1943-
  Bear Attacks II

ISBN 0-9698099-2-1
  1. Bear Attacks. I. Title.
QL737.C27S547 2001 599.78 C00-911337-1

Previous books by the Author:
Bear Encounter Survival Guide (1994)
Bear Attacks - The Deadly Truth (1998)

Pallister Publishing
Publisher contact: Julie Scheven
Horizon Productions, Box 355
Hagensborg, B.C. Canada V0T 1H0
Tel/Fax: 250-982-2936

Canadian Distributor: Sandhill Book Marketing Ltd.
#99 - Ellis St., Kelowna, B.C. Canada V1Y 1Z4
Tel: 250-763-1406 Fax: 250-763-4051

U.S. Distributor: Partners Publishers Group, Inc.
2325 Jarco Dr., Holt, Michigan USA 48842
Tel: 800-336-3137 Fax: 517-694-0617

First Printing: May 2001

Printed and bound in Canada

Acknowledgements

I would like to thank Julie Scheven, Angela Hall, Tracey Gillespie, John Thomas, Carolyn Foltz, and George & Cynthia Williams for once again assaulting one of my manuscripts with great vigor. Without their significant contributions, my books wouldn't have had the success they've had. Also, thanks to Dave Flegel for his editing suggestions regarding scientific material. In addition, thanks to Neil and Mary Ehrlich for reviewing the logical consistency of *Bear Biology as a Science* in the *Appendix*.

Front cover: This male grizzly was photographed at the bear viewing area of Fish Creek just north of Hyder, Alaska, by professional photographer Keith Douglas of Smithers, B.C.

Each year, nearly 40,000 people flock to the Hyder area to view bears. On July 15, 2000, a 41-year-old man from Ketchikan, Alaska, was killed and partially eaten by a 400-pound sub-adult male brown bear (grizzly) at Camp Run-A-Muck near the bear viewing area. Evidence at the scene indicated that the victim had probably been sleeping on the ground.

Back cover: Looking west at Mount Nusatsum from upper Bella Coola Valley. The author's home sits at the foot of this mountain.

Spelling

In my first book I used the combination of American and Canadian spelling that I had become accustomed to. In my second book, I used the British Collins Dictionary for my spelling reference. In this book, I made it easy on myself by using the QuarkXPress spell check. At least I'll have the consistency of each of my books using a different spelling standard. Note: Some italicized reports maintain their original spelling.

For the purpose of approximate distances referred to in stories, meters and yards are interchangeable. Many Canadians use both terms, and you'll also notice that Canadians use two different spellings for meters—metres, also, kilometers—kilometres.

This book is dedicated to my mom and dad, Grace and Bud, and to my brother and sisters, Bob, Geraldine, Phyllis, Carolyn, and Cynthia

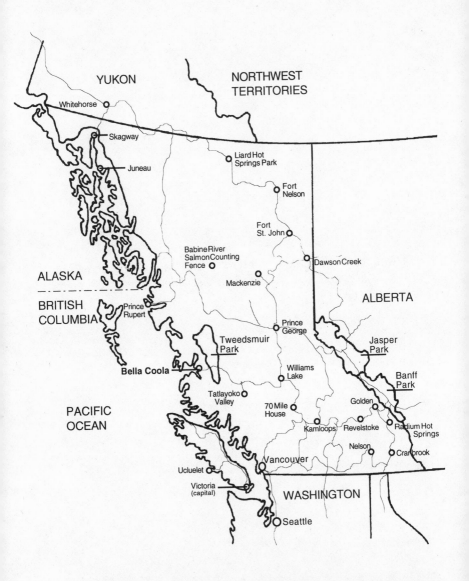

For those unfamiliar with Canadian geography, British Columbia (B.C.) is Canada's western-most province that abuts the Pacific Ocean. B.C. borders Washington, Idaho, and part of Montana to its south, Alaska to the northwest, the Yukon Territory due north, the Northwest Territories to the northeast, and Alberta directly east. Running parallel with the upper half of B.C.'s northwest coast is the Alaskan Panhandle.

Preface

T. J. could hear someone bellowing in pain, "Help me! Help! I'm being mauled by a bear!" He'd never heard any sound quite like the agonized cries he was listening to—then realized, 'That's me'.

He was shaken violently and flipped over as the pack was ripped upwards from his body. Horrible pain set in as the sow bit into his side. After several more painful bites, T. J. was flung downhill and landed with his back arched over a fallen tree. His head was hanging low, facing the bear. Through a red blur, he saw her bloodsoaked muzzle approaching and desperately placed his right hand against her throat—she stopped. He thought he heard other animals nearby, perhaps the cubs bawling, then suddenly the sow turned and ran off. It was finally over.

(For about 45 brutal seconds the sow had her way with T. J. A section of the skull above his right eye was broken loose, and most of the facial bones were crushed. He had deep lacerations across his forehead, the top of his head, and on the side of his torso. The top of his right hipbone had been broken off. Still, he was fortunate because during the biting process the sow had not pulled back; most of the tissue was still there, much of it hanging loose, but connected.)

———————

The Babine River salmon counting fence and compound was originally constructed in 1946 and was slowly expanded during its 54-year history. There have been few problems with grizzly bears at the location until recently. Last year there were many dangerous incidents that caused management personnel at the fence to question how they're going to maintain safety for their employees. The decision to build an electric fence around the compound and to install gun cabinets on the counting fence were excellent choices for dealing with safety issues.

We must ask ourselves: Why were there so few problems in the past? Why are there now serious problems? What's changed?

It is critical that Department of Fisheries and Oceans senior management understand we're entering into a new era in the way grizzly bears react to people. For a very long time we had levels of mortality and types of mortality on grizzly bears that suppressed their numbers and made them fearful of humans. During the last 15 years, that influence has been reduced to the point that most bear populations are increasing and many grizzlies no longer fear people. They are reasserting their position as a dominant species.

Craig screamed, "Bear," as he fumbled for the pepper spray. Grant yelled, "What?" This caused the animal to stop in its tracks 20 feet from Craig, as it now became aware of Grant, and turned its stare towards him. The bear was brown on the sides and looked shaggy. Its ears were up, but there were no aggressive signals—it had approached silently except for the noise of its feet hitting the ground.

Craig had the spray in his hand as Grant moved up beside him with the shotgun ready for action. The bear was just standing there, staring intently at the two men. Craig yelled, "Fire a warning shot." A split second later the slug whizzed a foot over the bear's head. The bear didn't flinch or react in any way. About 30 seconds later, it turned away and started circling downhill, out of sight.

The foregoing is a preview of what's to come. Good writing must be interesting as well as entertaining, and, equally important, it should be educational. Before we explore bear attack accounts and myths about bears, I ask the reader to carefully study the first part of this book. If you do, I believe you'll be rewarded with a clearer understanding of what follows.

Terms of reference

The following terms are extremely important for clarifying the broad range of information and issues I deal with in this book. The first objective of my writings is to educate people about bear attacks and how to survive them; the second objective is to explore the philosophical influences shaping our cultural belief system to determine whether those influences are creating biases, misconceptions, or myths regarding human/bear conflict and environmental issues.

There is significant confusion at this time as to exactly what conservationism is. Can the large number of nature enthusiasts and environmental groups with strikingly different and often opposing viewpoints all be placed under the banner of conservationism? No, they can't, because the various doctrines are so different in their purpose they require separate classifications to identify them. In general, there are two distinct groups: conservationists and preservationists.

Is it necessary to understand exactly what 'political correctness' is in order to make sense of present bear management policies? Yes, absolutely.

Based on the following definitions, I am a conservationist.

CONSERVATION theory began in the early 1900s and is based on the concepts that humankind is part of nature; that far more plants and animals are reproduced each year than can survive; that these excess plants and animals are natural resources to be harvested; but that mankind must be a steward that does everything possible and economically feasible to reduce human impact on nature.

ENVIRONMENTAL ideology synthesized between the mid '60s and early '80s and is based on a different doctrine: Modern industrial mankind is no longer part of nature; humans do not have the right to exploit or manipulate wild plants and animals for their excess material benefit; mankind must significantly reduce its exploitation of nature at every level.

PRESERVATIONISM took root in about 1985 by combining the two powerful philosophies of environmentalism and socialism with a new (neo) interpretation. 'Neo-environmentalism': Over millions of years, natural selection created individual plant and animal species that are adapted to particular niches resulting in a balanced, organized nature with a delicate, interconnected web of life. Modern humans are a threat to this natural order and must be restricted from using large areas of the world's surface. 'Neo-socialism':

Materialistic capitalism that developed during the last 10,000 years with agricultural expansion and is not part of the natural order. Governments must reduce and limit the free-enterprise system to a level that denies excess materialism to members of a society.

NEO-PANTHEISM is the new spiritual basis for the preservationist viewpoint that has significantly influenced our culture during the last 15 years. This belief system endows nature with balance, purpose, and justice, and identifies mankind as the spoiler of this natural order.

Most members of the more powerful environmental groups and some wildlife biologists appear to have embraced this new type of pantheism as a baseline for analyzing man's role in nature, and for determining how best to protect wild animals and the environment. This new spiritualism has not only influenced our cultural beliefs about nature but has also influenced many branches of science.

POSTMODERNISM is the 'cultural/political paradigm' that originated in the late 1940s as an antithesis to the Modernist period defined as the 'capitalist industrial age' (1900 to 1945). This new cultural movement took a significant departure from the previous views regarding technological science, materialism, and societal values. It began in the fields of art and architecture then slowly gained momentum as anthropology and the other social sciences embraced this new world view.

In more recent times, some of our best scientist/philosophers, such as Edward O. Wilson (*Consilience,* 1998), have rightfully broadened the definition to include some of the ideologies resulting from the 1960s counterculture revolution such as: social anthropology, socialist science, eco-feminism, multiculturalism, Afrocentrism, neo-Marxism, deep ecology, and a host of similar sub-philosophies. The newest sub-philosophy of postmodernism, preservationism, and its spiritual element neo-pantheism, are clearly associated with this cultural/political paradigm. The sciences of archeology, ecology, and wildlife biology are presently being altered by postmodernism, and may not survive long in their present forms.

POLITICAL CORRECTNESS is the expression of viewpoints pertaining to the propositions, hypotheses, and theories of sub-philosophies within the 'Postmodernist cultural/political paradigm'. For example: The following statement, "Native Americans lived as 'one with nature' and existed in harmony with grizzly bears," is politically correct because it's based on the postmodern hypothesis that Natives lived in harmony with nature. The contradictory statement, "Native Americans lived in significant conflict with grizzly bears and used snares and deadfalls to reduce grizzly populations," is politically incorrect because it's at odds with the above-stated hypothesis.

Politically correct propositions, hypotheses, and theories are elevated to 'politically correct truths' when repeatedly stated in various media over a long period of time without significant rebuttal. For example: If a computer simulation model designed to examine the correlation between land alteration and species extinction generates the conclusion that 2700 species are presently suffering extinction annually, and that statement is presented multiple times over television, in publications, and on the Internet, and no evidence is forthcoming to repudiate it, the hypothesis becomes a 'postmodern politically correct truth'.

HIGHER TRUTHS are the spiritual back-up position for postmodernists when politically correct concepts are challenged by contradictory facts or scientific evidence. For example: In 1996 when journalist John Goddard accused well-known Canadian writer, Farley Mowat, of significantly altering the facts in his books, *People of the Deer*, *Never Cry Wolf*, and *The Desperate People*, in order to push certain causes, Mowat responded with, "I never let the facts get in the way of the truth!"

Contents

1 Introduction...1

Section One: Prologue

2 The Natural History of Grizzly Bears...............................7
3 Bear Aggressive Behavior...19

Section Two: Bear Attacks

4 Predatory Encounters and Attacks.............................21
5 Carcass Defense...43
6 A Warning to Hunters..55
7 Spray Defense..75
8 Playing Dead..97
9 Dogs and Bears...113
10 Bear Attack Trauma...145
11 Defense Strategies..167

Section Three: Myth and Reality

12 Babine River Salmon Counting Fence.......................181
13 Bear Habitat Requirements......................................203
14 Bear Populations...213

Section Four: Epilogue

15 Cougar Attacks..223
16 Defending Reality...241
17 Conclusion..253

Appendix

Bear Biology as a Science..257
Postmodernism..268

I

INTRODUCTION

Between 1965 and 1985, I explored vast areas of untouched landscapes in British Columbia while hunting bears and other wildlife, while on backpacking trips, and while fishing many different river systems. From 1986 to 1989, I operated a guide outfitting business in Central Eastern B.C. During those 24 years, I had the great pleasure of learning about nature firsthand and to an extensive degree. But my education wasn't that of a passive observer; I was an active participant in the natural world with its many dangers—without the backup systems of our modern protective society. Most of my excursions started with a floatplane ride into a remote, rugged area. On many occasions, if I or one of my partners had slipped off a ledge while pursuing goats, or been swept away while crossing a river, or been injured by a bear, there wouldn't have been a rescue squad coming to save us.

During those years, I was able to discover both the beauty and brutality of what goes on in wilderness settings. And, eventually, I came to realize there is a vast amount of misinformation and mythology existing in our present cultural belief system regarding nature. I also became concerned about how bears and other wild species were being managed.

In the 1970s, I worked on bear conservation projects through the Bella Coola Rod and Gun Club and, in the 1980s, I became chairman of the Central Coast Grizzly Management Committee. This committee was co-chaired by Wildlife Branch Regional Biologist Darryl Hebert, and had members from all government ministries and other groups who were interested in grizzly bear management.

At that time, bears were not adequately protected, so we devised regulation changes and policies for reducing grizzly hunting kills and

The two pictures at the beginning are of the author in northern B.C.; above, at his cabin in the Coast Range Mountains; on the next page, snowshoeing into a moose wintering area east of Bella Coola.

problem bear kills, and initiated the protection of critical bear habitat. By 1985, a new concept about managing bears was put into place throughout B.C. This was due to the efforts of the Wildlife Branch, the BC Wildlife Federation, the BC Guide Outfitters Association, and many groups like the one I was involved in.

By the late 1980s, I'd had over 100 close-range encounters with grizzlies and black bears, had spent hundreds of hours observing both species, and had done extensive research into bear biology, evolution, and behavioral genetics. Many people in B.C. were becoming aware of my knowledge about bears and my abilities with firearms for defense against dangerous animals. As a result, I began receiving many requests for information regarding safety in bear country.

In 1989, the Mid Coast District Office of the Ministry of Forests asked me to develop a bear safety training program for their personnel that included bear behavior, bear avoidance, and firearms defense against bears. My course was immediately successful, and

I was soon providing training for other ministries as well. The next year, I was asked to create a similar course for people who don't carry firearms. After conducting research on available bear safety information, predatory black bear behavior, and pepper spray use against bears, I developed my avoidance/deterrence course.

I also spent two years as a member of the Central Coast Environment group. We were concerned about the rate of timber harvest and the need for better wildlife conservation. This activity led to the six years I devoted to the Bella Coola Local Resource Use Plan (LRUP) process. My main contributions were towards a wildlife conservation plan and the development of a declining rate of timber harvest in the LRUP area.

By the early '90s, my Bear Encounter Survival Training and Consulting business was flourishing and has now grown to an enterprise that takes up most of my time. During the last 12 years, my training program has not only given me significant research opportunity but has also provided continuous feedback from field personnel as to what strategies work well for bear avoidance and bear encounter survival.

In 1994, after my original research into bear behavior and bear attacks, I published my first book, *Bear Encounter Survival Guide*. That book, which is based on my training material, quickly became a safety manual for many government ministries and agencies in B.C. and Alaska.

It took two-and-a-half years of additional research and writing to complete my second book, *Bear Attacks - The Deadly Truth*, published in 1998. That book was intended to educate people about the danger of increasing bear populations and as a wake-up call for people exposed to bears by revealing the brutality of bear attacks.

It was great to see my second book on the British Columbia top ten bestsellers list for almost a year and also to see it sell so well throughout Canada and the U.S. It was also great to receive positive feedback from many biologists who accept and use my material. These researchers have acknowledged that my background and research methods are sound for probing the intricacies of human/bear interactions. They also understand that someone outside the biological community, without a career at stake, can successfully challenge government bear management policies that are lacking common sense.

It's difficult for a book to do well when it bucks the trend of prevailing views on a given subject. But I've suspected for a long time now that the general public is ready for a more realistic view regarding bears and nature.

This third book has an important purpose behind its inception in

addition to providing information about bear attacks and environmental issues. For many years I've tried to make sense of the continuous assaults taking place against the values that are important to
me—especially the governmental policies that seriously damage the
rural lifestyle. After 40 years of observing our society in general, and
after studying hundreds of books on subjects ranging from philosophy to economics, I've finally come to understand the underlying hidden forces altering our culture. That information is spread throughout this book, but is primarily presented in the *Appendix.*

Book Purpose and Organization

Section One has two chapters that are based on my most recent
research regarding the natural history of grizzly bears and bear
aggressive behavior. *The Natural History Of Grizzly Bears* documents how grizzlies came to this continent and provides information
about the past distribution of this species. Also, I carefully examine
the role grizzly bears play in ecosystem functioning and debunk the
claims made by many groups and individuals regarding that issue.
The *Bear Aggressive Behavior* chapter has new information that
improves my previous definitions as to why bears attack people.

Section Two contains numerous bear attack accounts that are categorized into chapters dealing with specific types of bear aggression. Each of these chapters has concluding statements that identify and explain the different aspects of the aggressive behaviors
involved and other factors influencing the outcome of bear attack
events. The *Dogs and Bears* chapter is a lengthy and badly-needed
piece of information about whether dogs should be used for defense
against bears. The *Defense Strategies* chapter is included at the
end. This second section is intended to broaden the bear attack
information in my previous works and to provide new insights regarding underlying causes for attacks.

Section Three provides chapters regarding the sub-title of this
book, *Myth & Reality.* In my previous two books, I had chapters
dealing with *Bear Management, Conservationism versus
Preservationism, Statistical Fallacies, Dangerous Beliefs,* and sub-
topics in other chapters that were all designed to shed light on how
and why certain political agendas are causing an increase in
human/bear conflict.
In the *Babine River Salmon Counting Fence* chapter I explore a
series of myths about bears and human/bear relationships that are
making it difficult to reduce human/bear conflict.

As the myths of preservationism continue to increase, there is a corresponding increase in the need for reality by those who actually have to deal with nature on a one-to-one basis.

The other two chapters in this section are intended to provide realistic information regarding bear habitat requirements and bear population status.

Hopefully, Section Three will help create a better understanding of the many bear issues that presently confront us.

Section Four has the *Cougar Attacks* chapter, the *Defending Reality* chapter, and the *Conclusion*.

Cougar attacks are increasing and are more difficult to survive than most bear attacks. I was fortunate to be able to document a cougar attack on a friend that demonstrates the amazing life and death struggle that takes place in this type of event. If you want to survive a cougar attack, you better have a powerful defense system.

The *Defending Reality* chapter demonstrates the activities I engage in while trying to provide realistic information to people regarding a wide range of nature issues.

I have used the *Conclusion* to state a credo regarding my approach to nature.

The *Appendix* deals with two subjects: science and postmodernism. I use the final part of this book to place the bear and nature issues I've written about into the broadest context possible.

Throughout this book I present many examples of biases, misinformation, and myths. But what about my biases? All people have biases relevant to the values taught them in their youth—values compounded by the lessons of life and the knowledge gained through the special interests they have pursued.

The primary task of one of my editors is to identify my biases and then make suggestions on how to either eliminate them or make them obvious. The standard I attempt to obtain is this:

1. While providing explanatory information, underlying hidden biases must not exist.

2. When expressing my viewpoint, the reader must be able to clearly recognize my biases.

Section One: Prologue

2

THE NATURAL HISTORY
OF GRIZZLY BEARS

North Americans have been fascinated by grizzly bears for centuries. The Spaniards had been interacting with the great bear of California for more than three decades before Meriwether Lewis and William Clark made their epic Journey of the Corps of Discovery between 1804 and 1806. Accounts of grizzlies and other animals were reported by the two explorers upon their return, and were published by many newspapers and journals. People within the newly formed United States, all the way from New Orleans to Philadelphia, were keenly interested in the stories about the western wilderness and its inhabitants.

However, before the European fascination for this animal began, Native Americans had lived with the grizzly for thousands of years. But the Native American relationship with grizzlies wasn't quite what's commonly believed.

The first European to see a grizzly bear was probably Spanish missionary Claude Jean Allouez. While traveling by ship along the northwest coast in 1666, he wrote about an indian tribe "who eat human beings, and live on raw fish; but these people, in turn, are eaten by bears of frightful size, all red, and with prodigiously long claws."

There are many accounts like that one, as you will read later, but that portrayal of grizzly bears doesn't seem to fit with the image we see on TV nature programs. How could those beautiful bears filmed at McNeil River Falls, Alaska, standing side by side, feeding on salmon, and ignoring the photographers on the hill above, possibly be dangerous to people? Well, if you were a Native American living in that area 4,000 years ago, with only stone tools in hand, and you badly needed those salmon to survive, you would've found out quickly and brutally about the danger of grizzly bears.

There are three main aspects to our continuing interest in this species: Firstly, grizzlies have always embodied the dangerous part of nature that mankind has little control over; secondly, and more recently, grizzlies have come to represent those areas of the continent where mankind's intrusion is minimal; and finally, there has been growing concern during the last 20 years regarding the decline in grizzly bear numbers.

One of the primary reasons I moved to the Bella Coola Valley on the remote Central Coast of British Columbia was because grizzlies and wolves still exist here. As a young man, I was determined to spend the duration of my life in a place where I could explore nature in an undisturbed form. I have accomplished that goal, and I sincerely hope that future residents of this area will also be enjoying that privilege a hundred years from now. Those who criticize my writings often claim that I am against bears and want to eliminate them. They are wrong. I have been involved in bear conservation for many years, but I now believe we are over-protecting bears to the detriment of people and our economy. We need to go back to the bear management policies that existed in the late 1980s before all the foolishness began.

This chapter is intended to provide an understanding of the natural history of grizzly bears in North America and also to examine the many claims presently being made by certain biologists and bear preservationist groups regarding the supposed decline of this species.

GRIZZLY BEAR PREHISTORY

Grizzly bears originated in Europe, not North America. The migration of grizzlies onto this continent is recent and complex. Grizzlies first migrated across the land bridge into Alaska at the beginning of the last ice-age, between 75,000 and 100,000 years ago, then south into British Columbia and the rest of North America between 10,000 and 12,000 years ago at the end of the ice-age.

On the next page are two maps that show the historic range of grizzlies when Europeans arrived, versus their present range. You can see that this species has lost about half of its original distribution.

Grizzly bear distribution at time of European arrival. Circa 1800.

Grizzly bear distribution at present time. Circa 2001.

Most people believe that the historic range of grizzly bears, based on where they existed when Europeans arrived, indicates a complete history regarding the North American distribution of this species. It doesn't, and it's time for the general public to have a more complete picture of the natural history of grizzlies on this continent.

During the last ice-age, Canada and most of Europe were covered by ice, but Eastern Siberia and much of Alaska were ice-free and connected by a land bridge. This prehistoric isolated area is known as Beringia, and, for 75,000 years, it had a complement of animal species of both European and North American origin. These animals were first cut off from their own species on each continent by the advancing ice sheets, then mixed together as ocean levels dropped and the land bridge formed.

Then, as the continental ice sheets melted, between 10,000 and 13,000 years ago, and the land bridge was cut off by rising seas, Siberian Beringian species mixed with European animals, and Alaskan Beringian species mixed with North American animals.

When grizzlies first entered Western Canada, they were not greeted by the beautiful forests we now have, but rather by an eerie, devastated landscape of glacial till and moraines where no life had existed for at least 75,000 years. There were no salmon in the rivers and there wouldn't be for thousands of years yet to come.

Based on lake bottom sediment fossil pollen studies, it took lodgepole pine 12,000 years to migrate the 2,200 kilometers from Washington State into the Yukon at a rate of slightly less that 200 meters per year. It took over 4,000 years for timber stands to migrate from Washington State to Central B.C., then several thousand more years to cover the province. Western Red Cedar didn't return to the Central Coast of B.C. during its northerly migration until about 4,500 years ago. The so-called 'Ancient Great Bear Rain Forest' of the Central Coast, in its present species mix and form, has existed for only about 3,000 years.

Let's now take a look at maps showing the history of recent glaciation (*After The Ice Age*, E.C. Pielou, 1991) and the distribution of grizzly bears (*Grizzly Bear Compendium*, The Interagency Grizzly Bear Committee, 1987).

Ice sheets 18,000 years ago.

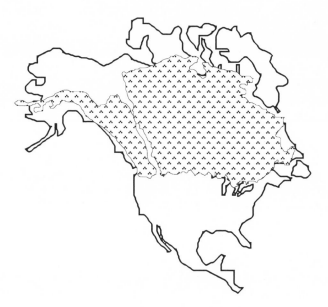

Ice sheets 13,000 years ago.

Ice sheets 10,000 years ago.

You can see by the maps that between 13,000 and 18,000 years ago, there was little change in the ice sheets. But, between 10,000 and 13,000 years ago, the ice sheets rapidly melted. This is when the mixing of Beringian and North American species took place, and is the same time interval of the extinction event that eliminated 57 of 79 large mammal species from North America (P.S. Martin, 1984)— such as the large-horned bison, ground sloth, American short-faced bear, woolly mammoth, camel, American mastodon, and saber-toothed cat, to name a few.

Let's now take a look at grizzly bear range distribution since the end of the last ice-age, based on grizzly fossil evidence found throughout North America.

When you look at the map showing grizzly bear range 7,000 to 10,000 years ago (p. 13), you might be surprised to discover that grizzlies originally ranged over most of North America, with the exception of the eastern seaboard. The second map, showing grizzly bear range at the time of European arrival, indicates a reduction of range by at least 25 percent.

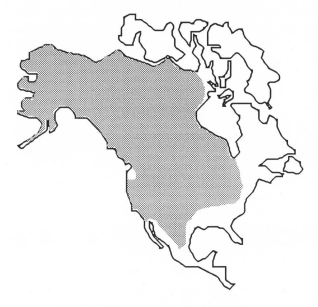

Grizzly bear distribution 7,000 - 10,000 years ago.

Grizzly bear distribution at time of European arrival.

Why did this reduction of grizzly distribution occur thousands of years before Europeans arrived on this continent? There are many groups and individuals who claim that grizzly bear reduction in distribution is caused by human population growth and human alteration to the environment. But that couldn't be the reason for a loss of grizzly bear distribution 7,000 thousand years ago. The answer to the question is this: Nobody knows. However, there is something we do know, based on the science of paleontology: The introduction of a new species to an area and its subsequent expansion in range is often followed by a contraction in range. Also, there is often extinction of other species during this type of expansion-contraction event. An earlier multiple species range expansion and extinction episode took place, before humans existed in this hemisphere, when the North and South American continents collided during the Pliocene Epoch. As the faunal exchange between the two landforms ensued, some species gained ground, but many vanished into the dust bin of history. This has been a common theme for millions of years, as evidenced by fossil remains of many species.

Now look at the maps again, because we need to consider the claim made by environmental groups and some biologists that grizzlies are a keystone species (a species that other species depend on for survival). You can see that grizzlies inhabited the Great Lakes Region 7,000 to 10,000 years ago, but were gone from that area long before Europeans arrived. Does that area now have an incomplete, collapsed ecosystem because grizzly bears are no longer there (the top-down theory)? Have all the other animals down the food chain that survived the extinction event disappeared from the state of Michigan? No, they haven't, because grizzly bears are not a keystone species nor are they an indicator species (a required species for ecosystem health) of pristine environments. As a matter of fact, in most areas, other predators and prey species have increased in numbers and prospered well after grizzlies were eliminated.

How could an animal that has been on this continent for such a short period of time become so important to the web of life? And how could a complex web of life with inter-related niche species exist when three-quarters of all North American mammals and hundreds of amphibians, reptiles, and birds became extinct between 10,000 to 13,000 years ago?

A more recent example of how quickly ecosystems can change has taken place right where I live. Approximately 300 years ago, elk suffered extinction in the Chilcotin Plateau east of Bella Coola due to the southerly intrusion of the sub-boreal pine/spruce forest that eliminated the vast grasslands that had prevailed in that area for several thousand years. Moose first arrived in the Central Coast area in 1921; there had never been moose here before, because they too, like the grizzly bear, are a European species new to this continent. And now, for the first time in history, Whitetail deer are migrating into the Central Coast. Do these events indicate a static unchanging nature? No, they do not.

Unfortunately, the North American faunal-assembly collapsed a long time ago. Many environmentalists claim that North America has a complex interconnected web of life, similar to that which exists in some marine environments. This is a myth that completely ignores the natural history of this continent.

Once again, look at the map showing grizzly bear distribution 'At time of European arrival' (on p. 13). There are many people who are also claiming that coastal grizzlies need ancient old-growth riparian (flat land adjacent to a river) forests for survival, with the implication that logging reduces populations. If you look at the northern, eastern, and southern areas of grizzly bear distribution on that map, you'll see that these areas are open-type habitats with few or no trees. Could an animal that is highly adapted to open-ground habitats become an old-growth dependent subspecies when it moved south into timbered areas, then evolve back to its original form after moving farther south or east back into open habitats? No, that's not what happened. Grizzly bears are a nonspecialized species that can successfully live in a variety of habitat types—they are not an old-growth dependent species.

GRIZZLIES IN HISTORICAL TIMES

There's another important point about the maps showing the reduction in grizzly bear historic range. We all know that grizzlies were eliminated from most of the Western U.S. and the Canadian prairies during European westward expansion. But the reason for that demise wasn't because of human population growth or habitat destruction, as some people claim. As a matter of fact, grizzlies were gone long before there was significant environmental alteration to the west.

Grizzlies and wolves were eliminated primarily for economic reasons. During the early Spanish settlement of California and the Southwest, grizzlies were heavily targeted by the Spanish army to reduce predation on livestock and to reduce danger to people.

Between 1840 and 1940, the people who moved westward from the Eastern U.S., like the Spanish, established the European agricultural economy based on domesticated plants and animals. These people survived hand-to-mouth by producing most of their own needs. There was no social security, welfare, or unemployment insurance. If livestock or plant crops were destroyed by predators or other animals, these people suffered terribly the following winter.

What they discovered was a brutal reality that most modern people are unaware of: Under the economic conditions they lived in, the settlers couldn't survive in direct competition with grizzly bears and wolves—those two species had to go.

By the early 1950s, grizzly bear range distribution in the Lower 48 States had been reduced primarily to the Rocky Mountain States, and by 1965 there were only small pockets of grizzly bears left in Yellowstone Park, Northeast Montana, Northern Idaho, and in the Washington State Cascade Mountains. At that time, alarm bells started going off within the biological community regarding the demise of grizzly bears throughout much of their former range.

In Western Canada, the prairie grizzly of Alberta was mostly gone by the 1940s, and the grizzly population of the Eastern Slope Rockies continued to decline until about 1980. In British Columbia, there was a decline in populations during the agricultural expansion years of the '40s, '50s, and '60s. Grizzlies were eliminated from the Central Okanagan Valley because of agriculture and human settlement, and were also eliminated from the lower portion of the south coast by over-hunting, intolerance, and human settlement. In most areas of B.C., grizzlies continued to decline at a much slower rate until about 1980, but still existed in large numbers in about 90 percent of their original B.C. range.

The grizzly bear populations in Alaska, the Yukon, and the Northwest Territories are mainly intact, and even though grizzlies have been eliminated near larger urban centers of the far north, populations aren't much different from one hundred years ago.

CONCLUSION

When I moved to the Bella Coola Valley in 1965, I saw the tail-end of the type of culture that was primarily responsible for the demise of predators. Many of the people here took a large part of their necessities directly from the land. There had been a 70-year war on predators, so there were fewer of those species then than there are today. But Bella Coolans, like most North Americans, now obtain most of their necessities from areas of the world where competitive plant and animal species have been eliminated—areas such as the Fraser and Okanagan Valleys in B.C., and places like California.

We can now tolerate much higher populations of these animals because the economic well-being of our families is not at stake. However, this is possible only because we are willing to let other areas of the world be significantly altered so that products can be produced cheaply, which makes it feasible to ship them long distances to us. If California and other prime agricultural areas of North America still had the full complement of insects, plants, and animals that originally existed in the 1600s, we here in Bella Coola would still have to take our survival necessities from the local land base and would still be trying to eliminate grizzlies and wolves, which would be a direct threat to our survival.

Historically, bear populations declined in Europe for thousands of years and in North America for hundreds of years. But the good news is this: Bear populations are no longer declining in those two areas of the world. Instead of walking around wringing our hands in guilt, it's time to face reality and disregard the fictitious claims that grizzlies are endangered.

Can grizzly bears survive in modern times? Yes, they most certainly can, but the human/grizzly equation must be managed carefully with an honest interest in also protecting people.

There will be much more information about grizzly bear habitat requirements and population status in Section Three.

Sow grizzly in Fish Creek at Hyder, Alaska.
Courtesy Keith Douglas.

3

BEAR AGGRESSIVE BEHAVIOR

Why do bears attack people? Before answering that question, it's important to understand that bears don't attack just people—they also attack other bears and other animals. Bears have genetically inherited types of aggression relating to predation, survival defense, and population regulation.

PREDATION: Black and grizzly bears are both omnivoristic predators that spend most of their time locating and eating the types of plant foods they can digest. But both are also opportunistic predators that kill a wide range of animals for food, including humans on some occasions.

SURVIVAL DEFENSE: Bears use aggression to defend themselves against other bears. This falls into two categories: competition aggression and home-range aggression.

Competition aggression pertains to bears slowly fighting their way up through the hierarchy of power until they don't have to run away from most other bears. Next, they must become successful breeding animals that pass as many of their genes into the next generation as possible. Male bears are very aggressive towards each other, especially during breeding time for this reason.

Home-range aggression pertains to bears defending personal space around food sources, bedding areas, and dens. This type of aggression is far more dangerous in grizzlies than black bears.

POPULATION REGULATION: Bears have a built-in mechanism limiting population, similar to that existing in most predator species.

Dominant breeding males often kill cubs, sub-adults, and sometimes complete family groups. This density-dependent behavior results in an increase of killing as the population density increases. A reciprocal behavior has evolved in female bears for defending their offspring that can be summed up in one word—ferocity.

This all boils down to five general categories of aggressive behavior: predatory, competition, home-range, cub-killing, and cub-defense. Three of these can be directed towards people: predatory, home-range, and cub-defense.

In a predatory attack, the bear is trying to kill the person for food. It takes significant resistance to survive this type of attack, and unknown to most people, black bears have a higher level of this type of aggression towards humans than do grizzly bears.

Home-range aggression pertains to defending high value space, usually a food source. This behavior is expressed as an intolerance of anything that gets too close. Grizzlies are much more dangerous than black bears in this behavior, especially during a close-range surprise encounter.

Cub-defense is the most common type of bear aggression towards people that results in injury, and it can be explosive, particularly with grizzly bears.

The final type of aggression has a chapter of its own dealing with the subject—carcass defense. The reason I don't list this type of attack as a separate category of behavior is because I consider it a part of predatory aggression. I do this because predator research in all parts of the world indicates that it's not enough just being efficient at killing animals—a predator must also be able to hold on to the carcass. I therefore class carcass defense as an important part of predatory aggression. Both black bears and grizzlies have this behavior, but walking up on a grizzly defending a carcass is probably the most dangerous encounter you can have with a bear.

The above descriptions of the various types of bear aggression are an abbreviated version of chapters in my previous books that give lengthy and detailed explanations of the subject. As you proceed through the following material, you'll see that each attack is categorized with the type of bear aggression involved so that the causes and factors become understandable.

Section Two: Bear Attacks

4

PREDATORY ENCOUN-
TERS AND ATTACKS

In August 1995, my wife and I travelled to Alaska on vacation. We were accompanied by my sister and brother-in-law, Carolyn and Dave Foltz. We were driving a SUV; they were pulling a trailer with their pickup.

We camped the first night at Bear Lake, B.C., and during the evening's conversation, we talked about predatory behavior in black bears, because I was just starting research for my second book. I explained to the rest that the Fort Nelson district had the highest incidence of this behavior, and that the next day we'd be travelling through that area.

About 4 P.M. the following afternoon we were heading north about 80 kilometers south of Fort Nelson. My wife and I were in the lead on a long, straight stretch of highway. About three hundred meters ahead, we could see a flatdeck truck on the left side of the highway, facing the same direction as we were travelling. A crawler tractor had just been unloaded and was moving out across a flat. The truck driver was gathering his holddown chains and another man was squatting and looking at one of the rear tires.

On the other side of the road, to our right, was a four-foot cut-bank and an open grassy slope that went for about 60 meters to a stand of timber. On the slope we saw a large black bear walk out of the trees and start a slow, steady walk towards the parked truck. The bear had made half the distance of the opening before the two men noticed it, and when they did, they immediately started moving towards the cab; we were now at about 100 meters distance. The bear was still moving forward, 5 meters from the top of the cut-bank, when the men stepped into the cab.

As we passed directly through the bear's line of sight, my wife and I both turned and looked into the bear's face, and so did my sister and her husband. As I looked in the right rear view mirror, I saw the bear stop and change its body posture five meters from the road. Our passing hadn't affected it in any way, and it never took its eyes of its intended victims. By this time, the truck driver and his companion had the door closed and were honking the horn. At the next pullout, we stopped to talk about what we had just witnessed.

Anyone who's seen the intense glare of those eyes, the stooped body posture, the lowered head, and the slow, steady, silent approach of a predatory bear, will never forget what it looks like. Some people might automatically sense what was taking place while others would not until it was too late.

The whole issue regarding predatory behavior in bears is an important one, because many North Americans don't know that a bear will kill and eat a person for food. This is because in the past, many predatory attacks have been interpreted as defensive attacks; additionally, many people are attempting to downplay this behavior in bears.

Fortunately, predatory behavior in bears is often identifiable, and being able to distinguish this behavior from defensive aggression is the key to surviving this type of attack.

I want to thank Conservation Officer Tobe Sprado for sending me the interview that the following story is based on. It's very obvious that Tobe went to great lengths in prying out all the subtle details of this attack for the benefit of educating and increasing the safety of field workers. I had Grant Swyers review the story to make sure nothing important was missing. This incident took place in a remote area south of Houston, B.C., near Whitesail Lake.

On the morning of June 23, 1998, Grant Swyers and Craig Nitschke, employees of TDB Consulting, were dropped off by helicopter to locate the boundary and to do other work regarding a proposed logging block. They were 15 kilometers from the nearest road. Grant was carrying a pump shotgun, and Craig had two cans of bear spray on his hip.

The two men split up to do different projects. After about one kilometer of locating a boundary and hanging ribbon, Craig came to the end of that line. He'd heard something following him for about 15 minutes; he didn't know if it was his co-worker or possibly a bear or a moose. Craig stood there for a few minutes, looking and listening to the loud noises not far away.

He started back down the line, looking for his compass that he'd lost somewhere along the boundary. Only 25 meters later, he saw Grant approaching and asked if he'd found his compass. "No," was the response. Craig was looking around on the ground when he heard something running behind him. He spun around and could see bushes moving not far away. He crouched and saw black legs moving through the thick brush, then a large black bear appeared running straight for him.

Craig screamed, "Bear!" as he fumbled for the pepper spray; Grant yelled, "What?" This caused the animal to stop in its tracks 20 feet from Craig, as it now became aware of Grant, and turned its stare towards him. The bear was brown on the sides and looked shaggy. Its ears were up, but there were no aggressive signals—it had approached silently except for the noise of its feet hitting the ground.

Craig had the spray in his hand as Grant moved up beside him with the shotgun ready for action. The bear was just standing there, staring intently at the two men. Craig yelled, "Fire a warning shot." A split second later, the slug whizzed a foot over the bear's head. The bear didn't flinch or react in any way. About 30 seconds later, it turned away and started circling downhill, out of sight.

Their supervisor told them to move south to the big swamp after Craig explained over the radio-phone what had just happened. That location would be safer as they'd be able to see all around, and the helicopter could land there.

As they moved through the timber, they could hear the bear behind them but couldn't see it. The swamp was about 300 meters across, and when they reached the other side, the black bear was just coming out of the trees on their trail. It was sniffing the ground and looking around. The bear crossed a small creek and stopped, then saw the two men, and, once again, ran towards them. Its ears were up, and it was not showing any aggressive displays.

Grant and Craig were standing about ten meters apart, waving their arms and yelling as the animal approached. They considered trying to spray the bear, but the wind was blowing hard against them, and they would have sprayed themselves. At 20 meters the bear halted, then looked back and forth at its intended victims. It started to move sideways when Craig yelled, "Shoot it!" Grant aimed and fired, but missed. The bear ran off through the swamp and into the timber. The two men listened intently for the bear to return during their 30-minute wait for the helicopter.

There was still work to be completed in the block. Because Grant was the only person with a firearm out of the crews working in the area, it was decided that Craig and Grant would finish the job.

The next morning at about 8 A.M., the two men were dropped off at the far end of the proposed cut-block. They worked all day across the block, doing GPS locations of creeks and contour breaks. By 3 P.M. they ended up within about 700 meters of where they had last seen the bear the day before.

Craig was ahead as the two men worked along on a bench. They started hearing noises below them over the edge of a break. They moved forward carefully, listening. Craig stopped to punch information into his GPS data logger. All of a sudden Grant yelled, "Bear!" "Where?" Craig screamed as he spun around. The black bear was only ten meters away. It was walking on a log over a small pool of water, slightly crouched, head down, staring intently at Craig as it inched slowly forward—it was completely ignoring Grant.

Grant yelled, "I'm going to shoot, get down." Craig jumped behind a tree and watched as the four shots exploded in rapid succession. The first slug put the bear down, but Grant kept firing because the log was propping it up. They approached slowly and made sure the bear was dead. It appeared to be a large male, but the lower part of its body was under water in the small seepage, so they couldn't tell the sex for sure. The hide was in good shape, but the body was thin.

The men worked for another half-hour to finish the work and were taken by helicopter back to camp.

The above story is one of the best I've documented for demonstrating what predatory behavior in bears looks like. The following series of stories will complete the picture.

This incident, as explained by Russell Atkinson, took place on September 19, 1999, approximately four kilometers south of Port Alice on Northern Vancouver Island:

John Johnson and I were timber cruising along a sidehill in an immature stand of fir trees when we had our first bear encounter. We had finished a coffee break and had worked for about 15 minutes. I was uphill 25 meters from my partner, recording tree heights. John was moving from tree to tree in our plot when he saw the bear only ten meters away.

He called to me, and I saw it immediately. It was about a 350-

pound black bear, and it was walking toward us. John joined me uphill from the plot, and we started yelling at it. It kept coming and coming as we yelled and threw sticks at it.

We both had bear spray, and pulled the cans out as we moved further uphill. The bear moved into our plot area and smelled at our hats and other clothing items and then kept coming towards us very slowly.

John and I stayed together, but started to walk very fast across the hill for 300 meters. We crossed a few gullies and headed downhill to the road. We kept our eye on the bear the whole time, and it kept pace with us all the way.

We were very scared, and at times, we considered climbing a tree or facing the bear with spray, but getting out of there won out. As we broke through the brush and onto the road, I looked back one last time and saw the bear about 15 meters away.

Our other crew was ten kilometers down the road with the truck and too far away for radio contact. We hitchhiked back to the highway and, eventually, made it back to town.

Other points of interest: There were no berries in the immediate area; we were near a very busy logging road—lots of traffic; the bear must have heard us up the hill and came to investigate; we wouldn't have seen him at all if it hadn't broken through some spaced debris where John could see it. If that hadn't have happened, who knows how close the bear would have come.

The next story was sent to me by Conservation Officer Jim Hart in Fort Nelson:

My name is Aleck Spracklin, I was born on November 16, 1972, and I've been a Forest Resource Technologist since April 1995. I started working in Northern British Columbia in August of 1995. I was asked to write this letter for increasing awareness of a dangerous hazard that all bush workers/recreationists eventually face—bears.

Bears are a common sighting in the Fort Nelson area. My coworkers and I see at least one bear a week, and often more. I've had only four potentially hazardous bear incidents before the two I'm going to describe. Thus, in my experience, a risky bear encounter can be expected about every four-and-a-half months.

I'd been working for two weeks on the Pine Plateau, approximately a one-hour flight by helicopter north-west of Fort Nelson. I was revising and finalizing some cut blocks for harvest in the upcoming logging season.

There were three people at this tent camp: a fellow full-time employee, a summer student, and myself. Throughout the camp stay, we had two encounters with bears coming through our camp and one encounter where a bear had cut off the student so he couldn't get back to camp.

On Thursday, June 23, 1997, my colleague had come down with some sort of stomach flu and had to stay in camp, so the summer student and I, followed by my colleague's dog, walked to a cut block approximately three kilometers away from our campsite. The student and I split up and went to opposite ends of the block, working towards each other.

At approximately 10 A.M., I was walking along a proposed road ribbon line when I heard a crash behind me. I turned around, pulling out my bear mace, and came face to face with a charging black bear. The bear was already only an arm's length away, and it breathed a loud "huff," which startled me, causing me to jump back and fumble with my bear mace.

My colleague's dog then charged at the bear, barking and snarling. As the two animals faced off, I turned and ran—I don't know for how long, but it seemed forever. When I stopped, I realized I was lost.

Not knowing what direction I'd run in meant I had no bearing to use to get back. I walked a long time in a spiral pattern trying to find a ribbon line to indicate where I was. While I was walking, all I could hear was the dog barking, trying to keep the bear away. The dog stayed by my side for the rest of the day, and I could see the bear through the bushes always circling me, trying to find a way past the dog to get to me.

This went on for seven hours. The bear charged me a second time, a mock charge that didn't come very close to me or the dog, before I finally got out of there.

When we finally met up, I out-distanced the summer student many times on the way back to camp, chain-smoking every time I stopped to wait for him.

My second bear incident occurred on December 22, 1997.

It was unseasonably warm for that time of year, and my colleague and I would soon be heading to camp for a Christmas break. That morning we went to a block about ten kilometers south of the Yukon border, where we split up and began painting the block boundary.

I'd just walked down off a hill, paralleling a creek, when I glanced back to check my boundary. Moving slowly down the hill was a black bear. I turned away and continued to paint along the bound-

ary before I realized what I'd just seen.

I looked back and, yes, there was a bear stalking towards me, three days before Christmas, when bears are supposed to be asleep! The bear darted towards me, so I jumped and positioned myself behind a tree.

My handheld radio was in my pocket, so after keying it, I yelled to my partner what was taking place. I dodged around the tree for a while as the bear chased me. The only thing I had in my hands was a can of blue spray paint, with which I sprayed the bear in the face, hoping to blind it.

I frantically pawed through my pockets searching for my lighter (spray paint makes a nice flamethrower), until I realized I'd left it in the truck. Since the bear was not going to leave me alone, I began dodging from tree to tree, moving away from the bear and towards the truck.

As I made my way back up the hill, the bear crawled down into a hole in the snow. At this point I realized I'd originally walked over the top of the bear's den. As soon as the bear disappeared into its hole, I put away my paint, pulled out my radio and my buck knife, and began to run towards the truck.

While running I radioed my co-worker and frantically described my situation. The bear caught up with me in a clearing just as I jumped over a large blown-down log. As it charged over the top of the log it immediately wrapped its paws around my leg. The bear then bit into my knee and rolled onto its side in an attempt to drag me down to the ground. I yelled in fright and stabbed my knife into its neck, causing it to let go of me.

My knee was burning as I watched the bear lap at the trickled blood coming from its neck. My co-worker was yelling support to me on the radio, but all I could think about was that the bear was now wounded and angry—as well as hungry.

I froze; my initiative had run out. I had tried everything, and the bear was still going to kill me. I couldn't back away any more on my own. I only moved when the bear moved, instead of the other way around. I still yelled and waved my arms at the bear, but I'd lost hope.

I don't know how long I was in this situation before my colleague finally got close enough to shoot off a bear banger. The bear hesitated, standing on its hind legs and sniffing at the air. I could finally move again and began backing away, but the bear began following me again. Finally, my colleague released another bear banger, and the bear turned and ran. I quickly moved off to the truck and was rushed to first aid.

The next two newspaper articles show a trend that started in 1997, where recreationists are now also victims of predatory attacks:

BASEBALL BAT USED TO FEND OFF GRIZZLY
with permission of the New Denver Valley Voice
July 20, 1999

Nathan Mooring and Sylvie Besinque are lucky to be alive after being mauled by a grizzly bear. They were attacked while sleeping in a tent at an old forestry landing near the Shannon Lake Forest Recreation Site July 19. They're not sure why, they had no food in the tent to attract its attention.

They had awakened earlier in the morning, felt chilled and put on their coats. Besinque woke again around six to see the silhouette of bear paws on the outside of the tent, around Mooring's head. The grizzly attacked, breaking a hole through the tent and grabbing Mooring's shoulder.

It was fortunate Mooring had put on a heavy coat earlier; the grizzly bit into it and his pillow, giving some protection to his shoulder.

"It felt like a hydraulic press," he said, remembering the sensation as the grizzly's teeth sank in.

Mooring stands six foot three inches, weighs at 235 pounds, and is a body builder. It would take every ounce of his strength for the two to survive.

"I kept hammering at the grizzly's nose. A bear's body is like a rock, it was like hitting a telephone pole."

The grizzly turned and came through the front of the tent. Mooring, realizing it was going after Besinque, started kicking it in the teeth as it tried to reach her. He still has teeth marks on his feet. Mooring grabbed Besinque and they escaped through the hole the grizzly had made. She has burn marks from the floor of the tent where he dragged her out.

"I don't remember a thing," said Besinque, "except for being outside the tent."

"If it hadn't been for the hole the grizzly made in the tent, we wouldn't have made it out," said Mooring.

He called friends who were sleeping in his truck to throw his baseball bat out to him. When one of the campers opened the door, the movement startled the grizzly, which was now at the passenger door. Mooring grabbed the bat and the grizzly ran around the front of the truck.

"I tried to look as intimidating as I could," he said; he took a swing at the bear, but missed.

"It ran 20 feet and turned around and lunged at me. I thought I was going to die. I thought I was going to be mauled to death, but I wasn't going to watch it maul Sylvie. I decided to fight."

When the grizzly was "just about right on top" of Mooring, he swung the bat with every ounce of strength he had, aiming between the grizzly's eyes. The bear went down and pawed at its nose where Mooring had hit it, then raced off down over the bank as fast as it could go. That was the last they saw of it.

In addition to their cuts and scrapes, the two have a souvenir—the wooden bat, with a huge dent in it.

According to the Ministry of Environment, the bear was a young one, in poor condition. They're attempting to trap it, and Mooring will try to identify it. If the right bear is found, it will be destroyed as this area is heavily used for recreation—there are two wilderness campsites nearby as well as the Forest Rec. Site.

Nathan and Sylvie.

Courtesy Valley Voice Newspaper.

BEAR ATTACKS BABY, MOTHER
with permission of the Calgary Sun
August 6, 1999

A baby boy is recovering at his home south of Calgary after a black bear gouged his head and bit his mother's leg during a terrifying attack while they were camping in B.C.

But Tammy Spencer, 24, said the attack on her, her son Chase Davies, one, her husband and four-year-old son could have been much worse if a neighboring camper hadn't sprung to their aid.

"Thank God he was awake," said Spencer, from the family's home in Champion, about 100 km southeast of Calgary.

"Otherwise, who knows what would have happened."

The 200-pound bear ripped through the tent where Spencer, hus-

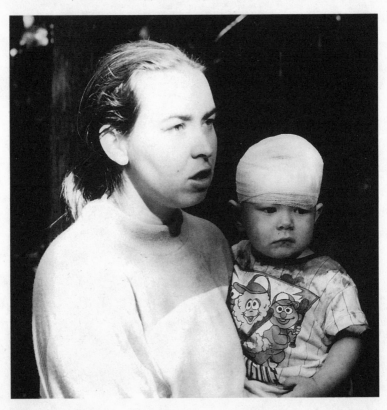

Tammy and Chase.

Courtesy Valley Voice Newspaper.

band Eric Davies and their sons, Chase and Malcolm were sleeping Monday morning in B.C.'s Roseberry Provincial Park, 300 km south west of Calgary.

The bear wasn't scared off by their shouts, said Spencer, but finally left after a camper they know only as Dawson beat it with a stick.

She said there was a harrowing moment when she and Eric couldn't find Malcolm—but they discovered he'd been pulled to safety by the other camper.

The mother and son were driven to nearby New Denver hospital, where Spencer's leg was bandaged.

Chase required nine stitches to two separate wounds on his head—one so deep you could see his skull, said Spencer.

"It was terrifying," she said of the attack.

"Those claws are razor-sharp."

Conservation Officer Jim Beck searched for the bear after the attack and put it down by shooting it in the head.

"All indications are it was a predatory attack—there was no food left out or anything, which would attract the bear," said Beck.

He said the claw marks on the tent match the bear he shot, and saliva has been sent for testing—along with the body to Nelson, B.C., to ensure the right bear was killed.

After the attack, the bear retreated to the woods, but returned a short time later, just three or four campsites from where the mauling

Conservation Officer Jim Beck with predatory black bear.
Courtesy Adrienne Mercer.

occurred.

"He walked towards another camper, but the camper retreated into his trailer," said Beck.

After finding a bag of garbage, the bear went off into the woods again.

Beck said it was the second attack in the area in two weeks.

In the last attack, a man was accosted by a grizzly in his tent, but fought it off with a baseball bat.

Spencer said the family will camp again, but said next time they'll take a bat or stick in case they need to beat off bears.

"You can't predict them. Nobody knows what a bear is thinking," she said.

"We thought we'd be OK, but we weren't."

In mid-October 1999, I received a call from the BC Wildlife Federation Hunter Safety Program Manager, Robert Paddon. He told me that there had been a death inflicted by a predatory black bear near Dease Lake, B.C., and that I should call Conservation Officer Gord Hitchcock to get the details.

I was able to connect with Gord in early November and interview him. He related the following:

The body of 71-year-old Helmut Weiland, a visitor from Germany, was found on October 7th by the owner of a cabin where the victim was staying. The incident happened on a remote stretch of the Dease River about 65 miles north of Dease Lake.

The COs and the RCMP flew by helicopter to the location the afternoon of the 7th and located the body. Evidence collected at the site indicated that the death was caused by a black bear attack. They didn't find any bear in the immediate vicinity and couldn't do a thorough search because of impending darkness. The body was flown out to the regional coroner's office.

The next morning, Gord Hitchcock flew back to the site and set a series of foot-hold snares around the attack area, then conducted an air search for the bear, but didn't see it. Later that day, a large, healthy, male black bear was caught in a snare 200 meters from where the body had been found.

Gord Hitchcock then did a field assessment of the track size and body size of the bear and concluded that there was a high probability that the snared bear was the offending animal. After dispatching the bear, Gord flew the carcass back to Dease Lake, and later, in consultation with the Wildlife Branch's provincial veterinarian, a

The black bear in a foot-hold snare.

Courtesy Gord Hitchcock.

necropsy was undertaken. Relevant samples were removed and sent for forensic analysis to determine if they'd killed the right bear. An autopsy was preformed on the German victim October 14th, and the cause of death was confirmed as a bear attack.

I asked Gord if the bear had fed on the victim, and he said that a fair amount of the body had been consumed. I asked if he was classing the incident as a predatory attack, and Gord stated that no conclusions had been made, and wouldn't be made, until all investigating was done and the final report finished. I tried to pry more information out of him, but he was very tight-lipped about the incident. He wouldn't tell me who the owner of the cabin was.

Gord finished by saying that this was the first bear attack investigation where the Conservation Officer Service played a role in all aspects of the inquiry and report. I could sense that the CO Service must have a new policy regarding how they handle press releases pertaining to bear attacks. I felt that that was fair enough, as long as the final report was available to serious researchers within a reasonable length of time.

I'm very careful not to read predatory intent into an incident if the evidence isn't there, but I've been dealing with people for a long time who do everything possible to downplay this behavior in bears. Most tourists who come to B.C. aren't afraid of black bears and have no clue that a black bear could stalk, kill, and eat them.

I knew from past experience that the official report would tell only part of the story. I needed to interview the owner of the cabin who was Helmut's friend and had found his body. But it can be a bad mistake to contact a person too soon after such a terrible event, and I'd heard indirectly that the person I needed to talk to was a 'no-bullshit' kind of guy who may not take kindly to someone prying into a personal tragedy like this one. I would have to wait for the right time.

On January 11th, I was talking to the general manager of the BC Guide Outfitters Association, Dale Drown, about bear management issues. He asked me if I'd heard about the bear-inflicted fatality near Dease Lake. I said yes, and that I'd started research on the incident but wasn't sure how to proceed. Dale suggested calling Guide Outfitter Myles Bradford and asking for help.

Myles was good enough to call his friend Pat Hickman (the owner of the cabin) and explain who I was and what I'm about. Without this introduction, I doubt that Pat would've talked to me, as he seemed to be a very private man.

When I called and talked to Pat, he told me that the cabin where the attack took place can be accessed only by floatplane or river boat. It is a beautiful place where the Hickman family has spent a lot of time enjoying nature.

They had known Helmut for 15 years, and he wasn't really a tourist; he'd been coming to B.C. for years and loved being out in the wild by himself. Over the years, he'd used their cabin in both winter and summer and knew a lot about the bush. Helmut enjoyed fishing, hiking, photography, snowshoeing, and watching animals whenever possible. He'd also travelled extensively and seemed to be familiar with many of the world's mountain ranges—he was fascinated by mountains. Helmut's career had been with the Berlin Symphony Orchestra. As far as Pat could tell, he didn't have any family back in Germany.

Pat had taken Helmut up to the cabin by riverboat about a month before the attack and had checked in on him every now and again. They both knew there was a bear hanging around, but were not really concerned about it. However, the day before Helmut's death,

The Hickman cabin on the Dease River.

Courtesy Pat Hickman.

while Pat was visiting him, Helmut expressed concern about the bear's behavior. Pat told him that he didn't have to stay there and urged him to move to another location for the rest of his trip. But Helmut didn't believe there was any real danger if he was careful.

The next day Pat flew his Supercub in to check on his friend. After beaching the aircraft, he noticed a paddle, a life jacket, and a fishing pole lying on the ground nearby. That seemed unusual, because Helmut was so particular in how he handled his possessions. Pat thought that maybe he was taking a nap, but when he knocked on the door and looked in the window, he couldn't see any sign of Helmut. A tree had blown over in the yard, so Pat was thinking about bucking it up as he walked away from the cabin and then suddenly realized that there was no smoke smell. He looked up, but there wasn't any smoke coming out of the chimney. Helmut always had a fire going. Pat went to check the stove; it was cold. The place looked normal, but now he was getting worried.

He looked around the immediate area, then checked the canoe in the slough. He then walked down-river, thinking that Helmut may have had a heart attack and was lying somewhere dead or incapacitated—but found nothing. Pat was thinking about doing an aerial search, but when he saw the equipment lying on the ground again, he suddenly realized that something had happened right there. Helmut wouldn't have left those items like that overnight.

Helmut couldn't be very far away, so Pat picked one of the many game trails heading into the tall grass across the slough. In about 40 yards he saw a hat and glasses on the ground. As he continued, he could see that he was now walking on a wide drag mark. He had gone only another 30 yards when he saw Helmut's partially buried body. Pat could see intestines exposed. The upper part of the body was covered. Strangely, he couldn't see any blood on the ground.

Even before he found Helmut's body, Pat suspected the possibility of a bear attack. Now that his worst fears were confirmed, he realized he had no gun, and the bear might be close by, protecting its kill. He had felt compelled to keep searching for Helmut until he knew for sure whether he was dead or alive. Now, the reality set in; he had no choice but to back off and leave.

After Pat reported the incident to the RCMP and the conservation officers, he wanted to go back in and kill the bear. The C.O.s asked him to work with them so they could do a proper investigation and make sure the right bear was killed by using DNA evidence. Pat agreed to their request.

Pat went on to say that when the bear was caught in the snare, it showed no fear of the conservation officers. And even though he's never really trusted government officials, he felt that all the officers involved did a good job in bringing the incident to a conclusion. This was extremely important because of his concern for his own family.

Two days after talking to Pat, I received a fax from him stating that he'd received a call from C.O. Gord Hitchcock, who said he was doing an additional investigation of the incident, and asked Pat many questions that seemed to be aimed at exonerating the bear, or at least justifying the bear's actions. I called Pat that night and told him that some employees within the Ministry of Environment have a bias that a victim usually does something to contribute to a predatory attack. This includes feeding a bear or leaving garbage out. Even though I didn't know if Gord had that bias, he was probably instructed to investigate all possible aspects of the incident. (See note at end.)

Pat said the attack was clearly predatory, and that Helmut had defensive wounds all over his body, indicating he'd fought the bear for his life. Also, the fishing gear was set down neatly, as if Helmut had seen the bear approaching and was probably walking back to the safety of the cabin when the bear charged after him. Pat went on to say that he'd been promised a copy of the official report when it was done, and he would send me a copy.

I decided to let the story sit until the report was available.

On May 23, 2000, I was in Prince Rupert conducting a Bear Encounter Survival Course for the Ministry of Forests. During a classroom discussion about predatory behavior in bears, I asked the participants if they had heard about the attack on a German visitor near Dease Lake the previous fall. About half of the people nodded yes, and a young man stated, "The guy had been feeding the bear, so what do you expect." Others in the class had heard the same rumor and seemed to be convinced that it was true.

When I arrived back home, I called Pat to see if he'd received the report—he hadn't. I then told him about the rumor I'd heard in Prince Rupert, that Helmut had been feeding the bear. Pat sounded quite perturbed about it and said the rumor was ridiculous. Even though Helmut would sometimes put out small scraps for the squirrels and birds, he wouldn't have been feeding the bear. I told Pat that if he didn't receive the report soon, I would use the *Freedom of Information Act* to get a copy.

About a month after talking to Pat, I sent in an official request for the report and received it on August 1st. After reading the report and all other material sent to me, I realized that the B.C. Conservation Officer Service had significantly increased the investigative requirements for completing an Animal/Human Attack Report. This probably resulted from the uncertainty as to whether the C.O. Service killed the right bear in regard to the deaths of Shane Fumerton and Bill Caspell in 1995 (*Bear Attacks - The Deadly Truth*, *Without Warning* Chapter).

The report was the most thorough bear attack investigation I've ever read, and made it clear how important it is for public safety and confidence that the identity of the offending wildlife be confirmed by the use of DNA technology.

Following are a series of statements from the first part of the report:

The victim was found on his back. Victim was wearing clothing and footwear suitable for the outdoor temperatures. Upper shoulder and head area covered with grass. The grass appeared to have been pulled in from the surrounding area of the victim. Bite wounds observed on hands, wrists, and forearms of victim. Cursory examination of the exposed wounds indicated an upper canine bite of approximately 50 mm from center to center. Bite impression marks noted on pants. Claw impression marks noted on jacket.

No major life-threatening injuries noted at this point. Pile of grass removed from head area. Extensive injuries noted. A significant amount of damage noted to the shoulders and neck area. No head observed on victim. Victim's head not observed in immediate area. The neck and shoulder area appears to have been fed on by wildlife.

The ground (wetland area) surrounding the immediate area of the victim was not conducive to track impressions. No distinctive wildlife tracks observed.

Returned to the location of the helicopter. A prominent trail lead-ing to the cabin noted at this location. The trail is adjacent to the river. The riparian vegetation borders a portion of the trail on both sides giving it a tunnel-like appearance. The cabin is located approximately 200 meters east of the helicopter. A single life jacket, paddle, and fishing rod was observed adjacent to the trail. The fish-ing rod and paddle were facing the canoe location. The canoe was in a stored state adjacent to the back channel.

In close proximity to the helicopter a trail was observed leading into the slough area in the direction of the victim. The grass was flat-tened indicating travel in a northeast direction. The trail impression appeared recent. The grass was flattened in the direction of the vic-tim. The trail was examined and followed for approximately 35 meters. At this location the trail opened into a circle-like impression and three items were recovered. One set of eyeglasses, one hat, and a buck knife. Blood evidence was noted on the ground at this site. The inside of the hat was blood-stained. The knife appeared to have originated from a leather carry case on the belt of the victim. The blade was in the closed position. A single black bear hair was observed on the knife. The hair sample did not include a root. The eyeglasses were intact. The immediate area surrounding the recov-ered items was disturbed and the grass flattened. The trail contin-ued in the direction of the victim. The trail was now wider. The grass was flattened in the direction of the victim. The impression of being dragged. The trail was examined and followed for another 16.3 meters. At the 16.3-metre mark a single gold neck chain was recov-ered on the trail. Bear scat was observed at this location. The bear scat was located immediately adjacent to the gold chain. The scat appeared to be a recent deposit. The trail continued in the direction of the victim. Noted the victim's final position to be approximately 12.7 meters from the gold chain.

This information indicates that Helmut had either left to go fishing or was returning from fishing and was approximately 200 meters from the cabin. At this point, he probably saw the bear close by and laid down the items he was carrying, readying himself for a retreat to the cabin. The bear probably tackled him to the ground and quickly started dragging him away parallel to the river. He would've received multiple bites as he fought the bear during the 35-meter drag.

The circular, disturbed spot where the eyeglasses, hat, and knife were found is probably where Helmut died, or was rendered helpless by bites to the neck. He may have been trying to get his knife in action. The drag mark was wider after this spot, indicating a limp body being dragged partially sideways by the hip or shoulder. The gold necklace may have just come off while being dragged, or the bear may have regripped at the neck.

The report stated that several small piles of carrot, onion, and potato peelings were found within 24 meters of the cabin, and that Helmut had been storing fish on the veranda in a cupboard attached to the cabin, and that he had told a visiting moose hunting party that a bear had been on the veranda at nighttime. The hunters noticed boards blocking off the entrance to the veranda and explained to Helmut that the bear was being attracted by the fish smell. One of these hunters saw a large black bear swim the river near the cabin on a day preceding the attack. The hunter yelled at it, but it showed no fear of him.

The film in Helmut's camera was developed, but there were no pictures of bears. Also, his diary was translated and a note on September 22nd, slightly more than two weeks before the attack, stated that a big black bear had been on the veranda in the morning and that he'd scared it away by banging pots together inside the cabin.

The report finishes off with the following statements:

No evidence collected to support a defensive attack.
No evidence collected to support a provocation issue.
No evidence collected to support a bear protecting a food source.
No evidence collected to support prior bear/man conflicts.
No evidence collected to support the issue of feeding bears. A suggestion may have been made to refrain from placing food items to attract squirrels and birds. No other attractants observed to have supported a Dangerous Wildlife Protection Order.
Evidence collected to support black bear activity in the slough area and near the cabin and on the cabin porch prior to the wildlife attack. The degree of habituation is unknown. This location is remote and the number of visitors is low and seasonal. There are no documented problem wildlife occurrences from this location.
Evidence collected to support the victim may have indirectly attracted the bear to the cabin by storing fish parts in the open porch area and leaving small portions of food items for the squirrels and birds.
The wildlife attack on the victim was extensive. A significant portion of the victim's body was damaged by bite marks and claw marks. A significant number of these appeared to be placed through the victim making defensive posturing. Wounds observed on the hands, wrists, and forearms of the victim. More wounds noted on the left

side of the body than the right. The pathology of the wounds indicated a significant number of the wounds were made in living tissue. A considerable amount of the victim's upper torso was fed on. This evidence may support a predatory type behavior. The bear mauling of the victim was significant. The impression the investigating officer received was that of a predatory black bear behavior as opposed to a neutralizing behavior.

There was not enough DNA material in the animal saliva swab sample taken from a puncture wound on Helmut's left thigh to confirm that they had killed the right bear. But the circumstantial evidence gathered strongly supports the conclusion that the offending bear was killed.

It's good that Gord Hitchcock did a thorough investigation regarding the issue of attractants and the possible feeding of the bear. If he hadn't, the rumors would persist and finally become the facts of the case.

There are many people, including some bear biologists, who would claim that the food scraps and fish parts were the cause of the attack. This view is illogical. What caused the attack is predatory behavior in bears and the availability of someone unable to defend himself. The food scraps and fish parts are factors leading up to the attack, but how important are they? What if Pat Hickman had years ago planted apple trees near the cabin that now produced fruit? Or what if there was a salmon run in the river or other natural foods that attracted bears to the area? These are the same types of factors that tens of thousands of North Americans who are exposed to black bears are involved with daily, including forgetting to clean the barbeque and putting it away, or leaving a dog dish on the back porch.

Note: I later had the opportunity to ask Gord Hitchcock about his telephone call where Pat got the impression he was trying to exonerate the bear. Gord stated that he was gone from Dease Lake for several days after the attack, and when he returned, there was a rumor circulating all over the north that Helmut had caused his own death by feeding the bear. Gord decided to reopen the investigation on his own, not because he believed the rumor, but because the investigation required that he be completely neutral and objective regarding any possible factor leading up to the attack. He asked Pat a series of questions in that phone call that were designed to root out any possibility that Helmut may have done something that contributed to the attack. As his report indicates, he didn't find any evidence that the bear had been fed. It was a clear-cut predatory attack.

I've told this story somewhat dispassionately because of the way the information came to me, and because I didn't interview the Hickman family in person and gain their perspective on the loss of a friend. But we must not for one second forget the horror and pain during the last ten minutes of Helmut's life.

CONCLUSION

Predatory attacks are now taking place in areas where they haven't happened before. Consider the following four attacks:

*A 16-year-old girl was attacked and seriously injured in the early morning hours of July 25, 1996 by a large male black bear on Mount Lemmon in Arizona. The bear had recently been relocated by an employee of the Arizona Game and Fish Department, and a lawsuit resulted.

*On August 9, 1999, at Long Lake in Wisconsin, a 14-year-old boy scout was attacked in a tent by a black bear and dragged into a ravine before his father successfully fought the bear off. It took 196 stitches to close up his wounds. Local authorities were baffled by the bear's behavior.

*A 50-year-old woman was killed and fed on by a black bear sow and cub in the Great Smoky Mountains National Park on May 21, 2000. A dozen hikers threw rocks and screamed at the bears for several hours, trying to remove them from the woman's body, but to no avail.

*In Glacier National Park, a 24-year-old hiker received minor injuries from a black bear on June 26, 2000. The bear circled the victim, then charged and attacked. The young man first played dead, then successfully fought the bear off.

During the next 20 years, there will be a continuous increase in predatory attacks on people by both grizzlies and black bears. I base this view on the increased frequency of contact between people and bears that is now taking place—just as an increase in the number of vehicles on roadways within a province or a state would result in a corresponding increase in vehicle accidents.

Bear populations are increasing all over North America, and there is an additional problem that the above statistical principle doesn't include. What goes with more bears is not just more encounters because of numbers alone, but more encounters because protected bears lose their fear of people and do not try to avoid them. Bears that do not fear people are more likely to be predatory.

Unfortunately, human death rates and property damage by bears will have to reach epidemic proportions before present-day policies are influenced. We should be asking ourselves this question: Is it really necessary to allow bears to reclaim all of their former range and their status as dominant species in order to guarantee their future survival?

5

CARCASS DEFENSE

The most common type of grizzly bear behavior that causes injury to people is female cub defense. But the type of grizzly behavior that has the highest potential for causing human death is carcass defense. Luckily, these events don't happen often, but each year there are one or two people severely injured or killed in North America under these circumstances. When I was young and foolish, I deliberately walked up on many grizzlies defending carcasses. I wouldn't consider such a thing now, but I learned much about this behavior.

I have several accounts of people encountering black bears defending a carcass, and even though the bears' reactions were similar to that of a grizzly, no injuries resulted because black bears are less likely to make contact when engaged in this behavior. It could happen—you could be killed by a black bear protecting an animal carcass—but it's much less likely to happen than with a grizzly bear.

Every once in awhile, we have an opportunity to look at the complex aspects of bear behavior without someone getting killed or injured. I was glad to receive the following account for this chapter, because it demonstrates some important points about the type of bear aggression we're exploring here.

Lawrence Rippel lives in Kelowna, B.C., and works for the Central Okanagan Regional District. On February 7, 2000, he faxed me an interesting story that happened to a friend of his, Randy Mueller. Randy explains the events of his first moose hunt in the following narrative:

Last fall, I had the great opportunity of going on my first moose hunt with my brother-in-law, Wilfred, and my father-in-law, Ed Fischer. We travelled to Dease Lake on September 24th and returned on October 9th.

We first hunted a few spots around Dease Lake and saw a lot of moose sign but were either too late to see a moose, or other hunters were there before us. On the fifth day of our hunt, Wilfred and I drove up what's called the microwave road, which leaves Highway 37 and winds its way to Alpine tundra, then back down on the other side of the mountain.

It took us 45 minutes to make the top with the quad (small four wheel ATV); I was driving, and Wilf was on the back. With no trees around, the wind was blowing hard. We saw lots of caribou sign in the Alpine.

After 35 minutes of driving down the other side, we came to timber line, and ten minutes farther on, I dropped Wilf off to hunt down the road. I planned to drive to the end of the road, then return up it and meet Wilf in the middle. But first we had coffee to warm up, then wished each other good luck and said, "See ya in awhile." The temperature was about minus 7 celsius; it was overcast, and there was about five to six inches of snow.

I slowly worked my way down the mountain for ten minutes or so and encountered two men on a quad. We chatted for a while, then carried on. It was around 4:20 P.M. Shortly thereafter I saw fresh moose tracks in the other quad tracks. I slowed down to a crawl, and in another 50 feet saw a bull moose on a small hill about 200 feet away.

I got off slowly, made several cow moose calls, loaded my 7mm magnum with two rounds, then made my first-ever shot on an animal. The bullet seemed to hit in the lung area, and I fired a second round for insurance, as I didn't want to just wound it. The bull moved about five feet and dropped to its knees.

Suddenly, I saw movement in my peripheral vision in the willows down in the ditch to my left, but I was too interested in what the moose was doing to be concerned about it. I was thinking that Wilf would be showing up soon to help me with the bull.

Then, an adult grizzly crawled out of the ditch about 35 feet away and immediately got my attention; my heart started to pound as I realized my gun was empty. I slowly put three rounds into the rifle, knowing full well that as close as the bear was, I may not get a chance to use it. I could now feel my heart beating in every part of my body. The grizzly just stood there looking at me—the two shots I'd just fired hadn't bothered it a bit.

After what seemed like a lifetime (about 30 seconds), the moose coughed and was obviously spewing blood from its lungs. I don't believe the bear knew the moose was on the hill, but may have been smelling the blood. Finally, after another 45 seconds of staring each other down, the grizzly turned and saw the moose—it immediately headed in that direction.

The bear was huge, and as soon as it was a safe distance away, I got on the quad and backed up the road a ways, then turned around and headed up the road to find Wilf. It took me a few minutes to calm down and explain what had happened. We both realized that I'd escaped from a very dangerous situation.

We decided to go back down and take a look at what was going on. We stopped at a safe distance and then snuck up into a stand of brush on the sidehill about 150 feet from the bear and moose. It was dead silent except for the sound of tearing flesh and breaking bones.

Then, I fell and grabbed a branch, which snapped loudly. The bear went berserk and came in our direction, searching for what had made the noise. It was pouncing up and down on its front legs as it rushed forward. What an awful feeling it was. After a short while, it couldn't find us and went back to its feast. We continued to watch it

eat the fat from the intestines for awhile, then carefully, quietly, we removed ourselves from the scene and headed for camp to calm down.

The next day the three of us decided to go back and see if we could salvage the hind quarters. When we arrived at the area, we slowly approached until we could smell a terrible stench. We were about 200 yards away, but could see through our binoculars that there were three bears near the moose. The single bear we'd seen before was obviously a sow, and was now accompanied by two large cubs. They weren't feeding; they had the moose buried and were guarding it. The bears knew we were there and were watching our every move.

Six days later, before heading home, we went back to the site with guns ready. The bears were not there. We quickly ran up to the kill, took some pictures, replayed the scenario, then retreated. What was left of the moose carcass was buried, and there were tracks and droppings everywhere. The smell was absolutely awful.

I recently read an article by a bear expert in the U.S. who claimed my contention about carcass defense behavior in grizzlies being extremely dangerous was an exaggeration, and what was really taking place under these circumstances was bears defending personal space—what I call home-range aggression. The gentleman is wrong. I've seen and heard many examples like the one above that shows the difference. When the grizzly crawled out of the ditch, it was only 35 feet from Randy, well within the bear's personal defense zone, but the bear didn't attack. What do you suppose would've happened if Randy had walked up to within 35 feet of the moose carcass when the sow was bedded next to it? The following incidents will answer that question.

I received a call from Christiana Wiens of the Terrace Standard Newspaper on October 19, 1999, regarding a follow-up article about a grizzly attack that had taken place earlier in the month. Christiana faxed me the following article and wanted my views on it:

Grizzly Bites Man

A Nass Valley man says he's changed his hunting patterns after a near death run-in with a 600-pound grizzly October 1st.

"I'll hunt when the bears are snoozing in winter," said Jim Gosnell. "I won't be going out in the fall anymore."

Gosnell survived the 20-second attack with only a five-centimetre deep gash to his left knee.

"I've got one big tooth mark in my leg," said Gosnell from his home Wednesday afternoon.

Describing the incident as "terrifying and then some," Gosnell was in the hospital here for three days.

Gosnell is now an outpatient at the Nisga'a Valley Health Centre in New Aiyansh, where he receives a daily antibiotics and rabies drip.

Gosnell and his brother Gerald were helping their cousin Eric Clayton retrieve two moose he'd shot near Dragon Lake, 10 miles northeast of New Aiyansh, the night before, when the attack happened.

Gosnell, 40, said he should have been suspicious when part of the moose carcass was missing.

But, he said, he didn't see the silver tip grizzly until it grabbed his leg.

The bear then tossed him into a nearby swamp and started munching on the moose again.

"He wasn't going anywhere," said Gosnell who had clamored to safety up a nearby tree.

"I didn't even know I could climb a tree - it didn't even have any branches," he said.

Gosnell said he called for help, while Eric Clayton rang three quick gunshots into the air.

The bear was scared off, long enough for Gosnell to run halfway out of the woods - before Clayton and Gerald Gosnell drove him out on their all-terrain vehicle.

"I didn't feel any pain until I was in the ambulance," he said.

Gosnell doesn't blame the grizzly for the attack.

Jim Gosnell was lucky; that particular bear let him off easy. I find it very interesting that a grizzly can be eating animal flesh, then remove a person from the scene and go back to its meal without considering the person as food. There are some cases where a bear adds a person to the food stash after a carcass defense incident, but usually their main interest is in eliminating any competitive predator that comes along.

The next story shows what unfortunately happens in many carcass defense attacks.

On the morning of March 15, 2000, I interviewed Sheldon Clare at his home in Prince George, B.C. Sheldon teaches English classes at the College of New Caledonia. He is an active outdoorsman and is the president of the B.C. Branch of the National Firearms Association. Sheldon was raised in Prince George and has lived there most of his life.

"It was quite a shock to this community when George Evanoff was killed by a grizzly," Sheldon stated. "I got to know him during the four years before his death, because we were both members of the Alpine Club. He and his family are highly respected, and he was well known as an expert woodsman."

I asked Sheldon about the cabin that George was hiking to when the attack took place. "The cabin is on Bear Paw Ridge in the McGregor Mountains about 70 kilometers northeast of town. George operated a backcountry ski and recreation service and occasionally used the cabin. George was involved with the local search and rescue program and had previously been a member of the ski patrol. Many of the people who helped search for George when he went missing knew him well, and some had received training from him in the past."

We talked for another hour or so about bears and outdoor recreation, and then I thanked Sheldon for providing me with background information about George for this story.

I received the Animal/Human Attack Report and the Coroner's report regarding George's death in April. Much of the information in the Animal/Human Attack Report was removed because of concern for the family. I had access to the eliminated material from other sources, but used only what was necessary to gain an understanding of what took place.

On May 24th, I talked to Dave King, who was a close friend of George Evanoff. Dave is the habitat section head for the Ministry of Environment in Prince George and has extensive bush experience. He was willing to explain what took place during the search for George.

George Evanoff, age 66, left Prince George at 7:30 A.M. October 24, 1998, to go for a day-hike to the cabin on Bear Paw Ridge. George had told his family that he'd be home by suppertime. At noon, numerous attempts were made from his cell-phone to call his family, but none were successful.

When George didn't arrive home as expected, his wife called Dave King to alert him of the situation. Because George was always reliable and punctual, Dave was immediately concerned. He started calling friends who could help in a quick search effort. One of the people called was a doctor—Dave asked him to come along in case George had been injured.

At 6:00 P.M., George still hadn't returned, so it was decided that a search was necessary. The group left town at 7:30 and had located George's truck at the trailhead by 9:30 that night. They had to use their headlamps almost immediately because of darkness.

The first part of the route was on a grown-in logging road and through two old clear-cuts. George's tracks were followed in the fresh snow to the end of the road and into the dense timber. Because there was no snow under the tree canopy and the tracks disappeared, it took a major effort by the searchers to stay on route and not become lost in the darkness. As the concerned friends moved along, they hollered and blew whistles, hoping to hear George's response.

The searchers reached the cabin at about 11:30 P.M. Because George wasn't there, and they'd seen fresh grizzly tracks a kilometer back, they now became very concerned. At midnight, Dave used a cell-phone to call their contact in Prince George and requested that he ask Search and Rescue and the RCMP to initiate a search response for the next morning.

After warming up with hot tea, the group retraced their route once again, searching, yelling, and whistling, and arrived at the vehicles by 2:30 A.M. They bedded down in sleeping bags but had a short rest as the RCMP and volunteer searchers started showing up about 5:30 A.M.

Two RCMP officers with a dog immediately hiked into the area to look for George as they didn't want the area contaminated with too many tracks. As a camp was being set up at the intersection of Bear Paw Ridge and Pass Lake Road, Dave and another person from the initial search party flew around with the search team leaders in helicopters to familiarize them to the area.

The first search group was flown in at 7:00 A.M. Dave went in with the second group and had the task of flagging a baseline through the area for maintaining search grids. The third team in had travelled only half of a kilometer from the cabin when they found a buried moose carcass with grizzly tracks all around. They also found George's tracks entering the area. Some of George's personal belongings were located about ten meters from the moose.

The RCMP were called and informed of what had been found. Shortly after the police arrived, they found George's body nearby. Radio calls were made to apprise everyone of what had been found. The search personnel retreated to the cabin area for safety concerns, as it was believed the bear was still in the area.

After the search crews were evacuated, three conservation officers were flown in. The RCMP and the C.O.s approached the site with caution, conducted an investigation, then removed the body. George's injuries seemed minor. He had canine puncture wounds to the back of his neck and shoulders. Evidence indicated that there were possibly two separate attacks—the first taking place within ten meters of the moose, and a second attack 25 meters from the moose. It appears that George may have been trying to call his family between the two separate attacks.

It was determined that the attack was a clear-cut case of carcass defense and not a predatory attack. A decision was made not to track and kill the bear based on a consensus of the conservation officers, the RCMP, and the family.

It was a very sad day for many of the residents of the Prince George area.

I received the following from Tony Rathbone in October 6, 2000. The attack took place north of Shuswap Lake in south central B.C:

Hi Gary,

I took the bear course from you through Fisheries and Oceans Canada in New Westminster on June 14, 2000. I have submitted this report to the Conservation Officer Service in Kamloops and turned the hide and skull over to them. They inspected the teeth and felt the bear was in excess of 20 years old.

On the morning of September 30, 2000, my hunting partner, Bill Wyett, and I departed from home to hunt deer in the area of Mt. Fowler. It was a long truck ride on a rough and brushy road followed by a quad ride, and finally, walking to our first hunting area.

We arrived at the Alpine slides around 11:30 A.M. We soon spotted a sow grizzly with a cub feeding on berries approximately 800 metres below us.

After watching the bears for about an hour, we left to hunt an area several miles east known as five-mile flats. We were heading into the Mag fire burn, which burned in 1987. The five-mile flat is a long bench at approximately 5,500 feet elevation, which has a block of timber approximately one mile square in the centre.

Normally, the timber block is a refuge for animals to bed down with very accessible food resources close by in the old burn and logged cut-blocks. We hunted for another three hours, me on foot, and my partner driving the old roads with the quad, checking for any fresh deer crossings.

We met again at 4 P.M. and decided to hunt around the south and west edges of the timber block. We parted at an old washout, with me heading down an old trail, which would eventually join up with the main road (only passable by walking), and this was to be our meeting place around 6:30 P.M.

I proceeded down the old road for about 300 metres. At this point the track runs along the low side of a 20-year-old cut-block. I opted to hunt along the edge of timber, as it looked promising for deer that might be moving out of the trees into the open to feed. The cut-block was covered with a variety of balsam trees one to five metres high, as well as waist-high fireweed, buck brush, and grass.

I noticed two or three bear scats as well as deer and moose sign. I was hunting slowly, stopping every few steps to look and listen. The slight breeze was mostly in my face, blowing downhill from the timber into the cut-block.

After about 300 metres along the trees, I decided to start swinging down towards the road. At approximately 5 P.M., I'd walked 30 yards away from the timber, and I again stopped to look and listen. I heard a small rustling noise to my right and looked in that direction. A large dark colored bear came out from behind some small balsam trees approximately 20 metres away.

Because of the cover, I could see only the bear's back and the top of its head. It proceeded out into an opening without stopping—I automatically yelled out, "Hey." The bear charged at me instantly, and as I was raising my rifle, I yelled again.

With my rifle at my shoulder, it was difficult to line the bear up as it was almost too close to use the scope. I remember thinking just, prior to firing, that it would be impossible to stop something coming that fast. I fired, and the bear's head dropped; he slid to a stop with his nose in the mud.

The bear couldn't move, but was now breathing heavily and growling. I shot again at the back of the neck area. Convinced the bear was mortally wounded, I waited 30 seconds or so then took the walkie-talkie from my pack and called my partner. By this time I was going into shock and had a serious bout of shakes.

I told my partner the story and arranged to be picked up on the road below the cut-block. The bear still hadn't expired, so I carefully walked up and shot it point blank in the back of the neck near the base of the skull.

I turned around and saw my first shell casing on the ground and paced off four moderate strides from where my first shot was fired to where the bear came to rest. There were also two small bushes in my line of fire, which partially blocked my small shooting lane.

From the time I first saw the bear until I fired my first shot, was no more than three to four seconds. I had time to raise my rifle and shoot as the bear charged, and there wouldn't have been time for a second shot.

The bear didn't make any kind of vocalization in these brief seconds as it came after me. I was very shaken by the incident. I started towards the road, but then decided to flag a trail, as someone would probably have to return and investigate the scene.

About 20 minutes later I met my partner on the road. After calming down somewhat, we decided to return to the site to piece together the incident. After inspecting the bear and finding it to be a boar, we carefully walked along the charge path and followed a worn trail towards the timber.

About 40 metres from where the bear had come to rest, a large and semi-decomposing moose lay in some alders. There were a large number of scats around the moose, some with berries and some mixed with moose hair and berries. The bear had apparently dragged the moose about 20 metres to where it now lay. We then left the area.

After arriving home, I phoned the Conservation Officer Service in Vernon and Salmon Arm, without getting an answer. I also tried the 1-800 number from the recording, but had no luck reaching anyone.

The following morning I tried the Conservation Officer Service in Vernon again and found that I'd taken down the 1-800 number incorrectly. I phoned again and told my story to the person at that number.

I felt it was lucky that the bear charged along a semi-open route, as much of the cut block had much thicker brush. I also feel it lucky that I was able to drop a bear that was moving so fast. (I've taken the shotgun-training course on moving bear-shaped targets through my employer Fisheries and Oceans Canada, from Glen Lario in Williams Lake.)

I was carrying a 338 Winchester Magnum with 250-grain bullets. My normal deer gun is in 270 calibre rifle, but fortunately, due to a scope problem on my 270, I was carrying the far more powerful rifle.

My final thoughts about the incident are as follows:

I'd just taken Gary Shelton's Bear Encounter Survival Course in June.

I've hunted extensively in the province for 28 years, having shot a variety of big game animals that were standing, walking, and running. I'm certain that if this incident had occurred early in my hunting career, the outcome would've been devastating. I have no doubt that this bear would've mauled or killed me if I had not killed it.

The bear appeared to be a mature boar in excellent condition with a layer of fat covering most of his body, in some places two to three inches thick.

The moose carcass was surrounded by a screen of alders and small balsam trees which made it impossible to see until within four to six metres.

The moose was a mature bull with antler tips recently broken— possibly indicating a battle with another bull. We speculated that the moose may have been injured prior to its meeting with the grizzly. The bull had large deep wounds in the back of its neck near the base of the skull where the bear had bitten it during the struggle. The moose first fell at the edge of the timber, which was a good ambush site for the bear. And, of course, with the moose rut being in full swing, the bull had cow moose on his mind, not grizzly bears.

There's a very good reason why carcass defense behavior is so dangerous in bears. Bears evolved from a true predatory ancestor to become omnivores that depend primarily on plant foods. But they have retained much of their original carnivore digestive system and supplement their usual diet with animal tissue they've killed or taken from other predators. Their predatory behavior is opportunistic in practice.

During years when plant foods that bears can extract fats from (berries, acorns, beech nuts, pine nuts, etc.) are in short supply, which happens on four- or five-year cycles, obtaining and holding onto large carcasses can mean the difference between life or death during the following hibernating and spring den-emergence period. For this reason, bears have evolved a high level of aggression for defending an important fat source.

Following is an excerpt from my second book, *Bear Attacks - The Deadly Truth.*

If you are hiking through bear country and see a ground distur-bance ahead— as if someone has used a large rake to pile up litter and soil—or if all of a sudden you get a whiff of rotten meat, or if you become aware of many noisy birds in one spot, be suspicious of a carcass nearby. Quietly back up at least 200 meters and leave the area.

If you ever walk up on a bear—particularly a grizzly bear—defend-ing a carcass, and you don't recognize the situation until it's too late, you better have a good defense system along or you might not sur-vive.

6

A WARNING TO HUNTERS

During the last 15 years, the preservationist mind-set has swept across North America with a compelling agenda to reduce, or stop entirely, bear hunting and other types of bear mortalities. As a result of the success of this campaign, bear populations are increasing and expanding their range distribution in many areas. Bears are also being re-introduced into some locations by provincial ministries and state agencies. Hunters will be encountering more bears—and more bears without fear of people.

In the west, hunters will have more chance encounters with grizzly bears while hunting and will have to defend themselves more often against a grizzly trying to enter a hunting camp after meat. There will also be more carcass defense incidents when hunters are handling game meat.

The following stories will demonstrate what hunters must prepare for.

This grizzly attack took place in late September of 1996, about half way between Elkford and Sparwood in southeastern B.C:

Jim Zimmerman and a fellow hunter had spotted the small elk herd the night before. After locating the elk the next morning, they proceeded up the sidehill. When they were within about 200 yards of where they thought the elk might be, they began calling.

A bull responded to their calls, but after about 45 minutes of trying, they couldn't get him to approach or move into an open spot. The two hunters decided to slowly stalk the elk downwind about 100 feet apart.

When they were fairly close, Jim stopped and gave a wimpy call, hoping to get the bull to come towards him. Shortly thereafter, he saw something brown in color move in the brush to his left, which he assumed was an elk.

All of a sudden, a large grizzly stood up on its hind legs and looked directly at Jim. Jim yelled, "Grizzly!" to inform his partner of what was standing before him. Instantly, the bear lunged three times in Jim's direction. It was within six yards when he got the first shot off.

When the bullet struck the bear in the left side of the neck, its right paw shot out and swiped a four-inch lodge pole pine, snapping it off. The grizzly hesitated for less than a second, regained its footing, and then came again with its body turned slightly sideways.

The second bullet hit the right side of the neck, which turned the bear sideways; it then turned across the sidehill and started running towards Jim's hunting partner. His third shot staggered the animal and caused it to veer downhill below the other hunter. As the bear disappeared, they could hear the elk taking off.

The two hunters came together in a small clearing, and after about five minutes, they followed up on the bear. It was only 35 yards downhill, stone dead. The big male measured 6' 7" nose to tail, but weighed only about 500 pounds, as it was very thin.

Jim states that there was a poor berry crop that year. He said the bear was probably stalking the elk by sound, but clearly saw Jim and knew what he was. He believes the attack was predatory.

This story comes from Rick Stickle of Healy, Alaska:

In 1985, I was hunting up Moody Creek, which is behind and to the east of Dora Mountain. This area is accessible by a five- to six-hour horseback ride. It's extremely rugged, with very tall mountains and a lot of spruce and willow trees. In the valleys, it's perfect sheep, moose, caribou, and bear country, although it's a fairly narrow valley downstream by the cabin where we stay. (This is a very beautiful little cabin, built in 1924 by Dr. McClowery.) The valley widens considerably farther upstream. Earlier that morning, my friend and I had bagged a 38-inch bull moose for our freezers (just the right size for packing out, not too big and not too small). As you probably know, it can become quite messy cleaning an animal of this size. By the time we returned to the cabin with the moose and hung the quarters under cover in case of rain, it was late evening. At this point, Doug, my partner, proceeded into the cabin to round up something to eat. But all I could think of was heading for the river to take a quick bath as I always manage to get blood all over myself. I shed my clothing except for long-handled underwear, bundled it all up, and walked to the river, armed only with a bar of soap. Rarely do I have my gun any where except by my side, but this time I left it behind.

It's approximately 20 yards to the edge of the river channel from the cabin, and unless it's storming, the water is only thigh deep. I had advanced about 50 yards from the cabin up along the river bed when out of the corner of my eye I caught a glimpse of something following parallel to me. I instantly froze behind a thick willow bush, but was still only half concealed. It was a silver tip grizzly bear, no more than 30 feet away. He had a black body with a light blond hump. His ears were back, and he started clacking his teeth together, looking directly at me. He was swinging his head back and forth, and would act like he was going to walk away, then turn back, like he was daring me to run. At this point I decided I'd rather take my chances with a dash to the cabin than try to bluff him out. When he turned again like he was going to leave, I made my move. I slowly backed up until I was completely hidden behind the willow bush, then broke into a run. I just about fell down by tripping over my shoe laces as I hollered for Doug to grab the guns and then yelled, "Bear, bear." I managed to get within 20 feet of the cabin door before Doug exploded out of the cabin, tossing my rifle at me. While wheeling around and jacking a shell into the chamber, I fully expected to be hit by the bear at any second. (Doug later told me that the bear was just about to clobber me when he came out the door, but it turned and fled as soon as it saw him.)

This was just too close of a call, and we both knew that we'd sooner or later have problems with this bear coming after our moose. We decided we needed to kill him for our own safety—after all, it was bear season, and we both had grizzly tags.

We eased into the riverbed to look for him, but he seemed to have disappeared. All of a sudden, to Doug's left, was the bear. He was just standing looking at us, with no intentions of leaving. Doug shot first, and I followed up with two shots. (I guess I was still pretty upset about almost messing my pants.)

The close call with the bear really did scare me; I've had a few previous encounters, but none that close. After the kill, we measured the bear to seven feet four inches; it had colored claws. The bear had at least two inches of fat on his back and rump, so we knew he was in prime condition for hibernation.

———

I've known Don Vallerga and Gord Hannas for years. It was several weeks after I first heard about this attack before I knew who was involved:

LOCAL MEN SURVIVE GRIZZLY ATTACK
By Angie Mindus
Williams Lake Tribune Staff Writer
Tuesday, September 29, 1998

Two Williams Lake men say they're lucky to have escaped with their lives after being attacked by a grizzly bear north of Fort St. John last week.

Gord Hannas, an investment dealer with Money Watch Consultants, and Don Vallerga, a sales rep for Lake City Ford, encountered the 450-pound sow and her two cubs while hunting for elk in the Sikanni Chief River watershed area the morning of September 21st.

"If it hadn't have happened in the sequence it did, we'd be dead," says Vallerga, who was knocked unconscious during the attack. "Only teamwork saved our lives."

Vallerga and Hannas recall walking along a grassy trail surrounded by willows and small trees shortly after 8 a.m. the fateful Monday morning.

The men were several hundred yards away from their ATV's and many kilometres from base camp when, Vallerga says, he noticed movement in the nearby shrubs.

Vallerga tapped his hunting partner on the shoulder and pointed out the sow and cubs who were walking parallel with the hunters.

As they've done in the past to avoid bear encounters, Vallerga says they yelled at the bears.

"She never looked up at us once. That's what I thought was so strange," Vallerga says of the grizzly's reaction.

"We gave them ample chance to go away," says Hannas, who was later mauled by the bear.

In the blink of an eye, one of the cubs turned and ran directly at Vallerga, veering off to the right just before him. Unfortunately, the sow grizzly charging behind her cub didn't change her course of direction.

"I don't know whether it (the gunshot) hit her or not, but she didn't stop," Vallerga remembers before being knocked out by the charging grizzly.

Hannas, meanwhile, could only stand as a witness during the frightening attack against his friend.

"I remember very clearly thinking I can't shoot because Don is underneath the bear," Hannas said. While about 30 feet away, Hannas took a step towards the bear to get at a better angle, knelt on one knee and positioned his gun as the bear turned her attention

towards him.

Hannas remembers thinking, "I'm only going to get one shot and I better make it count."

Hannas was able to get one shot off, wounding the grizzly in the chest before the weight of the bear sent him and his gun sailing through the air.

"When I tried to get up she had my arm in her mouth."

While Hannas fought to free his arm from the grizzly's powerful jaws, Vallerga says he woke up wondering where the bear was.

"Don't shoot! She's got me," Hannas yelled to Vallerga.

Hannas was able to wrestle himself away from the bear and run towards a tree before the sow caught up to him again.

"She grabbed my leg and yanked me right off my feet."

Once again Hannas was engaged in the fight of his life, struggling face-to-face with the bear and even, at one point, giving her a big bear-hug to pull her off his leg.

"They were tangled up. I couldn't shoot," Vallerga says.

While the bear was on its back, Hannas took a chance and pushed off the bear, rolling several times to get away.

"As I was rolling I yelled 'I'm clear! Shoot, shoot, shoot'," Hannas says.

Poised and ready, Vallerga shot the grizzly three times.

Hannas ended the battle with one more shot.

"I had no choice," Hannas says of the outcome. "Either that bear was going to kill me or I was going to kill it."

Hannas used duct tape to apply pressure to the deep wounds on his right leg before making the 15-kilometre trek by foot and ATV to where crews were working on a gas well.

Hannas was transported by air ambulance to Fort St. John where he was treated for his injuries while Vallerga collected their gear and drove out.

"Reality didn't set in until after Gord was airlifted," Vallerga says of the experience. "It was quite an ordeal."

Hannas is still recovering from his injuries and chalks up the encounter to being at the wrong place at the right time.

One thing for sure, they're both grateful to have been together at the time of the attack.

"It worked both ways, I saved him and he saved me."

This letter from Dave Atkinson is typical of many I receive each year. I've done a small amount of editing to save space:

Mr. Gary Shelton,
   I am writing to thank you for publishing your two books on bear encounters. I was loaned your second book, last year. After my wife and I read it, we purchased our own copy so all our family could read it. Recently, while I was away hunting, my wife purchased your first book, *Bear Encounter Survival Guide*. I've now also read it.
   I am a 58-year-old hunter and have hunted most of my life. My hunting partner, George Taylor, is 63 years old, and for the past nine years we've hunted together here in the Okanagan and in many other areas of the province. Last year, and again this year, I've taken a shotgun with slugs as a camp protection gun. Well, a little preparation paid off this fall.
   We were hunting 29 kilometers due east of Yahk, B.C. We had our 16-foot holiday trailer set up in the B.C. Forest Service Hart Creek Campsite. The campsite is about one kilometer north of the B.C./Montana border. There were two other hunters in the campground when we arrived on October 7, 1999. One pulled out October 8th, the other, Roy Churchill, was still there when we left October 14th.

   We were hunting deer and also hoped for a chance at a six-point bull elk. George shot a whitetail deer on October 9th, and we used Roy's quad to lift it onto our meat pole. On October 11th, a storm *blew through late in the day, so we were hoping for a good hunt the next day.*

Cool, rainy weather greeted us at 6 A.M. as we headed out. The rain turned to snow at the 3,500-foot level. I was fortunate and took a mule deer buck at 8:05 A.M., about 20 kilometers northwest of camp. On our way back to camp we had to slow down to let a bear get off the road. It really didn't care about us driving beside it and taking its picture at 30 feet; it was a small grizzly.

After arriving back at camp at 10:40, we parked the pickup beside our trailer. I went and changed clothes as I was soaking wet. When I came out of the trailer, I unlocked my shotgun, loaded it with slugs, and leaned it against a tree. We didn't hang the mule deer, as we were waiting for our neighbor Roy to return and use his quad again, so we both went about doing camp chores.

I went over to Roy's fire pit to split wood about 30 yards away, and George was outside organizing things in the back of the truck. I had just finished splitting an armful of kindling and was arranging it for a fire when George yelled, "Bear."

I looked at George and saw that he was looking behind me. I glanced back and saw a bear coming from behind Roy's camper. Its ears were flat against the head and it was walking methodically towards me. I exited the fire pit area, scattering kindling on my way—I heard a shot. I don't recall running to the trailer, but I got there pretty quickly because as George was shooting the bear the second time with the shotgun, I also shot it with my 300 Winchester Magnum rifle. I'd left it leaning against our trailer with the magazine clip in it.

Satisfied the bear was down, we both looked around to make sure it was alone. We waited about five minutes and then approached the bear. It was dead; it appeared to be the same small grizzly we'd passed on the road a half hour earlier. It had a radio on its left ear, indicating that the Montana Wildlife Department had tagged it.

I suggested to George that we both write out statements regarding what happened, in case the conservation officers came while we were out hunting, and it would be better to keep the facts straight as stories change with each telling.

We finished our statements, and Roy returned to camp and lifted up my deer. I skinned it while George made lunch. At 12:30 P.M. we headed into Yahk to call the Conservation Officer Service in Creston. My call was answered with a recording, so I gave my name and all the details of the incident, and asked for the C.O.s to come to our camp.

Let me tell you, it was one hell of an adrenaline high, and it took a whole 24 hours to come down. That night I hardly slept, as I got

to thinking, 'If I hadn't loaded the shotgun and put it outside'; 'If George hadn't looked up at the right time to see the bear going behind Roy's camper towards me'; 'If George hadn't been a very good shot, as he only had a three-yard wide shooting lane to shoot the bear'. . . I guess it just wasn't my time.

The C.O.s arrived at 5 P.M. After introductions, one C.O., James, said they had some questions to ask us. At this point I handed him our written statements. As James read them, the other C.O., Arnold, asked us to walk him through the event. I went and stood at the fire pit, and George indicated where he was when he saw the bear, where the gun was, and where he shot from.

Conservation Officer Arnold walked over and paced the distance from the fire pit to the bear's claw prints—8 1/2 yards. After the C.O.s talked privately for a minute, they stated it was a clear case of self defense and backed their truck up to load up the bear. It was a 250-pound female in good condition.

That evening over supper, Roy said he'd met the C.O.s on the road and they had mentioned that we were a couple of lucky boys; had the bear advanced a couple more steps, she probably would've pounced on me.

I phoned the Conservation Officer Service in Creston on October 29th, at 9 A.M., and spoke to Arnold and asked a few questions *regarding the bear. They had contacted the Montana authorities and found out the bear was three years old, and had been snared and tagged in May of 1999. Arnold then told me they'd returned the radio and hide to the Montana people. He also stated that if the current government policy on bear hunting continues, he expects some severe maulings or killings in the near future, as bears have lost their fear of man and there is getting to be more of them.*

I'm fairly well convinced that this bear had decided to make lunch out of me. She showed no fear of us on the road, and she must've heard us making noise around our camp. I was chopping wood, and George was banging around the truck—yet she came straight into our camp.

MAN DIES AFTER MAULING
Bear attack on hunter is second of week
By Karen Aho
Anchorage Daily News reporter
Thursday, November 4, 1999

An Anchorage man hunting deer near Kodiak Island was mauled by a brown bear and died, apparently after struggling through thick brush in an attempt to reach his hunting party.

The body of Ned Rasmussen, 53, was found at the bottom of a steep sidehill on Uganik Island on Wednesday, two days after his companions last saw him, Alaska State Troopers said.

It was unclear whether Rasmussen died from his wounds or from exposure to the cold, troopers said. Temperatures dipped into the teens Monday and Tuesday night.

Authorities think Rasmussen shot and wounded the bear. Searchers in a helicopter Tuesday flushed an injured Kodiak brown bear and two cubs from brush close to where his body was later found. The sow appeared to have an injured leg and was bleeding from the shoulder, Trooper Sgt. Darlene Turner said.

Troopers have warned area guides, but did not know whether state game officials planned to find the bear and kill it.

The bear attack is the second this week in the Kodiak Archipelago, where bears are facing dire conditions this year. In the other attack, Gene Moe, 68, of Anchorage was wounded Monday when a bear attacked him as he butchered a deer on Raspberry Island.

Berry production in the Kodiak area was poor this year, said Larry Van Daele, area wildlife biologist with the state Department of Fish and Game. Several salmon runs were weak. And deer populations shrunk 30 percent after last year's bad winter.

As a result, the islands' thousands of bears are having trouble find-ing food.

"We've got some hungry bears out there this year," Van Daele said. "What's amazing is that the bears don't do more damage."

Rasmussen's three hunting companions told authorities they last saw Rasmussen alone on a ridge top in the vicinity of a grizzly about 4 p.m. Monday. About 4:30 p.m. they heard a gunshot.

They began looking for Rasmussen the next morning, after he failed to return to their hunting cabin. By noon Tuesday they had alerted the U.S. Coast Guard by activating an electronic distress beacon.

The Coast Guard searched late into the night Tuesday using an infrared sensor that detects body heat, and flew in rescuers and search dogs to resume the search early Wednesday morning.

Searchers found Rasmussen's loaded rifle on the ridge Wednesday and his hat and some blood about 50 yards away. About a half-mile down the sidehill, on the other end of a steep dropoff, a dog picked up a blood trail and found Rasmussen's body nearly concealed in dense alder underbrush.

"The person who had the dog didn't see him that well," Coast Guard Chief Petty Officer Tod Lyons said. "She happened to glance in on a second tick and saw the leg."

The body was about a mile from the U.S. Forest Service cabin he had rented with his friends.

"He would have been heading downhill toward the cabin, going to the low area," Turner said. "My guess is he was coming down off the mountain."

Rasmussen knew the area well, his friends said. A highly experi-enced outdoorsman, he had been hunting deer on the island about 15 years, many times on an annual outing with the same group he was with this week.

"He knew that mountain," friend Greg Svendsen said. "That bear had to have gotten a hold of him and did something to him that killed him. Whether it killed him right away . . ."

Turner wouldn't describe Rasmussen's wounds but said they were consistent with those from a large animal. An autopsy is scheduled for today in Anchorage to determine the cause of death.

Rasmussen was assistant director of the Anchorage office of the federal Center for Disease Control and Prevention. He worked at the Alaska Native Medical Center.

He hunted every year and played hockey and tennis.

He leaves a wife, Diane, and two grown daughters.

Daily News reporter Craig Medred and The Associated Press con-tributed to this story.

I met Sam Pellegrino in the spring of 1999 when he and a hunting partner came to Bella Coola to hunt grizzly bear. He told me about a friend who'd been attacked by a grizzly in the fall of 1996 while hunting in Northern B.C. He said that I needed to document the story, because it was a doozy.

I didn't get an opportunity to stop in North Vancouver and look up Sam's friend, Marcel Gregori, during my training trips, but in the fall of 2000, Sam returned to this area to hunt mountain goats and had Marcel with him.

We sat down at my dining room table in the early afternoon of Sunday, October 8th.

Marcel was born and raised in Switzerland and came to Canada in 1987. He worked as a manager of a fish canning business for six years. Next he bought a retail fish outlet and operated a commercial crab boat. He's also worked as an assistant guide and recently bought a guide-outfitting operation in the East Kootenay Mountains.

I asked Marcel if he'd had any grizzly incidents previous to the attack. He said that in 1988 he killed a grizzly in self-defense near the Racing River. It all started when he overheard a conversation between hunters about a wounded moose. He decided to walk into the area the hunters had mentioned to find the moose and finish it off. As he was hiking through the timber looking for the moose, he heard a large number of ravens squawking and chattering ahead of him. He approached carefully, looking and listening, and suddenly a grizzly charged him. He was able to kill it before it made contact.

Close by was the wounded moose, which was now dead. Marcel had a grizzly tag so he skinned out the bear and kept it. Later on, he decided that he would never again walk up on a flock of squawking ravens.

In the latter part of September 1996, Marcel drove up to Fort Nelson, B.C., and flew southwest to Kluachesi Lake. He was supposed to be met by a pack-outfitter with horses, but the pilot told him that the packer would be delayed for two days. There was no one else on the lake when Marcel put his gear in one of the packer's tents.

The next morning Marcel, walked for three hours up into the alpine, hunted for the day, and shot a bull elk at about 6 P.M. He field dressed the animal and hiked back to camp. The next day Marcel hunted for moose as he headed back to the elk—he saw a legal bull, but passed it up and filmed it instead. At about noon, he arrived at the elk carcass. He butchered it, deboned it, and hung the pieces in cheese cloth, then back to camp he went.

The packer arrived the following morning with seven horses and a wrangler. The elk meat was packed back to camp and hung, then the whole outfit headed off on a six-hour ride to sheep camp.

Marcel took a stone sheep within the first couple of days, so they closed up the spike camp and headed back to Kluachesi. When they arrived, they found the camp destroyed by a grizzly bear. About a quarter of the elk had been removed from the cache platform. They knew that the bear was still close by. During the night, as it started to snow, the bear came back, but was chased off by the dog.

The next morning, Lukas, the wrangler, accompanied Marcel as he hunted for moose. They saw several bulls, but couldn't stalk up on any of them.

Marcel hunted alone the next day and told Lukas that he was going back to the same area they'd hunted the day before. He was carrying a 7 mm magnum with 165-grain bullets. It was September 28th.

By afternoon it was a nice, calm, beautiful day, but there was a feel of changing weather in the air. Marcel was walking up a slightly sloping area through a large, brushy burn. He was surrounded by small, dead, standing trees. As he stepped up on a short stump and started glassing the sidehill in front of him, he heard a loud snort and saw a grizzly stand up, then immediately charge toward him. He raised the rifle and shot, but there was no reaction from the bear. Marcel maintained his view through the scope as he quickly worked the action for another round; he knew that if he took his eye away from the scope, he wouldn't find the bear again for the next shot. The animal was whoofing and breaking branches as it raced down through the brush. Just before the bear's chest hit the end of the barrel, Marcel squeezed the trigger—but the gun didn't go off.

'THIS IS IT, I'M GOING TO DIE', surged through his mind. The momentum and impact of the bear against the rifle sent Marcel flying backwards; in a flash the bear rolled its head sideways and bit multiple times into his left thigh before he hit the ground. He felt horrible pain.

Marcel rolled to a face-down position and instinctively placed his hands on the back of his neck. The power and size of the bear was overwhelming—he was completely helpless—the bear had control over his life.

The grizzly ripped and tore at his day-pack, then chewed on his neck. Next it was biting on his skull—the teeth were grinding on the bone; it sounded like eggshells crunching. But there was no more pain; he felt numb. The bear was trying to crush his skull. For a split second Marcel saw his wife and kids, but they quickly faded—then everything went black.

When Marcel came to, his mind couldn't decipher whether he was in a dream or not. 'Am I dreaming; am I dying; is this real'? He slowly moved his hands up and wiped the congealed blood out of his eyes. He was trying to focus on the blurs around him. His jacket and binoculars were covered with blood. The top of his head felt like it was torn open with the brain exposed. 'Is this real?'.

Instantly his mind was flooded: 'THIS IS REAL'. The bear was lying to his left, on its stomach, with its paws outstretched. It was groaning and breathing laboriously. 'I hit the bear', ran through his mind. Marcel was lying on his side; he looked to the right and saw his rifle. He raised slightly as he reached for it, brought it to his side, and worked the action. The bear's head was now up and turning, the lips rolled back as the snarl began—and as their eyes met, BANG! The grizzly's body collapsed flat; it took in a deep breath, then expelled it, then silence. Marcel raised the gun and fired two more times into the air.

(Lukas and the packer figured that Marcel had caught up with his moose when they heard the first shot. They kept working on their chores, but when they heard two more spaced shots a full 15 minutes later, they were suspicious that he was in trouble. Lukas immediately took off in the direction of the gunshots.)

Marcel threw the gun to the side and started checking himself over for damage. He didn't dare touch his head, and he couldn't feel pain anywhere. His right leg seemed to be okay and unbroken. His left leg had open wounds with muscle and fat tissue hanging out. He didn't see any bones protruding, but wasn't sure whether it was broken. He got up carefully to test the leg.

He found a stick and propped it under his right arm, but couldn't find another crutch for the other side. Marcel knew that he had to be found today if he was going to survive, and he had to get out of the brush into an opening where he could be seen.

The torn and bleeding man started to move towards the packers camp on his single crutch. But now the shock was wearing off and the pain was setting in. Within a short distance, it became unbearable. Now he was down on all fours, crawling slowly, wincing with every movement. He was also getting cold and wet.

After an eternity of suffering, Marcel made it to the edge of a small clearing. It was starting to snow. He looked at his watch and saw that it was 3:50 P.M. As he lay there and glanced at his watch every so often, he realized that time had slowed down to a crawl. The blood smell was brutal and making him sick; he fought hard to avoid retching. He was also fighting to keep from passing out.

Marcel was tough, but he had never been a first-aid person, and he didn't know what to do to help himself—he wasn't prepared for the situation. As the snowfall increased, he knew he couldn't survive the night. His only chance was to be found quickly.

5:00 P.M. finally came, and the pain was as bad as ever. If someone didn't arrive before dark, it was over. He decided to muster what energy he had left to call out every so often in case someone was nearby. As he shivered and prayed, he yelled out. But there was only silence.

Every so often Marcel would yell as loud as he could, and finally, after what seemed like hours, he heard a human voice answer. What a wonderful relief it was to hear Lukas calling his name. As the wrangler got closer, Marcel could hear Lukas cursing himself for not going with Marcel.

"How's my head?," the injured man asked. "It's okay, it's okay," was the answer. Marcel still felt as though his skull had been broken open.

Lukas checked his shaking friend over, then took off his jacket and shirt to wrap around Marcel and placed a tourniquet on the bleeding leg. Lukas loaded his rifle and placed it next to Marcel, then took off on a run for help. The nearest people were at a guide-outfitters jack camp. When Lukas arrived at the camp, he explained what had happened. An assistant guide called the main camp and had them radio for a helicopter. As luck would have it, one of the American hunters in camp was a doctor.

The two American hunters and Lukas rushed back to Marcel. As the doctor started bandaging and reassuring his patient, a fire was built, then Lukas and the guide started cutting down snags for a landing pad on firm ground. The men continued to give mental support to Marcel, telling him that he was going to make it and would be fine.

Lukas and the guide went exploring in the direction where the attack took place. After they returned, Marcel could hear them saying that they had found the rifle, the pack, and the dead bear. And not far away, they had also found a moose carcass. Now everyone understood why the bear had attacked.

When the helicopter landed, the medics loaded Marcel on a stretcher, then cut off his boots and some of his clothing. As the machine lifted off, Marcel felt relieved, like he was going to survive the ordeal. But en route, he heard someone saying, "I've got a weak pulse, I've got a weak pulse." Then he wasn't so sure whether he was going to make it or not—he knew that he'd lost a lot of blood.

At the airport, he was placed into an ambulance and suffered a 20-minute bumpy ride to the hospital, where a surgical team was waiting for him. He was immediately given morphine, and as his head was being washed, he was given more. After stitching up his scalp, the doctors turned their attention to his leg, and two hours later he was being wheeled into a room. Small portions of the wounds had been left open to drain. The lights were dim, and the nurse's voice was soft; Marcel now felt safe, and the morphine had delivered him to cloud nine.

The RCMP came later that night to interview him about the attack. Before falling asleep, Marcel had decided that he would never hunt again. The next day a conservation officer stopped in to obtain information for his report.

It had turned cold and snowed for 48 hours straight. What luck it was to have survived the attack in the first place, and then to have gotten out in time. Marcel was thankful for all the people that helped and particularly thankful for Lukas's effort and determination to save him.

By the second night in the hospital, Marcel was thinking that maybe he would do a little hunting in the future, and by the time he flew home to North Vancouver, he realized that hunting was a major part of his life and that he'd continue to hunt, but very carefully.

During the six days that Marcel was in hospital, Lukas gathered up his gear and brought it out, and had the sheep and elk flown to Fort Nelson for butchering. Lukas was nice enough to drive Marcel's pickup down to North Vancouver for him with the meat and gear aboard.

Marcel didn't talk much about the incident during his recovery at home. But the newspapers found out about the attack, and soon the story was well-known in the Lower Mainland. Shortly thereafter he received several harassment calls where the parties stated that it was unfair that he'd killed the bear because it was just acting naturally, and it was too bad it didn't turn out the other way around.

Looking toward where the attact took place.

The wounded grizzly lay only a few feet away from Marcel while he was unconscious.

Marcel returned to the location of the attack several years later and found the moose bones.   Courtesy Marcel Gregori.

Hunters must be very diligent when pursuing game to make sure they don't become a victim of a bear attack. In areas where grizzly bears may be encountered, hunters should carry a rifle of at least 300 magnum power no matter what size game they're after. Hunters on the coast of B.C. and Alaska should consider the 338 Winchester Magnum as the minimum firepower to carry even if they are hunting Blacktail Deer. Following are a set of guidelines I developed in 1998 for B.C. hunters and guide outfitters:

*Keeping a clean camp is very important. If you have meat in camp, expect to have a nighttime visitor, and possibly even a day-time visitor. In those areas where grizzlies have learned to search for gut piles and are aggressively challenging hunters for animal carcasses, expect to have visits from bears even when there is no meat in camp.

*Erect meat poles 50 to 100 yards from camp in an open area with good visibility from tent openings. Go to the trouble of hanging your quarters high enough that grizzlies cannot reach them (12').

*Bow hunters should always carry two cans of bear spray, one on each hip, in holsters. Rifle hunters should consider the same, as you could lose your rifle during a struggle with a bear.

*When using a call to attract game, expect to have a predator stalk you from any direction, especially while wearing camouflage clothing.

*If you see a bear that is unaware of you, quietly leave the area if you feel threatened. Don't yell at a bear that has given an aggressive signal and is trying to locate you. It could trigger an attack.

*In some areas, grizzlies are responding to gunshots. It's quite possible that a bear could show up the same time you do, or shortly after killing an animal, or any time thereafter. I believe that it takes individual grizzly bears eight to ten years to learn what gunshots mean, and this behavior would most likely begin only in areas where large numbers of ungulates are being killed by hunters and where grizzlies have developed the 'gut-pile search behavior'.

*In areas where significant conflict is taking place with grizzly bears, hunters should stop their hunting activities in the afternoon, so that any game animal killed can be removed to camp before night-fall.

*Hunters must have firearms ready for defense against bears whenever approaching downed game, field dressing game, and packing meat. Remove all meat as soon as possible. If you have to leave meat overnight, move it to an open area away from the rumen, if possible. Then attach surveyor ribbon from each piece to the limb of a tree, or to the top of brush, so you can detect if the ribbon is broken by using binoculars from at least 200 yards distance. Leaving an article of clothing on meat overnight doesn't deter bears in B.C. any more like it used to.

*When approaching downed game that has been left overnight, or even for part of a day, do so carefully with at least two people. If possible, approach from uphill so you can have a good look around. Have firearms ready for defense, and start making loud noises at the 200-yard range, but be ready for a charging bear. Sometimes a bear will move a carcass from where it was left. Therefore, a bear could charge from a different direction than you are expecting.

*Grizzlies will often use aggressive displays when trying to take a carcass from hunters. But a grizzly could also quietly stalk hunters who are using a call, field dressing an animal, or packing meat, and then attack from close range as a predator.

*Do not argue with a grizzly bear over a carcass unless you have a large insurance policy and your wife is tired of you. Retreat slowly with your firearm ready when confronted by a bear. But do not retreat if you feel it would lessen your ability for defense. You have the right to defend yourself against a dangerous animal.

*When two or more hunters have rounds chambered during a bear encounter, extreme safety caution must be employed to prevent an accidental discharge that could kill someone. Keep barrels straight up unless pointing at the bear, and remove chambered rounds as soon as the danger is over.

*Even though black bears are usually less aggressive than grizzlies, treat them with the same respect, as some black bears are very dangerous when meat is involved.

*If you are forced to kill a bear, do not remove any parts from the bear, and inform the proper authorities as soon as possible.

7

SPRAY DEFENSE

This chapter is intended to add to the spray information in my two previous books. We must continually analyze this subject to gain a better understanding of how to use bear sprays more effectively.

There are many parks in North America where people can't carry firearms, and there are many people who wouldn't carry a gun even if allowed. Based on my research, the 'play-dead with a grizzly and fight-back with a black bear' strategy has had a low success rate since about 1990. Firearms are successful against bears about 95 percent of the time (not including grizzly attacks on hunters), and sprays about 75 percent of the time. You must have a defense system when exposed to bears if you want a fighting chance of surviving an attack.

The following spray defense against a black bear is similar to many anecdotal accounts I've heard. It happened to Brad Eddy in North Central B.C. and involves what was most likely a predatory bear:

The incident occurred near the Ospika Arm of Williston Lake on May 8, 1996, at approximately 11:00 A.M. I was working roughly 150 meters from my partner (Dana Robichaud) and had just climbed a creek bank when I noticed a movement to my left. When I turned, I saw a black bear about 40 meters away. The bear rushed toward me until it was at 20 meters. I froze for a second, yelled at it, and took a couple of steps backward. The bear had paused briefly, and I started to take my bear spray out of my vest. Again, the bear started to come toward me, but much more slowly than the first time. When I unfastened the velcro strap on my spray holster, the bear paused again. By the time I had my spray ready to fire, the bear was only about seven meters away. The first shot seemed to travel more toward the bear's front paws, but appeared to be effective. The bear turned and started to move away. I fired again, but the bear was moving away from me, and it probably didn't accomplish anything. The bear continued to retreat, coughing and blowing through its nose, and when I felt it was safe to do so, I hurried back to my partner. There was no sign of the bear for the remainder of the day.

The above account shows the type of success that often happens with spray, but in this chapter I'm going to concentrate on spray events that go wrong, or partially wrong, so we can see the complexities of using sprays against bears.

———

In the third week of June 1999, I heard vague details from a friend about a grizzly bear attack in the Yukon. I put a note to myself in my research file to contact *The Yukon News* in Whitehorse during July. The Yukon News has been very helpful in making people aware of my publications and in supplying me with bear attack news stories. They don't sensationalize bear attacks, nor do they downplay them.

In the second week of July, I received an envelope in the mail containing a newspaper article about the attack with a note written in the margin that said: Gary, a letter will follow. Ole.

I sent a short letter to Ole (Bruce D. Ohlson) stating I would very much like to document his story for my next book because this type of attack is one of the most difficult to survive. I also explained I was just leaving on vacation and would call him when I got back.

When my wife and I returned home from the western states, a letter from Ole was in my large stack of mail. His letter stated that when he was in Whitehorse waiting for his friend Phil to get out of the hospital, he came across a copy of my second book in the Fireweed Bookstore and read it. Later, he also visited my web site for additional information.

Ole's letter contained a description of what took place during the attack. Over the next few months, I talked to him several times on the phone, and he sent me a second letter with more details. The following is in Ole's own words:

Phillippe Vermeyen and I rented a canoe from Up North Boat and Canoe Rentals in Whitehorse, Yukon. We put in at Johnson's Crossing on May 28, 1999. Our plan was to canoe down the Teslin River to its confluence with the Yukon River, then on down to Circle City, Alaska—a distance of roughly 800 miles. We had four weeks for our adventure.

I had taught canoeing as the waterfront director in a boy scout camp and had worked the summer of 1992 as a whitewater raft guide on the New River in West Virginia. Although this was our first trip in a canoe on a major northern river, each of us had spent significant time visiting and working in Alaska and the Yukon.

I drove commercial bus tours from the Lower 48 to Alaska during the mid-1980s and had led an American Youth Hostels van tour of Alaska. On my own, I had bicycled thousands of miles throughout Alaska, the Yukon, and Northern British Columbia on two major bicycle trips. Phil had worked as a tour guide in Alaska for seven summers, and had traveled, hiked, and biked in the north on his own many times. We both knew how to handle ourselves in the wilderness; we knew what we were getting into. Phil was the brains of the operation as he had done the major planning and was the map reader. I had made the reservations and was the boat steerer. On a lark, I had purchased a can of Counter Assault bear spray in Whitehorse the day before we put in.

The preceding page shows Ole in the front of the canoe. Above, is a sweeping view of the Yukon River.

The fully loaded canoe at a rest stop. On the next page, Phil is setting up camp.

In the evening of our 13th day on the river, we landed and camped on Halfway Island. Someone had dug steps up a six-foot cut-bank and removed about a half-dozen trees for a clearing, but the site hadn't been used very much. Phil placed his tent by the river; I pitched mine 30 feet back in the timber. Our two tents and a small fire ring about 20 feet from the bank formed an equilateral triangle. After dinner we wrapped our 80-pound food stash in a plastic tarp and placed it about 60 feet downriver from Phil's tent.

At 5:30 A.M. the next morning, I was awakened by the sound of Phil yelling, "Bear in camp! Bear in camp!" I looked out through the screen door of my tent and saw an adult grizzly step back from Phil's tent, rear up on its hind legs, turn completely around 360 degrees, then fall forward onto the tent. Phil began yelling, "Ole, get him off me! Get him off me!"

I grabbed the bear spray from the wall pocket of my tent, peeled off the cellophane, pulled out the pin, unzipped the door, pulled on my shoes, and quickly walked the 30 feet to Phil and the bear. Phil was lying face-down on the ground and not moving. The bear was *holding him down with one forepaw and biting him. As I halted at three feet distance, the bear turned its head and looked at me. I extended my arm and gave it a two-second blast of spray; my mind was flooded with the thought, 'This might be the day I die'.*

The bear stepped back and released Phil. It was a grizzly all right; its head was massive. As Phil scampered away, the bear's body recoiled, and just as it was going to spring after him, I intercepted it with another dose of hot liquid pepper. The grizzly stopped, but didn't back off. We were now facing each other, just the two of us. I could see the red particles of the spray on the bear's face, but it wasn't choking or gasping, nor was it showing any anger. 'What should I do now?' went through my mind. I gave him another shot of spray, again at a distance of three feet, but there was no reaction. Five seconds later, I released the fourth blast; I could see the stream of red hitting him in the face. The bear still didn't back off. The can was now feeling awfully light. I turned and walked back to my tent where Phil was. I gave him a hug and said, "I'm glad you're still on you're feet."

The grizzly walked over to the fire circle, stood up on its hind legs, then started swaying back and forth looking at us. I walked about half way to it, raised my arms and said, "Go away," in a deep voice. Even at 15 feet, the animal towered over me. I figured there was one spray blast left, and thought I better save it until the bear was chewing on me.

The bear turned and dropped to all fours, then walked back to the wreckage of Phil's tent. It shot a glance at me over its shoulder; I again urged it to depart, and it ambled upstream along the top of the cut-bank.

I walked back to Phil and examined his wounds. Blood was oozing, but not spurting. "Buddy, we've got to get out of here," I said. Phil ran for the canoe as I grabbed my clothes bag and quickly followed. We untied and shoved off. To say that we were uncoordinated as we paddled down the Yukon would be an understatement. We landed about a half-mile downstream on the other side of the river.

I bandaged Phil's injuries as best I could. He had puncture wounds on his left side just above the pelvis, and on the rib-cage. I then helped him into my wool pants and polypro jacket. I pulled on shorts and a T-shirt. We were both trembling violently, more from the adrenaline than the temperature. We were about 100 miles from Dawson City, the closest civilization downstream that we knew of. All we had was the gear we had left in the canoe the night before—which wasn't much. Phil wanted to return to the camp. "We've got nothing," he complained. "No map, no knife, no food, no matches—

nothing."

I wouldn't hear of it. "We aren't going back to that camp without a gun." I forced the issue. We got back in the canoe and headed north. Of the two of us, Phil is by far the better map reader. He reads maps for pleasure and had done the major planning for the trip. From his position, lying on the bottom of the canoe, he explained what he remembered from the map about the route ahead of us. He said he didn't expect to remain conscious for the 24 hours he figured it would take us to get to Dawson City.

Roughly six miles down stream I spotted a boat pulled up on the bank. We knew that two Japanese men were ahead of us on the river. I thought that we might be able to get some food from them and a look at their map. The camp turned out to be owned and occupied by Linda Taylor of Dawson City. She was spending the summer with some of her children and grandchildren at her cabin on the confluence of Kirkman Creek. She immediately radioed for a helicopter; our prayers had been answered.

Ole explained the following in his second letter:

There is a difference between the story I have given you and what was recorded by the Yukon Conservation Officer [C.O.] that investigated the incident. The officer flew back to Kirkman Creek in the helicopter that evacuated Phil. We then flew up to Halfway Island and searched for the bear until the chopper was getting low on fuel. We landed at the camp site and the C.O. videotaped me walking around describing what had happened earlier that morning.

During the interview I calmly and confidently related the morning's adventure. I thought I had a handle on things, but it turned out to be an unedited series of snapshots of the action. After dropping me back at Kirkman Creek, the C.O. flew up the river and posted warning signs.

While he was gone, I started working through the sequence of events of the bear attack in my mind. I began to realize that I had related many of the events in the wrong order, and I had entirely blanked out the part where Phil was under the bear. When the conservation officer came back by Kirkman Creek that evening, I told him that I wanted to correct some aspects of the story. But, unfortunately, he stated that he would prefer to stick with the original report.

I was somewhat spooked by the whole incident and tempted to abandon the canoe and gear and ask for a ride out in the helicopter, but thought better of it. The next morning I left at 4:00 A.M. and paddled down to Dawson City. It was a long, lonely day.

So there you have it; my best recollections of the most traumatic day of my life. Except that the attack happened at all, we came out of it smelling like roses. It took only 20 stitches to close Phil's wounds, but they kept him in the hospital for a week on intravenous antibiotics. The problem was that the bear's teeth had pinched up the skin and connected. He had holes eight inches apart that drained as one. The doctor's main concern was infection. The teeth had just missed one of his lungs and one of his kidneys. Had either been hit, he would have bled to death before we could have made it to a hospital capable of stopping the bleeding.

I called Ole again on December 22nd to clarify some points. I asked him a series of questions:

1. Why were you carrying bear spray?

Ole explained that while on an around-the-world bicycle tour several years before, and while camped at Haines Junction in the Yukon, a bear entered his camp during the night, which scared him and his camp mate. The next day his partner went to a store and bought a bear banger and a can of spray. Also, just before this trip, he had read a chapter in a bear book that suggested having a knife and a can of spray in your tent while camped in bear country. Ole had bought the spray the day before leaving on their canoe trip.

2. Why were you sleeping in separate tents?

Ole responded that Phil had just flown in from France after leading a three-week hike for the Appalachian Mountain Club, and he had just ferried up the Alaska marine highway. When they met in Whitehorse and rented the canoe, they arrived there each with a small size tent.

3. Do you realize that having separate tents played a major role in your survival?

Yes, if we had been in the same tent when the bear did the body-slam onto the tent, or if it had attacked me first, things would have turned out completely different.

4. Did the bear make any noise or show any anger at any time?

No, it didn't. The best way to describe its demeanor was that it seemed to be puzzled by us and what was going on.

It took a while to catch up with Phil Vermeyen, but on the evening of January 13, 2000, I interviewed him by telephone at his home in Vista, California.

Phil explained that he woke up with a start and when he looked at the side of the tent, he could see the outline of a bear. He could tell it was only about a yard away. As he started yelling to wake Ole, the animal turned its head and looked in his direction, then stepped forward and started biting the tent.

Phil moved back as the bear explored the side of the tent. All of a sudden the bear stood up on its hind legs and fell onto the tent. Phil was then bitten on the elbow. The ensuing struggle created a hole that Phil quickly ripped larger so he could escape. But as he fought his way out of the tent, the grizzly pinned him down with a front paw and started to work on his back. Once the bear got blood in its mouth, it seemed to turn more serious about what it was doing. Phil received deep bites to his lower and middle back. The bear wasn't showing any anger—it seemed to be in the process of chewing and tasting him.

Suddenly, Phil was aware that Ole was spraying the grizzly—he could hear and smell the spray. The bear backed up and took its foot off him. Phil jumped up and raced over to Ole's tent. The next thing Phil saw was the bear moving off.

Phil stated he has no memory of the events between running to Ole's tent and the bear leaving. He didn't know until later that Ole sprayed the grizzly multiple times before it left.

I asked Phil if he got any spray on him, and he said that when he was lying in the canoe and Ole was walking up to the camp at Kirkman Creek, he started sweating, and spray from his forehead ran into his eyes and blinded him. He also remembers that his arms were stinging from the spray during the flight to the hospital.

Ole later recalled that his wrist stung for part of the afternoon because of the spray.

The official report by Conservation Officer Russell Hunter was very thorough and lengthy. He did his best to root out all the subtle details of the attack and the possible behavioral motivation of the bear. The report states that their food was properly stored and that the camp was very clean. Also, there were no significant attractants left by previous campers at the campsite.

Other important details were that the bear didn't explore the tarped food cache only 60 feet down river. And there was no recent bear sign in the area. Phil told C.O. Hunter that when he yelled "Bear in camp", his voice was high-pitched and the grizzly may have sensed distress. Phil didn't believe the attack was predatory as the animal had plenty of time to kill him if it had wanted to.

At the end of the report, two statements were checked off under 'Inferred Motivation of Bear':

1. Possibly predation; 2. Startled and attacking strange object.

The conclusion is probably right on. There are many accounts of

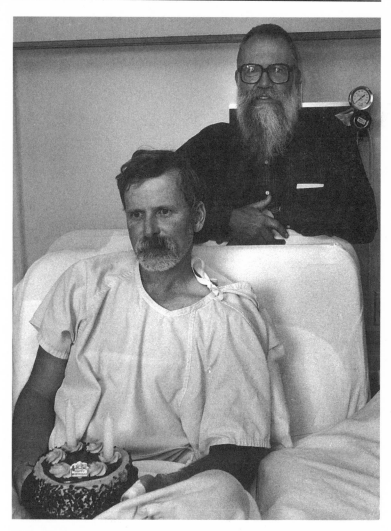

Phil and Ole at the hospital.

Pictures courtesy Ole.

similar attacks in national parks. A grizzly enters a camp at night in its normal exploratory food search behavior. It becomes aware of something in a tent and starts to paw or bite the tent. Next it discovers an animal moving inside the tent, emitting high-pitched screams, and proceeds to bite and test it. Once the bear has blood in its mouth and the normal predatory instinct is aroused, it escalates the biting of the head and neck area until movement stops.

In some cases, the bear then buries the victim; in others, it holds the body down with its front feet and starts ripping off and gulping down chunks of skin and flesh.

There's no way of knowing for sure if this bear would have gone into the final stages of predatory killing, and luckily, because of spray deterrence, we will have to leave it a mystery.

In late October 1999, I received a Seattle Times newspaper article from my brother-in-law, George T. Williams. The clipping was about a bear attack that happened at Yellowstone National Park in the previous month. The victim, T. J. Langley, is a resident of Seattle, Washington.

The following February I called T. J. and explained to him the nature of my training business and publications. I stated I'd like to use his story in my next book and that I'd send him copies of my first two books to read, so he would understand what I was about. Ten days later, I received a call from T. J. He said he'd read both books in a day-and-a-half and would very much like to participate in my next book. He went on to say he wished he'd come across my material before his trip to Yellowstone Park.

My sister, Cynthia, and her husband, George T., live in Sudden Valley just east of Bellingham, Washington. It's a wonderful place, with a forest of large fir trees and winding roads that climb and descend the small, steep hills in the area. T. J. was willing to drive up from Seattle and meet me, so I wouldn't have to brave the freeways and city streets where he lives. His sister, Joy, also came along. We met at a designated place in Bellingham, then drove out to George and Cindy's home. After introductions, we sat down at the dining room table and started the interview.

T. J. Langley (age 33) has been a strong environmentalist all his adult life. He was raised in Yakima with his two younger siblings, Matt and Joy. He began experiencing the outdoors very early in life. By age two he had been camping in Yellowstone Park, and at age four went on a camping trip with his family to the Shenandoah National Park in Virginia. On that occasion, a black bear ventured into camp, but didn't cause any serious problems. During grade school and high school, T. J. escaped into the back country whenever he got a chance.

After high school, T. J. moved to Seattle and earned a Bachelor's degree. After graduating, he travelled abroad extensively for a year-

and-a-half and learned much about other countries and people of the world. He considered this a great experience to have had before settling down to normal, everyday working life.

T. J. loves wild places and has been an avid backpacker for a long time. Most of his excursions have been three- to six-day events by himself. In the early '90s, he hiked in Glacier Park, Montana, and in 1996 spent five weeks exploring Alaska. In the late '90s, he hiked and camped in parts of Banff Park, Alberta. He saw five grizzlies while in Banff.

THE ATTACK

On September 6, 1999, T. J. drove into Montana and spent the first night of his Yellowstone trip camping by his car at a pullout. The next morning, he drove to Bozeman and spent most of the day visiting with a cousin, then travelled into the park that evening.

T. J had always had the basic belief about bears that 'if you leave them alone, they'll leave you alone', and he knew about the 'play dead with a grizzly and fight back against a black bear' strategy. His cousin had a can of bear spray and gave it to him to take along as an added measure for protection.

At the Mammoth Visitors Center, T. J. looked at all the trail maps and worked out a plan for his first hike. He'd read a lot about the re-introduced wolves in the park and hoped to see some of them. He next went to the back country ranger office to get a permit for his hike. A ranger explained that a section of the trail where he was going had been diverted around a grizzly on a bison carcass and to be sure to follow the flagging.

T.J. spent six days walking, camping, and enjoying the Lamar River and connecting loop trail, searching for the elusive quarry, but didn't catch a glimpse of any wolves. After hitch-hiking back to his car, he spent two nights at a campground in the Geyser region. Next, he did a one-day hike to Pelican Valley and back—but again, no wolves were spotted.

At the Old Faithful Visitors Center, T.J. obtained a permit for his next hike and was told by a ranger to be alert because a hiking party had used pepper spray against an aggressive sow grizzly with two cubs in the area where he was headed.

T. J. left his car at Black Butte trailhead and headed off for another adventure. This would be a two-day loop trip where he would once again come out at a different trailhead and have to hitch-hike or walk back to his car.

During the first night, T.J. could hear elk bugling all around—there must have been lots of them. The next morning, the elk were still at it, and he saw a cow. After watching her for a while, he headed out Skyrim Trail. He spent the morning climbing to the 9,930 foot summit of Big Horn Peak, then stopped for lunch where the long, slow descent to the other trailhead starts.

As T. J. sat eating and enjoying the wonderful, endless view, he pondered the fact that he hadn't seen any wolves or bears, only elk and bison. His spray was in an elastic holster on his pack chest strap, and he thought about putting it in his pack for more comfort. 'No', he thought, 'it would be Murphy's Law to run into a bear if I did that'.

At about 1:30, after an hour of descent, T. J. passed through an open sidehill and into a dense stand of timber. As his eyes were adjusting to the darkness, he looked down to his right and saw a bear only 20 yards away, then another bear—his mind instantly reflected on the ranger's warning about the sow and two cubs. Then he thought, 'where's the third bear?'

The bears started a looping uphill climb behind T. J. He stopped for a second, then decided that moving on down the trail would be the best strategy. He kept looking back over his shoulder as he moved along, hoping nothing would happen. At about 30 paces, he looked back again and saw a dreadful sight—a larger bear was coming down the trail, silent in its movement. Stunned, he noticed only the large head coming towards him.

T. J.'s mind slipped into disbelief and denial: 'It's a dog, it's a dog'. He snapped back into reality as he spun around and grabbed for the spray. He stuck his finger into the hole of the handle, thinking it was the safety clip, then pulled and pulled. The bear had been only five seconds away when he turned to face it, but by the time he realized his error in trying to get the clip off, it was too late.

He turned his pack towards the bear as he fell to the ground, but in a heartbeat the sow jumped over top of him, then attacked. Everything went dark as the first bite encompassed the whole upper part of his face. Then came the horrible sounds of raking teeth and bones breaking. T. J. was still trying to get the clip off the spray when disbelief set in again, then came a quick succession of terrible thoughts and images flashing through his mind: 'I'm going to die here'. 'This can't be right'. An image of his broken body flashed by, and he felt the anguish and heartbreak of his parents as they stood in the morgue identifying his remains. With the next bites and cracking sounds, T. J. could tell the bear was trying to crush his skull. He could see the proverbial light at the end of the tunnel, flashes of brightness behind his closed eyes—'Heaven?', he wondered. 'Why is it taking so long for her to kill me?' Then he opened his eyes and saw only red through the filter of blood. A strange thought of permeated his mind, 'Oh no, I see red, I'm going the wrong way, I'm going to hell'.

T. J. could hear someone bellowing in pain, "Help me! Help! I'm being mauled by a bear!" He'd never heard any sound quite like the agonized cries he was listening to—then realized, 'That's me'.

He was shaken violently and flipped over as the pack was ripped upwards from his body. Horrible pain set in as the sow bit into his side. After several more painful bites, T. J. was flung downhill and landed with his back arched over a fallen tree. His head was hanging low, facing the bear. Through a red blur he saw her bloodsoaked muzzle approaching and desperately placed his right hand against her throat—she stopped. He thought he heard other animals nearby, perhaps the cubs bawling, then suddenly the sow turned and ran off. It was finally over.

(For about 45 brutal seconds the sow had her way with T. J. A section of the skull above his right eye was broken loose, and most of the facial bones were crushed. He had deep lacerations across his forehead, the top of his head, and on the side of his torso. The top of his right hipbone had been broken off. Still, he was fortunate because during the biting process, the sow had not pulled back; most of the tissue was still there, much of it hanging loose, but connected.)

T. J. crawled up to the trail, then stood up and looked at his backpack on the ground. He did a systems check. He could see only out of one eye, but he could walk. He knew it was park policy that a hiker shouldn't leave a pack after a bear incident, but he couldn't possibly carry it the four-and-a-half miles to the road. He had to get moving, but hesitated for a moment and called out in case someone was nearby; there was no response.

A little way down the trail, T. J. drank a few handfuls of water from a creek, but almost passed out. He kept moving on the mainly level trail, calling out every quarter-mile or so, hoping other hikers would hear him. He felt terrible pain on his right side whenever he went uphill. Fortunately, the hour-and-forty-five minutes seemed to go by quickly and he was soon at the trailhead.

T. J. tried to flag cars down, but two passed him by. He then stood in the middle of the road and stopped the third car. The woman driver, who happened to be a nurse, helped him, using her cell-phone to call for an ambulance. The woman sat with T.J. as they waited for help.

A park ranger arrived and immediately started efforts to control the bleeding; he also administered oxygen. Another ranger arrived within a few minutes, just as the ambulance got there. T. J. was placed in the ambulance and asked by the medic if he needed anything. He requested a painkiller and was given morphine. "I guess I'm going to be all right?" He was assured, "We've got you."

A life-flight helicopter was summoned for evacuation. T. J. explained what had happened, but kept saying, "Don't kill the bears, don't kill the bears." A third ranger was now on the scene and she quizzed him about the location of the attack, so she could retrieve his backpack.

When the helicopter arrived, the nurse on board introduced herself and the pilot, but T. J. didn't get a chance to talk to them as he was airborne only a few minutes before passing out. The next thing he sensed was the click-click of the wheels on a stretcher, then into a cat-scan, and finally going under the anesthesia.

When T. J. awoke, he discovered that he was at the Idaho Falls Trauma Center. A husband and wife surgical team had performed hours of delicate repairs to his face while another doctor worked on his hip. Fortunately, the female doctor was a plastic surgeon. On September 28th, after six days in hospital, T. J. flew back to Seattle.

I asked T. J. if he had any lingering trauma from the attack. He said he didn't, and had only one nightmare where he was being chased by dogs. He went on to explain that he had one additional surgery to repair the eyeball support plate on the right side of his nose. T. J.'s right eyelid is still partially closed, and the eye doesn't yet track properly. But he has a good chance of regaining full use of his eye in the near future.

In July, I received the National Park Service Case Incident Record regarding the attack. It stated that shortly after T.J. was evacuated, a park helicopter was used to check the trail for other hikers in the vicinity of the attack. A landing was made near the site and the female ranger retrieved the backpack. Following are excerpts from that report:

Initial on-scene observations showed Langley's pack lying on the side of the trail approx. 4.1 miles from the trailhead. The back of the pack was covered with blood and long human hair, which was stuck to the shoulder straps. A blood soaked black fleece jacket was located next to the pack. Also in the immediate area of the trail was: a can of bear spray with blood on the body (not discharged), a fuel bottle, binoculars, and a pair of sunglasses with one lens gone. Due to time constraints, we loaded the pack and left the area. The location was marked with pink flagging for my return trip the next day. There was no indication that the bears were still in the immediate area, or that they had come back prior to our arrival.

On 9/24/99 myself and another NPS employee returned to the scene at approx. 1500 hours. Drops of blood were noted from the creek 3 miles in to the incident location. We noted recent bear diggings on the hillside above the trail just below the incident location. This hillside was covered with heavy timber and obvious squirrel caches which had been dug up. We continued to the scene and immediately noted half-eaten pine cones lying on the trail. We retrieved an older pile of bear scat, full of pine nuts, which was on the trail just below the incident. A number of logs along the trail had also recently been torn up, such as bears do when looking for food.

Closer observation of the actual contact point showed a 10" pool of blood located on the trail where the pack had been retrieved. We noted a large disturbance in the deadfall to the north (downhill) side of the trail. Numerous branches were broken, pools of blood, pieces of human clothing and bloody stubs were easily located. We collected both human and bear hair from this area stuck to the logs. Also located here were Langley's compass, sunglass lens, and chunks of hair. According to Langley, the second and third attacks from the bear took place in this deadfall area.

Further investigation showed where the adult bear had come down to make contact with Langley. It appeared that she had been 30 feet above the trail, digging on a rotted log. Due to heavy timber in the area, neither bear nor human would have seen the other until they were almost directly in line.

Later on, T. J. obtained more details about the previous attack that the ranger at the Old Faithful Visitors Center had warned him about. It had taken place just three-and-a-half weeks before his attack. On August 27th, a visitor from Sweden, who was accompanied by a woman from the U.S., had to defend himself by first spraying the cubs and then spraying the sow as he held her off with his foot. He received four claw gouges (two deep and two shallow) when the sow swiped at him with a front paw.

This is a difficult attack to analyze from a defense perspective. In most cases, you would be better off using a spray against a grizzly rather than 'playing dead'. However, during a sow attack where the cubs run away, lying face down and protecting the back of your neck can reduce injury. But T. J. heard another animal close by at the end of the attack—this must have been one or both of the large cubs. When grizzly cubs stay on the scene of an attack, as they did in both T. J.'s and the previous incident, the sow will not easily detrigger, and this is one of the variations in grizzly attacks where 'playing dead' does not work well.

In the attack on the Swede by this grizzly family, the cubs attacked first. In my previous books, I explain the behavior demonstrated in these two incidents as family-defense behavior in grizzly bears. I've convinced most B.C. Parks personnel that when they receive a report about an aggressive sow grizzly with large cubs that also display aggression, the area of the incident must be closed indefinitely, because that family group is very dangerous until the cubs go their own way in the following summer.

It is unfortunate that T. J. didn't get his spray operational.

There was a second horror to this incident. The hospital, doctors, and other expenses came to $114,000, and T. J.'s disability insurance had a one-event limit of $27,000. T. J. has been working very hard at paying off this debt and will probably have it down to about $65,000 by the time this book is published. He feels lucky to have had such good doctors and hospital care and wants badly to conclude this obligation.

A fund has been set up to help T. J. with his financial recovery. Anyone wanting to help with this cause can send a contribution to:

T. J. Langley Recovery Fund
c/o Arlene Spaulding
2131 - 10th Ave. West
Seattle, Washington 98119

T. J. wants to express a heartfelt thanks to all of those people who helped in the initial first aid, evacuation, and hospital care.

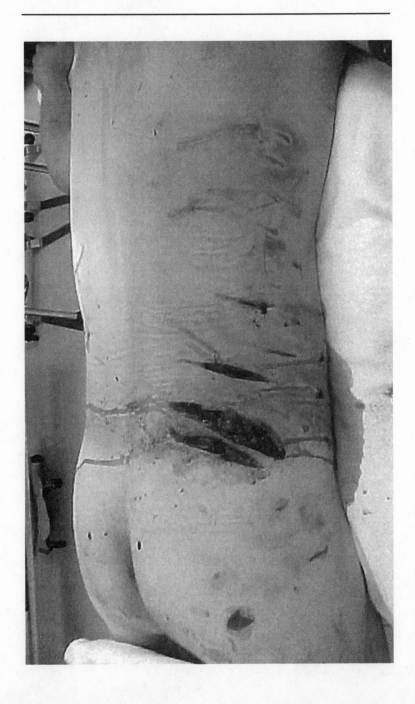

8

PLAYING DEAD

Each year, my bear encounter survival training is usually wrapped up by the end of June, but in 2000, the demand for training continued into the fall. There were two grizzly attacks south of Bella Coola during August on Department of Fisheries and Oceans (DFO) personnel that resulted in minor injuries. Shortly thereafter, I flew down to Genesee Creek DFO Camp for a day of training, and two days later up to the DFO Babine River salmon counting fence in Northern B.C. to do the same. While at the Babine River Camp, I was asked by management personnel to investigate their operation of the counting fence and to write a report regarding the best way to deal with the increasing grizzly bear problems at the site.

After that, I was asked by BC Hydro to provide training at Mission, B.C., near Vancouver, and also requested to do training for the Nicola Stock Breeders Association at Merritt. I decided to also pursue two bear attack interviews during this last training trip of the year. I also decided I'd work on the Babine River DFO report while on the trip.

September 24, 2000

After concluding the training for BC Hydro on the 20th, I drove down to Blaine, Washington, to visit family for three days, then back to the center of Vancouver on the morning of the 24th to be a guest speaker on a radio talk show. It was now afternoon and I was headed west on Georgia Street.

I was hoping to find a parking spot not too far away from Paul Courtney's apartment building. I always dread visits to downtown Vancouver, but on Sunday afternoons the traffic is as light as it ever gets.

I've always marvelled at the architectural design of the tall buildings on West Georgia that are supported at the first floor level by spaced round concrete pillars instead of continuous foundations. I was surprised when the street number I was looking for turned out to be one of these buildings, and there was good parking right in front.

The security guard pushed a button to let me enter the glass enclosed area between pillars, and asked who I wanted to see. Paul came down to the lobby shortly after the call to his apartment. After introducing ourselves, we decided to do the interview outside, because it was such a nice day.

We walked downhill three blocks north to the edge of the bay and found a nice bench to sit on adjacent to the yacht club dock. Individuals and family groups were passing by in front of us, and everyone seemed to be enjoying the warmth of the sun, as if they knew there wouldn't be many more days like this until the following spring.

We had a beautiful view of Stanley Park and the north shore, but the pleasant atmosphere seemed completely out of place for the task at hand, and I felt slightly uncomfortable. Fortunately, all the smiling people around us wouldn't hear the details of our conversation.

"Paul, I want to use your story in the 'Playing Dead' chapter of my next book." "Yes," he responded, understanding my meaning. I continued, "But before we go through the details of the attack, I need some background information about you and Christine." Paul nodded his head:

Paul was raised in North Delta just south of Vancouver. He has one brother, and his family still lives in the Lower Mainland area. Paul and his brother operate a custom brokerage firm that their father established. Because Christine's dad was in the air force, she'd lived in many different areas of Canada while growing up, and attended high school in Comox Valley on Vancouver Island. After high school, she'd obtained a degree in occupational therapy and was practicing in Vancouver.

They married in September of 1995 and were soon planning adventurous vacation trips. Christine had done a lot of traveling, including outdoor travel in remote regions of the world. Paul had less travel and outdoor experience but was picking up the traveling bug from Christine, and he was looking forward to many exciting outdoor excursions with his wife. They had hiked the West Coast Trail one year and canoed the Bowron Lakes Park another year. The couple were environmentalist, but not fanatical; they were middle-of-the-road. They didn't have extensive knowledge about bears and basically believed if you left them alone, they would leave you alone.

In the latter part of June 1996, Paul and Christine flew to Whitehorse, Yukon, for another adventure. After renting a car, they traveled around the territory looking at all the beautiful sights. They spent two days in Ross River visiting friends, then traveled southwest. They ended up at the Kluane Park Visitors Center on July 4th and obtained information for the hike they'd been looking forward to. They planned a two-day overnighter which would allow the right amount of time to arrive back in Whitehorse for the return flight home.

They watched the park 'Bear Aware' video that gave instructions on how to react during an encounter that included the 'play dead' strategy with a grizzly if attack seems imminent. A metal container for food is required for backpackers in the park, so they rented one.

Paul and Christine.

Courtesy Paul Courtney.

After parking the car at the trailhead and getting their equipment ready, they started up the trail. It was about 1:30 P.M.

Above, a view of the Kluane Mountains. On the next page, Christine took this picture of Paul about half way to their camp.

For several hours the route meandered along a small stream, then up into semi-open Alpine. They hiked for a total of five-and-a-half hours, then set up camp for the night and followed all the park rules when preparing dinner and storing their food. As far as they knew, there were no other people in the area. Paul felt slightly uncomfortable and vulnerable and didn't sleep well because their camp was on a sloping, brushy hillside, and because of his concern about bears. Paul felt relief to break camp at first light in the morning—they had made it through the night without a bear problem. They hadn't talked about bears, and Christine didn't indicate whether or not she also felt vulnerable.

The two hikers continued along the trail as it was a circular route that would take them back to their car later in the day. They were occasionally taking photographs as they discussed their return trip home, and both were relieved that they hadn't run into any bears.

After walking for over two hours, they rounded a bend in the track and saw a large bear walking towards them about 100 yards away.

It was brown in color, with a hump on its back, and its head was low—it looked like a grizzly. They'd both seen bears before, but not this close. The bear didn't react in any way, and they couldn't tell if it was aware of them.

In hushed voices, they debated what to do. Paul suggested walking into the timber, out of sight. Christine wanted to walk backwards slowly, letting the bear notice them, so it would leave. Finally, Paul convinced Christine to follow him into the trees.

About 20 yards along, they came to a small, sloping clearing. They looked back and saw that the bear was following them. As it approached, they decided to remove their backpacks. After dropping the packs, they started backing away downhill, hoping the animal would be interested in their offering. The grizzly was now only 15 feet away as it moved past the backpacks. It was slightly crouched with its head low and not making any sounds. Panic and terror was setting in when they decided it was time to 'play dead'.

The bear went out of sight as Paul hit the ground, rolled into a ball, and clasped his hands over the back of his neck. Every muscle in his body was rigid with fear; he couldn't assess the situation; he hoped the bear would leave. Paul thought he could hear slight noises, like the bear was sniffing him, but wasn't sure. 'Where is it?' 'What is it doing?' Then Christine yelled for help.

What a horrible sound it was to hear his wife's desperate plea. He was on his feet in an instant; then the terrible reality came into sight—the grizzly was biting and clawing at Christine. She was in a fetal position on her side, with her hands clasped around the back of her neck; the bear was standing behind her, biting at her neck.

Paul scrambled around looking for a weapon as the bear bit into Christine and slid her slightly downhill. He grabbed a four-foot branch, then charged the grizzly and started hitting it on the head. The bear was oblivious to his attack for about 20 seconds, then turned to face Paul. The grizzly lunged and bit him low on his left leg as he spun downhill and jumped behind a small tree. The bear paused for a moment, then returned to Christine. Paul ran back up the slope and started beating the bear again, but Christine quickly said, "Stop, you're aggravating the bear." "Should I go for help?" Paul responded. "Yes," was her quick reply.

'What to do?' What to do?' Paul's mind was racing—should he fight the bear more or go for help? He didn't want to leave her. What should he do?

The panic-stricken man limped downhill to an old road and started yelling at the top of his lungs. He had to get help quickly if he was going to save Christine. He ran in the direction of the trailhead; he thought it should be only about three miles away.

Paul was confused and lost as the road tapered into a path. Shortly thereafter, he entered into a small river valley and started moving downstream. He crossed the river back and forth many times to avoid bad terrain. His leg was now bothering him much more; he was trotting with a bad limp. He kept looking uphill and yelling as he moved along, out of breath, thinking that the main trail should be right there, somewhere. He was yelling as loud as he could, hoping someone would hear him.

Suddenly, he saw a single hiker come out of the woods a short distance away and realized the trail must be nearby. He rushed up to the young man and tried to explain what had happened. But the hiker was responding in a deep German accent and didn't seem to understand what Paul was saying, and acted as if he was being unnecessarily held up.

Finally, the German tourist sensed that something was seriously wrong and helped Paul back down the trail to the parking lot. Then, several other hikers took over and drove Paul to the visitors center. Paul ran into the main building looking for a warden. It didn't take the park personnel long to figure out what had happened. Paul was questioned about the circumstances and location of the attack, and shortly, he saw two men leaving with guns in hand. Several park employees stayed with Paul in a back office, trying to console him. After what seemed like a long, endless hour, he heard two helicopters arrive, then quickly depart.

Within about 20 minutes, one of the helicopters came back and Paul was asked to fly with the wardens in order to find the location of the attack. They couldn't see Christine or the bear from the air, and Paul couldn't identify the exact spot, but he helped them find the general location. By now Paul was feeling ill and was in shock. He was flown back to the center and given sedatives.

Paul was asked to lie down in a back office. Two agonizing hours passed as he lay there, wondering, going over the attack in his mind. Had he done the right thing, or should he have fought the bear longer? Why was it taking so long for the helicopters to get back? Then he was told the worst: They had found Christine's body. She was dead—the bear was in the process of burying her when it was killed. Paul had never had a feeling in his throat and chest like he was experiencing. Nothing in his life had prepared him for the mental anguish and physical pain he felt. The parks personnel were doing their best to help him, but no one could ease his pain.

Not long after Paul learned about his wife's death, he was put on a stretcher and flown to the Whitehorse Hospital. Christine's parents heard about the attack on the radio and were immediately afraid that it was their daughter. Later, the terrible news was confirmed to them—Christine was dead. Their friends in Ross River came down to help, and after an overnight stay in the hospital, Paul flew home.

Paul went back to work as soon as possible because he couldn't stand to sit around and think about what had happened. He was a severely distressed for about a month and occasionally felt suicidal. His workmates were very supportive and carried most of his work-load until he started to recover. A friend suggested trauma coun-selling, and shortly after his loss, Paul received excellent therapy. He was able to explore why he did what he did during the attack and learned about the fight-or-flight response that humans and animals have. He also learned that the terrible guilt he was feeling was nat-ural, but unreasonable.

Christine's parents felt compelled to make sure their daughter's death was not in vain. They had a memorial plaque made up and requested that it be installed in the park as a reminder to other park users about the danger of bears. They insisted that it be located right at the trailhead into the area where the attack took place.

I asked Paul, "What kind of demeanor did the bear have as it approached just before you laid down on the ground?" "Like a cat stalking its prey," he answered. "And how exactly did the bear bite you?" I continued. "I don't know—take a look at the scars," he sug-gested.

Paul turned his left leg sideways. About five inches above the ankle on the outside of his leg were two parallel marks a half-inch wide and slightly more than two inches apart. "Those are canine teeth puncture wounds," I stated, "and you must have been spinning as the bear turned its head sideways to grab your leg, because the teeth tore grooves across the side of your calf, but there are no cor-responding canine teeth marks on the other side."

After walking back up to Paul's apartment building, we said good-bye and I started the drive from one end of Vancouver to the other. I was glad that the traffic was light, because I couldn't keep from being distracted by Paul's story. I wondered what I would have done in his situation, but couldn't come to any conclusion.

I made it to the town of Hope by 8 P.M. and spent the night in a motel room. I was up early and, after having two cups of coffee, I started the long haul to Pincher Creek, Alberta.

————————

It was 12 hours later when I pulled into the hotel on the outskirts of town. When I was settled in, I called Patricia Derksen in Taber, Alberta, to confirm our meeting two nights later in Pincher Creek. Pat had suggested we do the interview at Otis Handford's home so that as many people as possible who were involved in the incident could be there.

I spent the next two days working on the report for the Department of Fisheries and Oceans regarding their grizzly problems at the Babine River salmon counting fence. Fortunately, I had my computer set up on a small table by the window, and right in front of me was a beautiful expanse of the Rocky Mountains. Every time I grew tired of writing, I just looked out at the snow-capped peaks surrounded by blue sky and was instantly reinvigorated.

By Wednesday afternoon I had most of the work done, and I realized the DFO report had given me an important opportunity to present a large piece of new material that would hopefully expose a number of myths that make it next to impossible to solve human/bear conflict problems.

I had already driven around town the day before to make sure where Otis lived, so it was easy to arrive right at 7 P.M. As I walked up the driveway I could see a woman sitting on the steps, a middle-aged man sitting on the rim of a flower bed, and a young man leaning against a pickup truck.

"Hi, you must be Pat?" I asked. The woman stood up with a broad smile and said, "Yes, how ya doing, Gary?" "I'm doing fine," was my response. "This is Otis, and this is my nephew, Warren Tyshkewich," she said. "Glad to meet all of you," I replied, as I shook their hands.

As I sat down on the steps next to Pat, I asked, "Well, do you want to do the interview outside or in the house?" After ten minutes of casual talk, we went inside. I was offered a beer as Pat, Warren, and I sat down at the dining room table. After Otis handed me the can, he went around to the other side of the peninsula cabinet and leaned forward on it—waiting for me to begin.

After I explained how I conduct interviews and how important accuracy of the account is, Pat said she'd invited Warren so I could obtain details from him as well. I asked Pat for background information about her and her husband.

Christopher John Kress and Pat had lived in Taber for 12 and a half years. They usually spent two weeks a year camping and fishing somewhere along the front of the Rockies. Pat was a horse person, so occasionally, they'd have a horse trailer in tow. Chris would also go out with "the boys" for a little additional fishing now and then. They both really enjoyed the outdoors.

I asked both Otis and Warren about their histories. Otis was born and raised in Pincher Creek and had worked mainly at guide-outfitting and heavy equipment operating. His hobbies were hunting, fishing, camping, and horseback riding. Warren stated he'd lived in Pincher for five years and before that in Calgary. He'd mainly worked in the 'oil patch', and like the rest of them, he enjoyed doing most everything related to nature.

"Where exactly did the attack take place?" I enquired. Otis responded. "In the southwest corner of Alberta near the junction of South Castle River and Scarpe Creek; right next to Waterton Lakes National Park." "And who was in camp?" I asked. "There were 11 people of three family groups, with six dogs, and three horses," Pat answered, then continued. "We had arrived the night before at the end of the road where the trailhead starts. We had three wall tents set up and had the horses in an old corral. During the night, Chris heard something heavy walk next to the tent and asked me to look out at the corral to see if any horses were loose. But I could see all of them—none were loose."

For the next hour of the interview we pieced together the events during the day of the attack:

By 10 A.M., most everybody in camp had finished breakfast. Pat saddled up a horse and went for a ride. Chris took out his favorite fly rod and prepared his gear for a morning of trout fishing. Otis asked him if he wanted to take a gun or a dog along. "No, I'm just going up the creek a short ways, I won't be far from camp," Chris answered.

As the day progressed, the kids started using a chainsaw and hammers to build a fort. Others were riding the motorbikes they'd brought along. Not far away, in another camp, people were shooting high-powered rifles for practice. There was a tremendous amount of noise being made in the area, including dogs barking.

When Pat got back from her first ride, Warren was up and ready for action, so the two of them went riding together. The other couple in camp, Kim and Christine Davidson, went for a hike up the trail at about 2 P.M.

When Pat and Warren returned from their ride shortly before 4 P.M., Pat inquired if Chris was back from fishing yet, but no one had seen him since morning. This concerned Pat, as Chris should've been back by then.

At about 4:15, Kim and Christine were walking across an open sidehill, next to the river, on their way back to camp. They noticed their dog kept stopping and looking at something up-river. They assumed that Chris was still up there fishing. Christine then noticed something orange in the middle of the river. As the two of them visually searched the area, they saw a bear standing on al fours, sniffing the air, and also saw a pair of green waders sticking out from under the bear.

As the two of them charged into camp, Christine shouted, "We think we saw Chris." She ran right past Otis and started looking for her kids, to make sure they were all there and to get them inside a pickup. Kim explained to everyone what they'd seen.

The rest of the kids were rounded up and put into vehicles. Jeremy Davidson, a 15-year-old without a driver's license, drove a panic-stricken women out over the treacherous road to the nearest telephone to get help and to notify the authorities. The three little boys in camp had to ride in the back of the pickup, bouncing and banging all the way. Otis, Warren, Kim, and Otis's wife, Kizzy, stayed in camp. Kizzy is a nurse, so it was decided that in case Chris was still alive, she needed to be there. They all knew that they had to quickly determine whether Chris was alive or dead.

Warren and Kizzy stayed in camp as Kim started up the trail—Otis grabbed his rifle and followed. When they reached the spot where the bear had been seen, they could see Chris lying against the bank on the other side of the river. They were about 100 yards away and 100 feet higher. Their friend looked as if he was lying on his side, sleeping—they strained their eyes, hoping to see movement. Then they saw the bear lying in the sun 20 yards from Chris.

Otis steadied the gun on the limb of a small tree. He was having trouble lining up the open sights. He'd killed plenty of animals before, but never a grizzly. He wanted to make sure he didn't let it get away wounded. Otis kept checking the alignment of the sights with the center of the bear's chest. Kim put his hand on Otis' shoulder and said, "Kill the son-of-a-bitch, it's killed a human being." As the horrible reality set in, Otis finished the squeeze. The bear didn't even move as he emptied the gun, reloaded, and fired twice more.

In order to get to Chris, they walked about half-way back to camp and waded across the river, and then up the other side. They approached slowly and carefully, first making sure the bear was dead, then they checked Chris. What a gut-wrenching sight lay before them. Earlier that morning their friend had left camp in wonderful spirits, and everyone else had enjoyed the beautiful day, not knowing the horror that was taking place a short distance away.

Chris was stuffed against the river bank with dirt pulled down over him. His abdominal cavity was open with much missing; one arm had been eaten; most of the skin and tissue on his head had been ripped off; it looked like the bear had been trying to break into the skull for the brain. There were also severe neck injuries that probably had killed him.

The two men stood in paralyzed anguish, trying to make sense out of their ordeal.

Christine had called 911 when they reached the nearest phone at Beaver Mines on the main highway. The police and conservation officers were dispatched. Pat kept up her hope that Chris was still alive as Christine drove her to Kim and Christine's house in Pincher Creek. Otis and Kim raced out on the motor bikes to let the authorities know that Chris was dead and that the bear had been killed. The police were already at the highway when they arrived, and 20 minutes later, a helicopter landed.

By this time Otis was suffering from exposure and shock, because of the bike ride, wading the river, and, of course, because of what had happened to his campmate. The medics treated him for exposure. At first they weren't sure if Otis could handle going back in, but it was decided that he was needed to guide the police. Jeremy was sent in with the ambulance crew to provide directions on how to get there.

Otis mustered up his strength and flew back in with the RCMP and a bear specialist from Environmental Protection. They landed near the campsite on the other side of the river. The police loaded their guns and followed Otis up to the attack site. The pilot flew up over the area, checking to make sure there were no other bears.

Chris's body had to be carried about 200 yards upstream to where the helicopter could land. The body was flown out to the ambulance, then the rest were flown back to the highway at Beaver Mines. As Pat waited for word at Christine's house, her mind kept jumping back and forth between hope and despair, but deep inside, she knew Chris was dead.

A policeman called and requested information for identifying Chris's body, because they couldn't state he was dead until they had a positive identification. Pat told Christine to tell the RCMP to look in Chris's front pocket for his wallet. At 6:15 P.M., Pat was told that her husband was dead. Christine suggested to the police that they have his body examined for bullet wounds as a nearby camping party had been shooting in that direction during the time of the attack.

All Pat could think of now was that she had to inform the family of her husband's death before they heard about the attack from some other source. She called her boys and asked them to pick her up at Warren's place, but she didn't tell them anything until they arrived. Otis, Warren, Kim, and Alan Tyshkewich went back to retrieve the horses and equipment. That night, after Pat returned home to Taber, one of her sons stayed with her and they talked way into the night.

I asked everyone if the kids had been affected by the event. "No, we were careful to protect them from what was going on. None of them seem to have been affected," Otis answered, then added, "But I couldn't sleep the whole following summer." Pat stated that Chris must've been killed in the first hour from camp because he'd taken two cans of Pepsi with him and only one had been partially consumed. Otis said that the fishing rod was broken, but the line was still outstretched in the water. The bear might've taken him by surprise from behind, or Chris may have dropped the fishing rod and held the bear off for a while by lighting and throwing the firecrackers he always carried. Chris was a catch-and-release fisherman, so he wouldn't have had any fish on the bank. Warren said the event had taken the shine out of many things he enjoyed doing.

I asked Pat how her life had changed after losing Chris. She said at first it was overwhelming—she felt so lonely. And all her friends changed; it wasn't the same any more. Pat hasn't been camping since.

Otis explained that something happened several days after the attack that really bothered him. A newspaper article about the death gave Otis's name and stated that the bear needed to be killed. In the next edition of the paper a letter to the editor stated that the bear shouldn't have been killed because the people involved were invading its territory and it was only acting naturally. The letter was extremely upsetting, and Otis was agonizing with the prospect of writing a rebuttal, but didn't really feel like it.

Pat asked me if I'd be able to obtain a copy of the official government report regarding the attack. I told her I'd get it and would provide copies for all of them, because they had a right to know what is in it.

Three months later, I received the bear attack file from the Alberta Government. Some portions of the material were deleted for protecting other people's privacy, and the RCMP didn't release any of their investigation reports. Following is an excerpt from the Bear Response Team Leader's Report:

. . . *Our examination of the scene revealed the following. We located several beds in the area and four in a clump, 128 feet southwest of the victim. The vegetation in the immediate area included horsetail, thimble berry, lowbush cranberry, and cow parsnip. The area was cool and shady, the wind had been from the west. Immediately upstream of the victim was a part-full can of Pepsi. The victim had taken two cans with him that morning. Two grizzly prints were found* headed downstream on a sand bank just opposite the Pepsi can. The victim's fishing rod was lying broken just off the bank near the victim. In the river gravel a clear drag mark led 31 feet to a disturbed area in the gravel in the center of the river. Several personal items were recovered along the drag mark in the river. Several other personal items were located in deadfall in the river further downstream of the victim. I would surmise that the victim may have been sitting in the shade of a large spruce drinking his Pepsi when he observed the bear approaching along the bank on his right, from upstream. This would have been a distance of 20 - 30 feet. He then may have thrown his Pepsi can at the bear. (How would it get upstream?) The bear came around the large spruce on the bank and Mr. Kress' rod was broken in the initial contact. I believe Mr. Kress then managed to get to the center of the river where the attack took place. I believe the bear knocked him down on his back and very quickly . . . deleted . . . The bear then . . . deleted . . . the bear lay nearby to guard the site. The examination of the bear and the evidence at the scene indicate a predatory attack. Mr. Kress was also a competent fly fisherman who may have handled several fish over the course of the morning.

Next is a statement from a follow-up report by the Natural Resources Service regarding the attack.

A post mortem conducted on the bear found that the bear was generally in good health with no injuries. However, this bear was estimated to be 5-1/2 to 6-years old and about 170 pounds, which is unusually small for a male grizzly of this age.

There are two statements of importance in the autopsy report: 1. The injuries associated with vital reaction (injuries most likely inflicted before death) were on the neck, head, and hands. 2. Examination of stomach contents from the bear found at the scene revealed portions of bowel and scalp consistent with tissues missing from the decedent.

The investigation by the RCMP pertaining to people in a nearby camp shooting firearms during the time of the attack was not released, but that issue must have been a dead end or Pat would've heard about it from the police. Also, Otis thought that the shooting sounds they heard might've been Chris setting off firecrackers in an attempt to stop the bear, but Warren felt sure that what he heard was gunfire.

Chris and Pat.

Courtesy Pat Derksen.

CONCLUSION

I'm sure it's obvious to the reader that the two attacks described in this chapter are cases where 'playing dead' during a grizzly attack didn't work in the first, and wouldn't have worked in the second. But there is much more to the picture than this.

During the 1960s and 1970s, it was believed that almost all bear attacks were defensive-aggressive where bears were defending cubs, food, or their immediate space. It was also believed in those days that bears rarely attacked unless provoked. The general strategy that resulted from these concepts was that people should back away slowly during an encounter with a bear, and if attack seemed imminent, fall to the ground, curl up in a ball, and protect the back of their neck with their hands. There were many attacks where this strategy worked quite well.

When bear biologist Stephen Herrero published his book *Bear Attacks - Their Causes and Avoidance* (1985), based on research done between 1967 and 1980, he suggested that this strategy be amended to: Play dead during a grizzly attack and fight back during a black bear attack. The reason for this new strategy resulted from his statistical analysis of bear attacks that showed most attacks by grizzlies were defensive-aggressive, but that the deadly attacks by black bears were almost always predatory attacks. This amended strategy saved many lives in the late '80s, but unfortunately, during the '90s, there was an increase in predatory attacks by grizzly bears as well as an increase in predatory attacks by black bears where fighting back bare-handed didn't work.

Approximately half of the grizzly bear-inflicted deaths during the last ten years involved predatory behavior or some variation of attack where playing dead didn't work or wouldn't have worked. But there were also many attacks during this same period where people 'played dead' and reduced injury, and a few cases where people fought back against a grizzly and stopped the attack.

It's not that the 'play dead/fight back' strategy is wrong for some types of attacks. Rather, it's that there are now too many attacks where it doesn't work well or it doesn't work at all. I'm suggesting that the more powerful alternatives of firearms and sprays should always be used.

I'll never forget a reaction I received from a participant in a training course in Fort St. John several years ago. This gentleman didn't want to use firearms or sprays against bears. He just wanted me to give him a set of guidelines he could follow during an encounter that would eliminate the chance of a bear making contact. He said that the other safety courses he'd taken regarding other subjects had provided him with clear rules to follow, and he couldn't understand why the same couldn't be done with bears.

My answer was this: "I'm going to give you something much better than the customary rules or guidelines: I'm going to give you reality. There is no magic formula for surviving a bear encounter that goes wrong—so use the most powerful system of defense you have available."

9

DOGS AND BEARS

During the last three years, I've been providing a larger segment on dog use in my bear safety training program and telling people that if the present policies to over-protect bears in B.C. continue, dogs may be the only way of dealing with so many bears that no longer fear people. I give the participants examples of cases where dogs helped and cases where they didn't help or made the situation worse.

I was drawn into the dog issue in an unexpected way during May and June of 1999. I had a training session scheduled on May 18th for the Ministry of Forests (MOF) district office in Clearwater, B.C. Four days before that date, while travelling and conducting other courses, I received a message from Max Tanner at the Clearwater office that one of their employees had been attacked by a black bear. He was saved by his dog, but it was against district office policy for employees to use dogs in the field. The staff wanted to hear my views on this subject during the upcoming course.

The day before the Clearwater course, while providing training in Kelowna for B.C. Gas and Riverside Logging, another bear attack story surfaced involving a dog. This one happened to a Riverside employee. Then, about a month later, when I was at home, I received a call from a contract forester who had also been involved in a human/dog/bear interaction.

Let's take a close look at these three events in the order I first heard about them:

Jimmy Biagiona (age 26) is a forest technician at the MOF office in Clearwater, B.C. At 10:15 A.M. on May 10th he was walking up a skid trail near Mulliett Creek with his dog Bandit. His work project for

113

that morning was to inspect a series of completed salvage logging blocks.

They'd passed through two harvest openings, and as Jimmy left the timber and entered a third harvested patch, a sow black bear with two small cubs came into view about 150 meters ahead on a sidehill. Bandit was off to the left over a break, out of sight from the bears. Jimmy has had many encounters like this, with the bears always leaving when he yelled.

All of a sudden the sow came at him in a dead run. Jimmy yelled "Hey hey!" but the bear didn't stop. He yelled again, louder, but the bear didn't even hesitate, and she was covering ground fast. Jimmy turned and ran like hell. Within 15 seconds, he could tell that she was gaining on him by the sound of the growling and the paws swiping the air. When he turned his head to see how close those claws were coming to his behind, he tripped over a pile of debris and fell face-down—he cringed as he waited for the teeth and claws to start their work. The dog ran over Jimmy first, then the bear; neither of them could stop as quickly as he had.

As the sow spun around and took a swipe, Jimmy rolled, grabbed a small log, and hit the bear in the side of the head. Unfortunately, the log broke. As Jimmy lay defenseless, Bandit went after the bear's rear end. This gave Jimmy time to scramble to his feet and grab another chunk of wood. He hit the bear in the head again as it charged him. Even though this weapon also broke into pieces, the blow, plus the dog's persistent chewing on the bear's hind end, stopped the attack on Jimmy. Bandit now had the sow's attention, and she went after him.

The two animals were going around in circles right in front of the beleaguered man. As the dog tired, the circles grew smaller. Jimmy was yelling at the bear as he had been throughout the attack. He got hold of another piece of wood debris, moved into a good position, and 'smoked' the enraged sow directly on the snout. She was instantly stunned; growling and swiping at the air, she stumbled backwards about five meters and stopped. Jimmy and Bandit started backing away slowly. The bear was now on a pile of brush, in a daze, but still growling and snarling. When the man and dog backed up far enough that they could no longer see the sow, they turned and ran for the truck.

Jimmy was lucky. He had two claw gashes to his left hand, a gash on his right hand from a stick, bad scratches on his left forearm, and bruising in the abdominal area. Bandit had puncture wounds on the belly and shoulder and some minor bruising.

When the pair got home, Jimmy bandaged Bandit's wounds then cooked up two steaks. As the dog gulped down the special treat, his partner tied into a beer. The next day, when Jimmy returned to work, he received a cake and a basket of dog treats from his co-workers.

Later, Jimmy made the following statement: "If it wasn't for Bandit that bear would've been totally focused on me. I don't blame the sow for her actions, as she was just being a good mother. But she's probably got a migraine headache and a sore butt about now."

Later in the fall, Jimmy told me that Bandit is a well-trained, obedient 65-pound Coyote-Shepherd cross. I asked him if the ministry still had a policy of no dogs in the field. He said, "Yes, they do." I then asked Jimmy if they could carry spray. He said they could, but he personally didn't like or trust bear spray and preferred his dog. He went on to say that one of their office staff, Max Tanner, had successfully fought a campaign to obtain approval for some of the district employees to carry firearms in certain areas at certain times of the year for defense. I was glad to hear that.

In the afternoon of April 28th, Russ Ferguson, an employee of Riverside Forest Products, was working by himself 14 kilometers up Bald Range Mainline logging road west of Kelowna, B.C. He was accompanied by his 13-year-old Black Lab.

Russ was putting in a boundary and blazing stations for a small logging block. He was in a low elevation semi-open fir/pine forest. About halfway through the project, he stopped hanging ribbon and took a walk in order to find a way of hooking up the boundary to the mainline. Russ moved uphill to a ridge, then started down the ridge to where he'd hung the last ribbon. He heard a noise that sounded like branches breaking, but wasn't sure. As he continued along about 20 meters, he heard branches breaking again and a scratching sound. As Russ stopped he saw a black object at eye level in a clump of trees 20 meters ahead—his first thought was that it must be a porcupine.

Russ started yelling for the dog to come to him. Suddenly, a black bear came out of the clump of trees and headed towards him at a fast pace. Russ quickly pulled his ax out of its sheath and started waving his arms as he yelled as loudly as he could. He immediately sensed that he had to face this bear and not run. The dog was a short ways to his left but wasn't barking at all.

The bear halted a meter-and-a-half away; its head was low, with its ears pinned back. It made no sound at all. Russ kept yelling and waving his arms as he took a step backward. The animal stepped forward. Another step backward, followed by another step forward.

Russ repeated the slow retreat six steps, and each time the bear matched his movement—it stayed low and silent.

When the black bear took a step out of turn, Russ swung the ax as hard as he could, and connected with the left side of its head. The bear turned hard right and loped uphill 15 meters, then spun around and glared. Russ started moving backwards fast; he could see lots of blood on the bear's face as it started to move back towards where it had come from—it was bawling loudly.

Shortly thereafter, Russ heard the bear up on the ridge, moving parallel to him. When he was about halfway to his truck, Russ took the portable radio from his vest and called a member of a nearby work crew to explain what had happened. When he arrived at the truck, he jumped in and drove down the road to where Cec Harder and two other Riverside employees were waiting for him to show up.

This bear was acting as a predator as evidenced by its behavior. Its intention was to kill and eat Russ. But this forester has years of experience in the bush and knows that sometimes you have to use quick, vigorous aggression to survive. Later on, in a phone conversation, Russ explained that his dog had stayed behind him during the incident and hadn't helped at all. But he said it wasn't the dog's fault—it was a 13-year-old Lab-Collie cross that was almost completely deaf.

Russ went on to tell me that this event was the second serious bear incident he'd had. The previous attack took place in the second week of October 1995. He was mapping a riparian zone in a proposed logging block on a snowy, wet day. He was accompanied by his dog, Hailey. As he headed up the side of a ravine, he saw a grizzly 50 meters away coming at him full-tilt—it wasn't making any noise. He yelled for his two-year-old Border Collie as he turned to run.

The dog was barking furiously as Russ headed up the other side of the ravine. He hadn't made it far when a small cub went tearing past him—it too was silent—and now he knew what was going on. Nothing quite invigorates the desire to live like discovering that you're between a sow grizzly and her cub.

Russ hesitated and looked back; the sow was close, but his trusted dog had her stopped. Russ put his feet in high gear and made his get-away. When he ran out of breath and started slowing down, his thoughts turned to concern about Hailey. Was she dead by now? It was a relief when Russ saw her coming up behind him. They kept moving, and when they were about 500 meters from the ravine, Hailey turned around, started barking again, and headed back towards the bears. Russ put it into high gear again when he realized the sow was still coming.

It was a great relief to make it unharmed to the truck and to have his dog show up shortly thereafter.

The next day, Russ went back to finish ribboning the riparian area in the block, and when he went past the spot where his truck had been parked the previous day, he and Hailey examined the area where they'd come out of the timber. They found tracks indicating that the sow had followed them right to the truck and was accompanied by two first-year cubs. This time, Russ had a gun with him.

———

On the evening of June 22nd, I received a call from Colin Champagne of Okanagan Falls, B.C. This small town is about an hour's drive south of Kelowna. Colin gave me brief details of a bear incident that had happened four days earlier and said he'd fax me a copy of the company report. Several days later, after reading the account, I called Colin and recorded his story:

Colin is a forest technician and was doing a snow-free check of a proposed logging cut-block that had been laid out the previous winter. He was carrying a shotgun with slugs.

Colin was just finishing up a snack as he and Sage, his two-year-old female German Shepherd, were walking along the west boundary of the block. As they came to the southwest corner, they heard a grunting noise, then lots of branches breaking. They were on a flat pine bench, and just ahead was a steep downslope. The noise was coming from over the break, out of sight. Colin assumed it was an animal, probably a moose, and the sound they were hearing was it running away. Whatever it was, it had sensed them before they had sensed it. Colin started yelling, and Sage started barking.

All of a sudden, there was silence. The dog ran forward to the edge of the bench and hesitated, then started barking again as it took off down the hill. When Colin got to the edge, he could see Sage and a large black bear fighting on the slope below. At this point, he realized that the bear hadn't been taking off but instead had been tearing up logs and ripping at the brush in anger.

Now the bear was chasing the dog in circles—Colin was glad Sage wasn't running back to him. He quickly removed the gun from his shoulder and fired a shot into the air. The bear immediately stopped pursuing Sage and took off. Colin called the dog—she bolted up the hill and sat down behind him. Thoughts of a quick retreat were formulating, but before Colin could move, he saw the bear charging up the sidehill.

It was moving fast, but Colin seemed to be seeing its actions in slow motion. The wild look in its eyes was beyond description. Colin chambered a round, aimed the gun, and fired. The bear came to a screeching halt at 15 meters and immediately defecated on the ground. It then ran to the nearest tree and began to climb.

While the bear was up the tree, Colin carefully moved forward and looked for blood. There wasn't any, and the bear didn't act as if it was hit. There was no sign of cubs, nor any carrion smell. The bear's droppings, which it had involuntarily purged when the gun went off, were green plant matter. The bear looked like an adult male, probably weighing about 300 pounds. Colin quickly took his camera out, snapped a picture, then took off.

Colin later speculated that Sage may have made the bear more angry, but the bear seemed awfully mad before it even saw them. If, however, he'd known it was a bear and had called the dog back

Colin and Sage.

Courtesy Colin Champagne.

before it ran down the hill, the whole thing might have been avoided.

After carefully examining the complexity of these accounts, and after reflecting on the many requests I was receiving for information regarding dog use against bears, I decided that a thorough indepth research project was in order for shedding light on this topic. I started gathering more dog/bear stories and spent most of my spare time during the first half of 2000 doing theoretical studies.

We are going to look at many more bear attacks involving dogs, but first, let's go back in time and see how the dog/bear relationship began.

WOLVES AND BEARS

Most people have seen the fascinating films showing the endless battle between African lions and hyenas. These two species compete for control over a dead animals until the carcass is consumed. This is an age-old war where hyenas often chase female lions off a carcass and will sometimes injure or kill them. The large male lions take revenge by killing hyenas whenever possible. Neither species can afford to let the other get the upper hand; at this point in time, they seem to be in an evolutionary stalemate.

Wolves and bears in North America and elsewhere have had a simular struggle for millions of years. Most black bears will retreat up a tree when approached by a wolf pack, but not always. Because grizzlies evolved in the treeless subarctic environment, they developed an open-ground defensive aggression and have a far more antagonistic relationship with wolves.

When I was in Denali National Park, Alaska, in August of 1995 with my family, we took the 89-mile bus trip on the restricted road through the park. At one point, the bus driver stopped and pointed at a side-hill to the north. He said that the year before, they'd witnessed a pack of five wolves harass a sow grizzly until she could no longer defend both of her first-year cubs. She moved off, straddling one cub, as the wolves ripped the other apart and ate it.

On June 20, 1998, I held a bear safety course at Bella Coola for International Forests Products. Two BC Parks personnel also attended the course. One of them, Jesse Jones, told me the following story:

He and Parks employee Tony Siala were doing trail work in Mackenzie Valley in the Rainbow Mountains near Bella Coola. In the early afternoon, they broke camp and headed up Octopus Lake Trail. When they arrived at the pass where the trail starts a descent to the lake, they set up camp. As they were cooking dinner, Jesse took out his binoculars and started glassing the Alpine area above them. He spotted a caribou about 300 meters away, and within a few minutes the animal starting acting nervous and headed over the hill. Jesse swung his binoculars in the opposite direction to the south and spotted a grizzly, about 500 meters away, walking in their direction. The bear travelled a short ways, then stopped and started digging vigorously.

Jesse and Tony stalked up to within 250 meters of the grizzly without it knowing they were there. The two men watched in amazement as the bear flung dirt and large boulders in all directions. It took only about 15 minutes for the medium-sized grizzly to catch the marmot it was after. All of a sudden Tony said, "There's a wolf." Jesse looked downhill and saw a large, greyish-white wolf loping along below them. He immediately thought it must know they were there, but it didn't look at them.

They couldn't quite believe how little time it took for the wolf to trot over to the bear. Then two more wolves of the same color appeared out of nowhere near the grizzly.

The threesome started harassing the bear by darting in and trying to nip it on the tail. The grizzly was making ferocious charges at the wolves, but they could easily move out of harm's way with little effort. The bear was holding the marmot in its mouth as it expended tremendous energy fighting its adversaries. But within a few minutes, it dropped the prize as it took after one of its tormenters. Immediately, one wolf grabbed the marmot, then trotted uphill and sat down to watch the fun. The bear soon lost interest in the battle and started to run southwest. The wolves chased it for at least two kilometers. The two men perceived the bear to be a four- or five-year-old.

The next morning, Jesse and Tony spotted the same bear across the basin. As they were watching it, another grizzly, about the same size or maybe slightly larger, charged downhill and chased the beleaguered bear out of sight. A little later, before moving on, Jesse and Tony saw the two bears only a foot apart, with the first in what appeared to be a submissive posture.

Wolves and bears have been deadly enemies for eons. And their main squabble is the same as lions and hyenas—holding onto a carcass until all the valuable meat and fat can be eaten. Wolves usually get their way with black bears and often kill and eat them. But they don't have it so easy with the grizzly. Observations in Alaska and other areas of North America indicate that grizzlies usually win the battle against wolves over a carcass, but not always. There are also other types of interactions between the two when wolves have the upper hand.

Both species will go out of their way to harass, attack, and, if possible, kill the other. This behavior, as well as the African model, is part of the evolutionary wars. Our own species was involved in an evolutionary war against other hominids for a very long time—we won out. Some scientists speculate that our victory resulted because we developed a symbiotic predatory/defense association with wolves. But how could that have happened?

FROM WOLVES TO DOGS

For a long period of time, it was believed that various dog breeds could have been developed from wolves, jackals, coyotes, or wild dogs. However, the most recent DNA analysis proves that the primary dog ancestor is the wolf. This makes sense, because all dog breeds can theoretically mate with wolves and have fertile offspring, and also because of all the wild canids, dog behavior is most similar to wolf behavior.

Several hominid (human-like) species and several canid (wolf-like) species interacted as competitive predators for at least 100,000 years in Eurasia. These species, and other predator species, would have been in continuous contact with each other, often fighting over food sources and sometimes killing each other.

Primitive human hunters would have known the location of most wolf rearing dens in their hunting territory and probably killed wolf pups in the springtime, whenever they had the opportunity, in order to increase game numbers. At some point in the distant past, at least 20,000, and possibly 50,000 years ago, primitive humans brought live wolf pups back to camp. At first it was probably done for novelty, or bringing something back for the kids to play with, or to raise as a future food source. Humans eventually became aware that wolf pups would bond to people, then later, as adults, would treat their own kind as an enemy.

For thousands of years, the experiment of capturing and rearing of wolves took place. In some cases, wolves would have been successfully tamed, in other cases not. There were probably many times when the captives escaped and returned to their rightful place. But, eventually, humans zeroed in on unique aspects of wolf behavior that made it possible to tame, dominate, and train a species with superior sensory powers to be a subordinate hunting companion and encampment guard.

I was once asked, "Why would a wolf enter into such a relationship?" The only answer available has to do with genetics and evolution: To express their genetically-inherited behaviors. Wolves simply had no choice in the matter.

In the first 12 weeks of life, a wolf pup bonds with whatever is feeding and nuzzling it. The trick was to provide the necessary milk, then provide more human nuzzling than mother wolf nuzzling. It might have been that the first real success in taming the wolf was to capture a mother wolf with pups.

Early wolf trainers must have recognized the animal's need to bond to a group, so humans became the adopted pack. The wolf's inherent nature, a willingness to live as a subordinate of the pack, was crucial. Challenges for dominance were beaten down until the wolf accepted the lesser role.

Primitive humans then utilized the wolf's natural hunting abilities and acute sensory for locating, stalking, and bringing down game. Two or three sibling wolves would have made life much easier for hunters and could also be used as a food source in times of great hunger.

At some point, humans recognized their companions' territorial behaviors: First, the extreme sensitivity for encroachment into their space; second, a willingness to die for the pack. As a result, humans tied wolves to sentinel posts on the perimeter of encampments. No bear, lion, or a myriad of other predators could get close without the alarm going off. And, of course, these sentinels would eventually become the defenders against the most dangerous of all creatures—other humans.

Ancient people soon realized that most other predators were afraid of wolves. If they came across a grizzly with a fresh kill, humans and wolves working in concert would have had a much higher success rate in obtaining this type of food source than working separately. The humans would have had to beat the wolves back after taking a carcass, then have someone hold them at bay as chunks were cut off and shared with them. The rest of the meat could then be butchered and packed back to camp.

By 15,000 years ago, many human groups were perfecting the rearing-bonding and training of wolves. But they were not dogs. They were still wild, dangerous animals that were merely tamed. Under these circumstances, people probably killed and ate those wolves in their charge that had behaviors unsuitable to be good companions.

There are some dog experts who disagree with the theory just presented on how humans and wolves became associated—they consider this explanation as quaint and hunter-biased. These experts suggest that wolves were first tamed by humans around settlements because wolves would have acted as scavengers on human waste products. They're dead wrong. Our present cultural view about wolves is a myth. Primitive humans wouldn't have ever tolerated wild wolves nearby. Since 1981, there have been a series of attacks on children by pet wolves and wolf-hybrids that have resulted in 15 deaths, 6 arms ripped off, and 25 serious injuries. In 1998, a 19 month-old boy was attacked by a wolf in Algonquin Park, Ontario; in 2000, two wolf attacks occurred, one on a boy in Alaska and one on a young man in B.C. The recent circumstance in India where wolves are killing and eating children in some rural areas demonstrates my point. These cases are more representative of what the primitive relationship between humans and wolves was really like. We will experience many more events like these during the next 20 years. The only reason we don't have serious problems with wolves right now is because we have trained them to fear us with modern weaponry—and because of the wolf's supreme intelligence in dealing with other competitive predators.

In the beginning, we developed a 'symbiotic predatory/defense association' with wolves because of our similarities, but the eventual creation of the human/dog symbiosis had to do with selecting unnatural traits for augmenting agriculture and sport hunting. Wolves were already excellent hunters and camp guards, but not good for herding and defending livestock or retrieving birds for their human masters.

DOMESTICATION OF THE WOLF

The domestication (selective breeding) of wolves on a large scale didn't start until human groups developed permanent settlements at the beginning of the agricultural age, approximately 10,000 to 12,000 years ago. This created the necessary condition for genetically isolating tame wolves when people started eliminating wild wolves to protect livestock and children. There would have been a significant need at that time to selectively breed tame wolves for traits augmenting agricultural activities.

People at that time wouldn't have known anything about genetics or the ability to speed up the evolutionary process. But they surely would have recognized the variations in physiology and behavior of individual wolves, as they would have also recognized that humans within a family group had traits in common. To them, this would have simply been characteristics of the bloodline.

If they had a dozen female and a dozen male tamed wolves, they were careful to breed only those with behaviors they wanted. This would have been easy to do, because wolves, unlike modern dogs, breed only in late winter. The primary keys in the domestication of the wolf was selective breeding and the rearing-bonding of each successive generation of pups, with the corresponding elimination of animals having unfavorable traits.

An interesting experiment by Belyaev (1979) in Siberia demonstrated what Darwin called "the mysterious laws of correlation". Belyaev's purpose was to develop characteristics in farm-raised silver foxes that would make them more manageable. He selectively bred for tameness within a large population from many different farms and, in a mere 20 years produced, an animal that was not only tame, but had many other dog-like features such as droopy ears, curled tail, black and white coat, and biannual estrus (breeding twice a year). None of these traits exist in any wild canid, and further experimentation has demonstrated that these changes were not controlled by recessive genes. Darwin went on to say that "if man goes on selecting, and thus augmenting, any peculiarity, he will almost certainly modify unintentionally other parts of the structure."

Genes seem to influence a whole range of behavioral and physiological attributes that we would think of as unconnected. Selecting for tameness may well disrupt the genome and create novel new gene combinations that can then be selected for.

Between 4,000 and 10,000 years ago, humans in different areas of the world selectively bred wolf/dogs for a variety of physical and behavioral traits. In some areas, hunting and guarding were still the important tasks. In those places where agriculture was developing, herding and livestock protection became pre-eminent. By 3,000 years ago, special breeds of dogs had been created for augmenting a whole range of human activities—some for hunting only fox and being small enough to enter a fox den; others for herding and livestock guarding; still others for human defense and war. And, eventually, some breeds were developed solely for beauty. An interesting aspect that developed in dogs is barking as the primary sound element during an aggressive display.

Eventually, as dog breeds became significantly different, crossbreeding hybridization became an important tool for creating new potential breeds with unique characteristics.

As people in past cultures were selectively breeding dogs for particular traits, unknown to them, they were manipulating not only genes and gene groups controlling specific attributes, but also genes controlling mechanisms, the most important being that of paedomorphosis. See if you can make sense of the following definition:

Heterochrony is the general term used in evolutionary biology to embrace the change in relative timing of ontogenetic events that underlie phylogenetic transformations of morphological [or behavioral] features. In general, a feature might begin to develop either earlier or later in the ontogeny of the descendant than it does in the ancestral taxon. (Macro Evolutionary Dynamics by Niles Eldridge.*)*

This is the type of material I often have to plow through when doing research. Of course, it's written that way for very good reasons. And if you can work your way through 300 to 400 pages of this stuff with the dictionary of science in hand, you can find endless gems of relevant information.

The important point here is this: Selective breeding of dogs over thousands of years retarded the onset of mature wolf behaviors. In other words, dogs maintain wolf puppy and juvenile behaviors into adulthood (neoteny). This makes them more obedient, more willing to please, more willing to be subordinate, and less aggressive. Anyone who's been around an adult tame wolf (in an urban setting) will immediately understand the importance of this part of dog behavior. Dogs don't usually have the aloofness or reactive unpredictability of an adult wolf.

The end result of all this controlled breeding is very complex in relation to dog breeds and individual dogs within a breed. A wolf goes through a series of five stages of behavior development from birth to reproduction: 1. Search, attach, and suck nipple. 2. Submit, food-beg, and socialize. 3. Eye, stalk, chase, and pack participation. 4. Bite, kill, dissect, and consume. 5. Dominance, courtship, scent marking, and parenting.

All dogs still have the main component wolf behaviors of #1, #2, and an altered #5, but most breeds have retarded or arrested #4 behaviors, and some breeds have variations in retardation of #3 behaviors. But within a breed, individual dogs can also vary. For example; only about 50 percent of some livestock guarding breeds have the necessary retarded wolf attack behaviors and won't injure animals in their care. Those dogs that do injure livestock are quickly sold by herdsman for pets or show dogs. But no matter what stage of behavioral retardation exists in a breed and a particular dog, it only exists as a potential. If proper socialization for tameness and training for reinforcing certain traits doesn't take place by humans, most dogs will ascend to some aspect of adult wolf behaviors.

MODERN DOGS

The approximately 400 breeds of dogs are broken down into six groups (using the 1950s model): sporting, hounds, working, terriers, toys, and nonsporting. The variations in size, speed, and behaviors of the breeds and groups are significant, resulting in some being much more effective for dealing with bears. I've seen even the lowliest mutt make a pretty good bear dog. However, if good training is expended on a dog with the best possible genetic characteristics, the results are usually spectacular.

In general, most breeds in the sporting and working groups are good, and a few of the larger terriers also have possibilities. There are many more breeds suitable for black bear encounters than are suitable for grizzly encounters. Many types of dogs will make the mistake of closing in on a grizzly bear and weren't bred for dealing with this animal. There are breeds that require more training than others, and some that make good bear dogs but not good family pets. But let's make an important distinction.

There are five different ways in which dogs are used against bears in modern times:

1. For keeping bears back from a home area by barking and charging at the intruder.
2. For defending livestock against bears.
3. For hunting bears.
4. For bear avoidance and defense.
5. For hazing bears out of parks and other people-use areas.

Some dogs are good for two or three of these categories, but not all five, because the behavioral pattern needed between some categories is different, or is mutually exclusive. For example, a good yard dog might bring a grizzly right back to you during an encounter in the bush, like one of my German Shepherds did. Also, dogs that are trained for hunting or hazing will push a bear too hard and too quick for proper avoidance, forcing the bear into a defensive-aggression charge response.

The thrust of this chapter is to identify dog traits that fit #4, avoidance and defense, but also to shed light on other aspects of dog/bear interactions.

NECESSARY CHARACTERISTICS

To boil all of the above material down to its most useful form for our task at hand means this: The dog breeds having the best traits for the types of behavioral expression to meet our requirements for both avoidance and defense are those with retardation of adult wolf behaviors at the #3 level of eye, stalk, and chase. These are the Setters, Pointers, Retrievers, Shepherds, Collies, and larger Spaniels; also the Airedale in the Terrier group. If we were selecting for defense only, then the Huskies, Siberians, Malamutes, and Karelians are the best. But this last group (northern breeds) have behaviors more similar to adult wolves, and training them for bear avoidance techniques—staying close and heeling on command— can be difficult if not impossible. These dogs can be very independent and sometimes become fixated on hunting squirrels and other small animals. These northern breeds are excellent dogs, but are not for everyone. This is not intended as a complete list, but it should give you an understanding of what is needed.

AVOIDANCE AND DEFENSE

To understand the importance of dogs for bear avoidance and defense, you must realize that the main reason people and bears have so many close-range encounters is because both have limited sensory abilities compared to most other animals. In the last 34 years, I've walked up on hundreds of bears that didn't know I was there. On the other hand, I've seen only five wolves in the bush, during that same time span, that were unaware of me.

You must think of human senses as being significantly handicapped. Our hearing and smelling senses are miniscule compared to most animals. Our visual capabilities are exceptional, but often impaired while in the wild. Bears have poor eyesight and average hearing. Their sense of smell is phenomenal, but down-wind or cross-wind situations totally negate that important sensory.

When trying to reduce the potential of a close-range encounter or a predatory stalk by a bear, the introduction of a third animal with superior sensory, speed, and aggression is what's needed.

Your dog must be trained to heel and stay close. It should travel ahead of you no more than 15 meters (50 feet) and continually check back to adjust its movement to yours. Your dog must not chase game or be overly sensitive to small animals. Ideally, it should be a good barker that stands its ground, but doesn't move forward without your command.

If a dog positions itself between you and the bear, then stands vigorously barking without charging the bear, you have the best situation. This gives the bear a chance to retreat without invoking its natural aggressive charge response—especially if it's a sow trying desperately to move her cubs out of harm's way.

If you take a dog into the field that you're unsure of, or a dog being trained, keep it on a leash and release it occasionally. If it starts to bark, leash it quickly. Let it move the length of the leash in the direction it wants to, and always bring the incident to a conclusion by petting and rewarding your dog when things calm down.

A dog must be willing to fight the bear if it comes after you. In most instances, the dog functions like a rodeo clown—it takes the brunt of the attack and is fast enough in most cases to stay away from the bear, giving you the time to escape. But there is no way of knowing how a dog may react if it has no experience with bears, or is a young dog in training. A novice could make a retreat right past you, then come back, or keep heading for the truck, or it might get killed. And, of course, this is why you'd also have your spray or firearm ready for defense, just in case the dog disappears.

Many people have remarked to me that they were surprised how well their dog reacted during its first bear encounter, as if it already knew what to do.

Dogs are natural enemies of bears because of their wolf ancestry. They are born with instinctive knowledge about how to deal with bears. But there's more to the picture. When wolves fight their own kind during dominance combat, they appear to be genuinely angry. But when wolves fight bears for food sources or simply to antagonize them, it's done in a matter-of-fact and business-like fashion that seems to be devoid of any real anger. On the other hand, I've seen many situations where a dog has gone after a bear in an extreme fit of anger. This exaggerated defense-aggression for protecting people has surely come about through selective breeding and probably relates to territorial defense in wolves.

Dogs don't always react the way we want in their first encounter with a bear, especially if a grizzly goes right after them. I had a six-month-old German Shepherd ruined for life during its first meeting with a grizzly bear. After that, he would take off on a run for home when a bear was detected.

If there is any possible way you can carefully expose your dog to bears without creating a dangerous situation for yourself, do so. This used to be easy before most garbage dumps were fenced.

In general, male dogs are more aggressive in most breeds towards other predators. This makes males better for defense, but more difficult to train for staying put and just barking without aggressively advancing, which could make things worse. I believe that both sexes are good for different reasons; I'll leave the decision up to you.

I'm not going to delve into all the particulars of training dogs, as there are many good books available. My task in this chapter is to show you, through example and explanation, what you want a dog to do and what not to do. But I'm going to cover one more important subject that is often overlooked by people before we examine more human-dog/bear interactions. The following is based on many research projects regarding the rearing of wolf and dog pups.

CHOOSING AND BONDING TO A DOG

If you want a good bear dog, don't buy it from a pet shop. A puppy has psychological needs that must be met if it is going to evolve into a well-adjusted adult. And there are also bonding requirements that must be done in a particular way.

You need to know about the mother and father of a pup to insure that they're of the right breed and have the traits you want, and that neither parent is aggressive towards people. The pup should not be handled by humans in the first three weeks, but progressively handled from the fourth to eighth weeks. The pup can be removed from the litter at eight weeks, but, if possible, let it occasionally visit its mother and/or littermates.

From eight to 12 weeks, spend a lot of time grooming your pup to complete the bonding relationship, and also let it interact with other people and animals that it will be around in adulthood, such as cats, horses, ducks, etc. This is the period that requires the first mild discipline to stop the pup from chasing the cats and ducks and to stop it from chewing everything in sight. From 12 to 24 weeks, it must learn all the do's and don'ts, as well as beginning the more formal training of staying close by when in the woods and to heel on command.

If you obtain an adult dog, make sure you find out about its history and behavioral traits. This is usually easy to do in rural areas, and I've seen many occasions when people had to give away excellent dogs because of changing conditions in their lives.

After years of living in a rural location with neighbors who have livestock, I prefer a female dog that is spayed at six months. It's easy to teach females to stay in their home territory, and they tend not to roam long distances looking for mates like males do. On the other hand, if you keep your dog in at night, or if a male is neutered, there is nothing wrong with a male dog.

MORE BEAR ATTACKS

In July 1999, I received a phone call from a friend, Dennis Clausen, who said his daughter had a serious incident with two grizzlies in June. He gave me brief details, then said he would call me again in October to let me know when Kathryn had returned home.

I caught up with this young woman in early November and interviewed her over the phone:

Kathryn Clausen was working with a herd of 900 sheep in a brush control project in North Central B.C. The sheep were penned up each night in a temporary corral in an area that had been logged. Each day they were moved out into the slash to feed on the deciduous brush that is competing with the planted conifer trees. When the sheep were moved to a new area, it was done in such a way that they would trample smaller competing plants as well.

The sheep fed for four hours each morning, then rested for four hours, then fed for another four. After each 12 hour shift, back in the pen they would go.

The herding was done by two people and eight dogs of two breeds—New Zealand Headings and Hunterways. The guarding

Kathryn and Steve.

Pictures courtesy Kathryn Clausen.

responsibilities fell on five Turkish Akbash. The herding dogs are middle sized; the guards are large.

Kathryn was headed for camp when the attack took place. Because it takes only one shepherd to drive the sheep back to camp, she'd gone ahead to prepare a meal and was accompanied by three herd dogs. Her co-worker, Steve Marett, and the other dogs were about 15 minutes behind with the herd.

As Kathryn came around a bend on a skid road, she saw two adult grizzlies about 50 meters away. She stood there waiting for them to leave, but the larger of the two started sniffing the air and walking towards her, with the smaller bear right behind. As the dogs went ballistic, the larger bear stopped. It stood up on its hind legs about 30 meters away, then went back down on all fours.

The smaller bear ran into the trees and then back out as if it were trying to lure the other bear away. But the larger bear reared up again, came down, and charged the woman and dogs—chomping and grunting as it came.

Kathryn made the fastest dash of her life. She saw a small tree beside the road and barely beat the bear to it. As she flew up through the limbs, she looked down and saw the swiping claws only a meter from her feet. The dogs were in full attack mode—charging in from all directions and nipping at the bear's hind end. As Kathryn moved frantically higher, the grizzly started up the tree, climbing on the limbs, just as she had. But the dogs were not about to let their favorite person down. As soon as the bear's rear end was off the ground and the weaponry headed towards Kathryn, the dogs would sink their teeth into the less dangerous part of the bear. Back down it came to chase its antagonists. Then the other bear came back out in the open and the dogs went chasing after it. And as soon as the dogs put their attention elsewhere, the larger bear started up the tree

Here's our heroes: Large tan dog on left is Den, black dog under is Luke, Queen is on right.

again. Kathryn called the dogs, and once again they harassed the bear back down the tree.

Kathryn knew that Steve and the Akbashs were several minutes behind; she started yelling for them to hurry up and get there. Five more times the grizzly tried to climb up to the terrified young woman. But the dogs knew exactly when the bear was exposed and vulnerable, and they used maximum effort to jump as high as they could to bite and torment the enemy.

It had been an endless 15-minute battle when the Akbashs showed up, but they didn't do a thing—they first retreated, then just stood watching, as if it was free entertainment. Finally, the bear started to feel out-numbered when the man and the other herd dogs arrived, and slowly, reluctantly, it headed back where the other bear was. The faithful herd dogs escorted both bears far off with triumphant barking.

Kathryn felt that she wasn't given adequate education on how to deal with a bear encounter for her job, and she wasn't issued bear spray. She went on to say that in an incident later that year, the Akbashs redeemed themselves by chasing off a grizzly bear. Also, Kathryn stated that when she went back by the spot where the attack occurred, she couldn't find the tree she'd climbed, and none of them had limbs low enough for her to reach. Even though she doesn't remember it, she must have either made a huge jump or shimmied for a short way before climbing on limbs.

Tanya De Groot lives in Quesnel, B.C. Like many British Columbians, she picks pine mushrooms in the fall. The following attack took place in October 1996:

It was just another day picking mushrooms in the woods, what I call moss lands. The terrain was semi-open with swamps and glacial eskers. As the navigator, I would look for elevated parts of the land in order to get past the low, wet areas. I was accompanied by my husband at that time, Gordon, and my female German Shepherd, Keela. Keela was 11 months old and about 55 pounds.

As we were walking along a ridge, we came to a place where a bear had been digging for roots. Gordon and I had seen this bear sign before, but to Keela, this was something new, and she spent quite a bit of time checking out the strange smell. After crossing a swamp, we climbed onto another small hill to finish filling our packs with mushrooms.

It was around 3 P.M. when we decided to call it quits for the day. We'd be travelling back through the same area where we saw the digging, and it would take about two-and-a-half hours to walk back to the road and our truck.

When I came across more digging on the way back, I decided that making noise would be the best strategy, so I yelled back to Gordon that I'd found more fresh digging and that a bear was nearby. I was on a steep sidehill, and after taking two more steps, I looked up and saw a large black bear in mid-air coming straight for me. The front paws were outstretched and aimed at my neck and shoulders. The impact lifted me off the ground, and after flying backwards about ten feet, I landed hard on the center of my back over a log—crushing the mushrooms and bending my packframe. I remember my right hand running through the bear's fur as it passed over the top of me, but I didn't grab onto it.

I had let out a major scream that brought Keela and Gordon running from 100 feet back. The bear wasn't on top of me, so I rolled off the log and grabbed my bear spray. I had time to pull the safety clip off before it came after me again, but when I sprayed, it dove its head into the moss and avoided most of the blast. The bear recovered and was ready to spring on me again when Keela sunk her teeth into the bear's rear end. The bear swung around so fast to bite the dog that Keela was completely airborne for a second, but she didn't lose her grip. Instantly, the two animals were fighting each other off to my side in a Devil's Club patch.

I heard Gordon yell at me from a knoll a short ways back. He told me to come up to him. As I did, I yelled to him that a bear had knocked me down. Gordon asked, "Where's Keela?" "She's fighting the bear in a swamp," I responded as I arrived at Gordon's side.

Ever so often we'd catch a glimpse of the bear and Keela spinning amongst the Skunk Cabbage, and we could see Devil's Club plants bending in all directions. We could hear the roars of a very mad bear.

After a while, we saw Keela running towards us all covered in mud—she was springing stiff-legged as she came. She was all pumped up, and so was I; I could still feel the effects of the adrenaline. As the three of us stood there, we spotted the bear a short distance away, ripping up ground moss in anger.

We had to make a quick decision as to which way to go to get out of there. We swung around to the other side of the swamp and crawled through mud up to our knees. Then we had to fight our way through a patch of blowdown. But we all made it back to the truck okay. As we came out, Keela was on constant guard watching behind us.

Tanya holding pine mushrooms with Keela at her side.
Courtesy Tanya De Groot.

At the time, I didn't realize I had a serious back injury. Several months later I had to have surgery to remove a crushed disc. I now suffer from nerve damage and have constant back pain. I still pick mushrooms in the same area, but pack more protection than bear spray, and, of course, I always have my trusted Keela with me.

Tanya came to a bear safety course in Quesnel that I presented for the Ministry of Forests. I had her tell her story to the class, and after, she stated it is important to have a good bond with your dog, and that after years of experience with a particular dog, you can pretty well tell by a dog's actions whether an animal is approaching or leaving and what level of danger there might be.

I've met many young women in B.C., like Tanya, who use dogs in the field when working. Most of these women work in forestry-related jobs. They all tell me that there is no way in hell they're going to be exposed to bears without their dogs along, no matter what policies a ministry or company may have regarding dog use.

The next incident involves a crew of foresters who were out in the springtime working on a proposed logging block. This story has many strange twists:

Chessie saves pair from bear
By Frank Peebles
Prince George Free Press Staff Writer
May 30, 1996

Civilization was a 25-minute helicopter ride away, but that's the way Trevor Stephen likes it. He's a timber cruiser. He was on a four-member crew dropped into a remote block north of Fort Nelson two weeks ago, where they made base camp and then snowshoed in to lay out a block. They were three kilometres from camp when the four of them heard a rustling in the trees. Standing only 20 metres away was a black bear, teeth bared. Twenty metres and closing!

Brock Campbell was the closest forester, and the bear was making tracks for him when Chessie decided she would take one for the team. Chessie is a three-year-old Chesapeake Bay Retriever, and Trevor's closest companion. She snarled out in front of the bear while Brock, Trevor, and their two compassers went for the shotguns they always carry. Well, usually always.

"We had decided to leave our guns back at the camp," says Trevor. "We had no protection at all. Chessie was all there was between the bear and us. The bear took a swat at her, Chessie ducked out of the way but stayed in close. The bear took a few more swipes and then bit her in the rear haunches near the spine. It had her good and she was yipping and screaming."

That's when Trevor got brave (read that "stupid") and went in to save his dear canine friend. He started kicking the bear and yelling at it while it wrestled with the wounded dog. Brock threw him a hatchet and he proceeded to pound on the bear's head with the blunt side (he had the good sense to know the blade would be useless against the tough skull) until the two compassers could move in with their bear mace. The stinging spray did absolutely no good.

Finally, the bear hesitated, and the dog broke free. The four men decided a retreat was in order, and they headed for camp.

"The bear didn't stop hunting us all the way back to camp," Trevor says. "He kept right behind us, and Chessie somehow kept up to us. She was torn up really badly, especially on one rear flank. I knew she could make it though. We called for the helicopter to come, and we went for the vet. It took us 12 hours to get Chessie to medical attention."

The vet was able to save the furry hero, even though she was in critical condition. Her recovery has been quick, however. Her stitches were out within a week, even though her muscle damage will take months to recover. She can already run and swim. Trevor considers himself even more fortunate.

"I have no doubt in my mind that she saved our lives out there," he states. "Brock will say the same. That bear was hunting, it spotted food, and we were going to be it. Chessie is the only thing that kept that from happening.

"Now don't get me wrong," he continues. "I don't think all bears are killers, and in all the years I've been in the bush I've never been attacked before. But bears are hungry when they come out of hibernation, and with all the cold weather this spring, the vegetation is set back two weeks. The bears are just really, really hungry this year. They're in predatory mode, and a human is fair game. I urge everyone who has to be in the trees, especially tree planters, to be very careful."

I compared this newspaper article to the carefully written report that was given to me by Wade Sjoden of TDB Consulting. The article was quite accurate but the company report had additional information. Following are statements that start just after Trevor hit the bear with the hatchet:

After a ten minute stand-off, the crew decided that their only chance was to retreat back in the direction of the camp. After starting off, the bear began to follow. The crew walked the first 500 meters without snowshoes as they had removed them in the initial confrontation. The bear charged several times within this interval of the return journey. The crew repeatedly yelled at the aggressor and this seemed to cause some confusion in the animal to the point where it would stop its pursuit for a second or two. About this time the crew arrived back near a seismic line where they put their snow-shoes back on and continued their retreat to camp. The bear con-tinued its same tactics for the whole journey back until the last 500 meters or so where it became even more aggressive and tried to out-flank the crew and get in front of them.

The crew beat the bear back to camp by 25 - 30 meters to spare wherein both Brock and Trevor got their shotguns (out of the tent) that were filled with the legal limit of rifled slugs, and waited for the bear to come into camp. This finally occurred in about 25 minutes, and the bear was shot to death just west of the camp.

It was agreed by all who experienced this encounter that had it not been for the dog, the incident could have become tragic for one, if not all, of the crew.

There are two additional interesting points in the company report: The bear seemed slow to react in the beginning, as if it had just came out of its den; when they examined the bear's body, they found it to be a lactating female.

This is one of only three aggressive stalking accounts I know of that involved a female black bear. It's different with grizzlies, but almost all predatory attacks by black bears involve males. This bear may have left its cubs in the den and come out in a defensive-aggressive mode, but was then triggered into opportunistic predato-ry behavior by some factor, such as the men looking vulnerable because of their difficult movements in the deep snow.

I've known Bruce and Nancy Colpitts for about six years. Both were born and raised in New Brunswick and moved to the Bella Coola Valley as newlyweds in 1991. Bruce is the operations forester for International Forest Products, and Nancy works in the planning section for the Ministry of Forests. I spent several years working with Nancy on the Bella Coola Local Resource Use Plan when she was chairperson of that committee. I had the good fortune of going on a five-day backpack mountain goat hunt with Bruce and Dave Flegel in September of 1999. Bruce is a great guy to be with out in the bush.

I sat down with Bruce and Nancy at their home on the evening of December 1, 2000. After catching up on each other's latest activi-ties, I started the interview:

On August 28, 1999, the Colpitts family, including Chandler (3) and James (1-1/2) took a hike on the Saloompt Interpretive Trail. The trail leaves Saloompt Road and meanders southwest towards the

Bella Coola River, then runs to the east along the river, then loops back north to the road again. Fortunately, there was another family member along on the hike—Sam, the family's seven-year-old male Golden Retriever.

The parents were teaching Chandler how to identify different tree species and showing both boys the wonders of nature. As they neared the river where the trail turns left, Chandler was out in front about ten feet searching for rocks, and James, who was just learning to walk, was struggling alongside Nancy. Sam was running back and forth on the trail, but staying within about 30 meters of the family group.

Chandler found an interesting pebble and rushed back to show his mother, who stopped to inspect the treasure. Bruce was now out in front about 15 meters and could hear a rhythmic splashing in the river just over the bank. He immediately thought that it was a low cedar limb being pulled back and forth by the current. He started past the sound as the trail turned left, but then thought maybe he should check it out.

The dog had gone on up the trail to the left, out of sight. As Bruce took two steps off the trail towards the steep brushy bank that descended into the river and was still 20 feet from its edge, he stopped when a thought jumped into his mind: 'This is stupid! What if it's a bear?'

The black snout appeared first, coming up from behind the bank, then the huge head. The bear stopped moving when Bruce could see it from the shoulders up. Bruce turned his head and yelled to Nancy, "Bear—grab the kids and run like hell." When he turned back, the grizzly was standing 15 feet away, rocking back and forth and blowing aggressively.

Bruce began talking to the bear as he slowly turned sideways and started inching back. As his feet made the trail, the bear moved forward. Bruce took off on a dead run on the east section of the trail, away from his family. Nancy was in a state of panic as she picked up James and grabbed Chandler by the hand. She saw Bruce disappear out of sight; the bear was lunging no more than three feet from her husband. Her mind was flooded with emotion: 'I'll never see him alive again!'

Nancy's motherly instinct to save her children kicked in, but terror was crippling her body. She tried to run, dragging Chandler, but her legs felt like chunks of lead that would barely move. Time was passing by in extreme slow motion. Visions of horrible bear maulings were flashing through her mind. The effort it took to move along was bizarre. It was, she said, like one of those nightmares in a movie where a person is being held back by some invisible force.

Bruce had made several long strides when he looked back over his shoulder—the grizzly was so close he could see only its rear end going up and down. Sam the dog was coming down the trail silently. Bruce knew that the bear was about to make contact; his left arm shot out automatically to the side and hooked a small cedar tree— he instantly flung himself off the trail. As he spun to the other side of the tree he could see the bear slowing down; by then, the bear and the dog were nose to nose. Bruce didn't stop his momentum and kept moving in a run back towards Nancy and the kids as the bear redirected its anger at the dog.

Within seconds, Bruce caught up to Nancy and scooped up Chandler to help with the get-away. Chandler's hat fell off, and as the Colpitts family moved along, the three-year-old started to scream that his hat was gone. Bruce was afraid that the bear might hear the noise, so he put his hand over Chandler's mouth, but that made it worse as the offended child really began to wail.

The trail was now swinging to the east, so they were moving closer to where the dog and bear had been headed. All of a sudden, Nancy saw Sam to the right, running parallel with them in the timber. Bruce had everyone stop and go silent so they could listen for the bear. They heard nothing, and began moving again.

When they arrived at the truck, Sam wasn't there. Bruce got the family inside the pickup and called for the dog. Within 30 seconds Sam ran up, trembling uncontrollably, and was also put inside.

There was another vehicle parked nearby; Bruce became concerned that someone may have hiked in on the other side of the loop and would be heading for the bear. He grabbed two cans of bear spray from the truck and headed back in. When he got to the spot where he could retrieve Chandler's hat, he yelled out to see if anyone was anywhere on the trail system. But there was no answer.

I asked Bruce if he thought the bear was the same sow with two cubs that had acted aggressively towards several different people in the same area during the two months prior to their incident. He said that it was a single large grizzly. When Bruce pointed at the other side of the room and stated that the top of the hump was higher than the top of the back of the couch, I knew that they had encountered a large male.

Bruce went on to say that he believes the bear was aware of their approach and was trying to find an escape route, but ended up cornered. Also, the dog had passed by the bear without detecting it, and throughout the whole ordeal, Sam never barked once.

I finished the interview by saying that the dog's timing had been a fortunate piece of luck.

The Colpitts family, including Sam.

Courtesy Bruce Colpitts.

No one in the Colpitts family was injured or killed because their dog took the brunt of the attack when the bear was about to tackle Bruce from behind. The prospect of any of these four people being mangled by a bear is something I don't even want to think about.

Sometimes a bear will take revenge on the dog clan. The following incident took place in Alaska on November 16, 1998:

Musher struggles with memory of eight dogs killed in grizzly attack
Reprinted with permission of The Associated Press.
Fairbanks—Musher Sepp Hermann says the grizzly bear that killed most of his dog team charged without hesitation before turning its

ferocious attention to him.

Herman survived the attack Wednesday without a scratch. But eight of the nine dogs in his team died in the attack near Wiseman. And he is struggling with the painful memory.

"They trusted me," Herman told the Daily News-Miner. "It was the first time I told them somewhere to go and I couldn't protect them."

Herman, who ran the 1991 Iditarod, was training about five miles south of Wiseman for his first Yukon Quest International Sled Dog Race. He lives in Fairbanks and traps in Wiseman, a remote community about 200 miles north of Fairbanks.

Herman was mushing up a hill at about 3 P.M. when the bear came tearing down the trail at breakneck speed.

"It was very aggressive, nonstop, ran right into the team," Herman said. "It jumped right into the team and started killing them ... there was (dogs) screaming all over the place."

Herman said the bear went from dog to dog, pushing each down then biting it to death.

Herman could not bring himself to flee. "I couldn't just sneak off and leave my dogs with this bear," he said.

While the bear had its back to him, Herman reached for his ice hook, the closest thing to a weapon he had. But the bear noticed Herman's efforts.

The grizzly charged him, putting both paws right on his shoulders. "I screamed at him, he didn't even care," Herman said.

At that point, one of Herman's dogs bit the grizzly on the rear. "The dog paid for it with his life," he said.

Herman sneaked off towards the Dalton Highway, about a quarter mile away. "Over the next 20 minutes I heard the screaming of my dogs," Herman said.

Shortly after he reached the haul road, a woman from Coldfoot gave Herman a ride into Wiseman.

Herman returned a few hours later with several local residents who were armed.

"The bear was still there eating dogs," he said. "It was like a whole dog team, strung out all dead."

One of those with Herman shot and killed the bear.

Zula, one of Herman's lead dogs, heard his voice and started wagging her tail among the carnage. Her stomach had been torn open, and half a leg was ripped away, but she was alive.

"I'm so happy to have Zula, it's a reason to celebrate," he said.

Zula is recovering and was able to eat a bit of meat on Saturday. Herman said the bear was large, but thin.

Both Herman and five-time Iditarod champion Rick Swenson had never heard of a musher and his team being attacked by a grizzly bear.

Swenson has known Herman for a number of years. *"He's a really good musher, a wilderness guide,"* Swenson said.

Herman has mushed for 20 years and never before lost a dog. *"Now I have a whole team dead, it was a good team too,"* he said. Herman now has a total of six dogs left.

He is not ruling out the Quest, since he has put in so much time preparing for the race and figures if he does not run the race this year he never will. But he would need to obtain good dogs from other mushers.

Herman also needs time. Sights like his bloody harness dim his mushing zeal.

"I walked out on the trail and saw the tracks of my dogs," he said. *"I don't feel like riding or running dogs."*

CONCLUSION

Dogs and bears are age-old enemies because dogs have become a surrogate for wolves in an evolutionary war for dominance. Primitive humans used tame wolves for hunting and defense for thousands of years before actual domestication started. Selective breeding of wolves started with permanent human settlement at the beginning of the agricultural age. By 2,000 to 4,000 years ago, a large number of dog breeds had been developed for augmenting a wide range of human activity. While selecting for tameness and other desirable traits in dogs, humans unknowingly manipulated a mechanism that reduced or eliminated the onset of mature wolf behaviors (neoteny). Certain dog breeds have a level of neoteny, plus additional characteristics, that make them much better than other breeds for bear avoidance and defense.

There are many people who are opposed to using dogs for bear defense—some because they genuinely believe that dogs make things worse during a bear encounter; others because they believe that bears should not be harassed by dogs. My research has convinced me of an extremely important point: THE NUMBER OF PEOPLE INJURED OR KILLED BY A BEAR WHILE ACCOMPANIED BY A DOG IS EXTREMELY SMALL COMPARED TO THE NUMBER OF PEOPLE SAVED BY A DOG FROM INJURY OR DEATH. But, we must use well-trained dogs wisely so they don't make a bear encounter more dangerous.

I could have included many more accounts of dogs saving people, but I had to limit this very lengthy chapter to incidents that demonstrated important points.

In closing, I want to acknowledge that in the modern context, our relationship with our trusted symbiont goes far beyond the practical features I've described here. Dogs provide a type of unconditional love that most of us experience only for a brief period during childhood. Just remember this: No other domesticated animal or pet can save you from a bear or a human intruder. Dogs provide more than rewarding relationships; they also protect us, and have done so for thousands of years.

10

BEAR ATTACK TRAUMA

This chapter is not intended to be a scientific treatise. I don't claim to be an expert on Post Traumatic Stress Syndrome. This viewpoint about bear attack trauma is based on direct interviews. I offer this information as a practical guide for anyone interested.

Most people in our modern North American culture feel they have significant control over the events in their lives. When some unforeseen accident happens, or if we are assaulted by somebody or something, we lose temporary control over our well-being. Afterwards, we try to find remedies that will prevent the terrible event from happening again.

I'd never thought much about debilitating stress resulting from bear attacks until doing research for my second book, *Bear Attacks - The Deadly Truth*. After interviewing many bear attack victims and family members of people killed by bears, I've come to believe that bear attack trauma is an important subject worth exploring. I can clearly see there are peculiarities about this type of trauma that the general public, the biological community, and the medical profession (rehabilitation services) are unaware of.

There were four particular cases in my second book that had trauma stress or grief counselling ramifications:

1. Lisa Dunbar told me that the counselling she received didn't help because the two different counselors she consulted were not emotionally equipped to handle the details of what she'd gone through when fighting the bear that killed her four-year-old son. But the worst trauma Lisa and her husband Dave faced was the blame people put on them for having an attractant that supposedly brought

the black bear into their yard in the first place. (*Lisa* chapter).

2. The bear attack trauma that Ray Bartrum felt during his grizzly attack was mainly due to his belief at the time that all bear attacks were predatory—he thought he was about to be killed, ripped to pieces, and eaten. He didn't know that most bear attacks involve aggressive-defensive behavior and was surprised when the bear left without killing him. However, his long-term stress was mainly due to the other three bear incidents he had after his attack—in two cases he was treed by aggressive bears. His residual stress forced him to find a place to work where there was no possibility of encountering grizzly bears. He never received any counselling of any kind. (*Terror by Tooth and Claw* chapter).

3. The severe stress that Fred Kowark felt six months after his attack was primarily related to the deliberate traumatizing behavior of the sow grizzly (she ran circles around him, ripping brush out and smacking trees), plus the fact that he was still continually exposed to grizzlies in his work. The important point here is that bears have evolved a behavioral pattern of deliberately traumatizing an intruder during a defensive-aggressive attack. This type of mental trauma might eventually fade in someone who was a rare visitor to bear country, but would thrive in the mind of someone who has to make a living in the bush. (*Terror by Tooth and Claw* chapter).

4. Carey Fumerton explained to me that she made very little progress after her husband was killed by a grizzly until she received the appropriate kind of help (for her) from the third grief counselor she tried. He was religious, as was she, but most importantly, he outlined a plan that gave her the different stages of recovery (*Without Warning* chapter).

Some aspects of bear attack trauma are similar to trauma of other near-death experiences; there is residual stress, disfigurement anguish, and fear of the incident happening again. There are also four additional aspects of bear attack trauma that I believe are unique or misunderstood.

1. A gentleman who lives in Terrace, B.C., told me about being on a four-man crew walking single file through the bush when the lead man was instantly attacked by a grizzly. He stood 30 feet away in frozen, shocked horror as his companion was assaulted by the bear. The bear wasn't just ripping and tearing at his work mate, it was bellowing and displaying a ferocious anger. Several weeks after the incident, this man came to realize that he may have ended up with more trauma from watching the attack than his friend did from being mauled by the bear.

2. Most modern young people who have careers that require working in the field have university degrees. In many universities, like the

ones in British Columbia, these people often obtain a viewpoint about mankind and nature that is incorporated into their beliefs about life. One principle in that viewpoint is that animals attack only when people have wrongfully intruded upon their space, and if you obey the rules of retreat, animals will back off as they don't really intend you any harm.

In some types of bear attacks on a person with such beliefs, where the bear exhibits behavior contrary to that belief system and the person is severely injured, their psychology of belief is also injured. This may sound minor in significance, but considering that this type of person is often someone who has embraced nature pantheism, the resulting trauma can be deep, lingering, and hard to diagnose.

3. One commonly-heard statement is that bear attack deaths are rarer than lightning strike deaths, or that you are 160,000 times more likely to die from a bee sting than a bear attack. These statements are nonsensical because they pertain to all North Americans, including the 95 percent who never go into bear country. Does someone who lives in New York City have the same risk of a bear attack as I do living on the B.C. Central Coast? This is what the bear-attack-to-lightning-strike comparison implies. Statistical statements about risk are sensible only when applied to individuals within certain geographical areas.

According to B.C. vital statistics, between 1985 and 1998 there were 12 people killed by bears in British Columbia. During that same period, three people were killed by lightning strikes and nine people killed by wasps, yellow jackets, and bees. Also, there were three deaths caused by cougars.

When counselling trauma stress, it's always a problem to deal with the fear a person has about the incident happening again. If you are telling someone from New York City who was attacked by a bear in Yellowstone Park that the likelihood of them ever being attacked by a bear again was nil, your reasoning would be sound. However, if you are counselling a B.C. field worker who has bear attack trauma, and you tell him that his fear was baseless, you would not be helping him. Almost all B.C. field workers are aware that the bear population has increased, and all through the summer they hear weekly stories from co-workers about the latest close calls with bears.

4. The last point I want to make is something I discovered during ten years of providing bear safety training, and relates to the fear many people have of being attacked by a bear: People have significantly different levels of fear about different types of danger that are unrelated to the degrees of risk. Everybody knows that it's far more dangerous for most people to drive a car than to be exposed to bears. But even someone who's had a serious car accident will

almost always have a greater fear of being attacked by a bear if they are having repeated bear exposure.

Nobody ever becomes used to the idea of having a bear take them down and remove half their face, no matter how low the risk. You can improve your driving skills and learn defensive driving; you feel that you have a degree of control over the risk of car accidents. But what control can all those people have who don't carry firearms and also don't trust pepper spray?

ATTACKS RESULTING IN TRAUMA

In November 1999, I received a letter from a gentleman who lives in the city of Coquitlam just east of Vancouver, B.C. He stated that he'd just finished reading my two books, which had been given to him by a friend, and that he appreciated my material because he'd recently been attacked by a sow grizzly in October. The letter contained a brief account of the incident.

I called Dave Nelmes shortly after receiving his letter and he gave me a more detailed explanation of what had happened. I asked if he had suffered trauma from the event, and he replied that he had. I requested that at some point in the future, when it felt right, to please write the events down, including the details of his trauma. He affirmed that he would. The last question I asked was what he did for a living. He said he was a Vancouver city policeman.

I appreciate Dave's willingness to let us glimpse the psychological impact of ending up in the jaws of a sow grizzly. I hope the reader will realize how difficult it would be for most men to share their innermost feelings as indicated in the following account:

I've hunted moose in the Prince George area for the past 15 years. Even though Limited Entry Draws have been less than plentiful in our group, we usually bring home game. I've had the same core partners for years, and we all know the country well. Each year we arrive around October 10th and set up for a two-week stay. Many other hunters we've met in the past also arrive during this time, and we rekindle old friendships.

In the last five years, bear encounters have increased, and all of these incidents were with grizzlies. We had a bear roar at us from the bush at less than 50 feet away, one crossed in front of our ATV during the dark morning hours as we drove to our stands, and we've had our game dined on at night.

Two years ago, a grizzly walked into our camp at 1:30 in the afternoon. This was a particular surprise as there were about seven guys at camp, and we were talking and running motors. This bear had cir-

cled twice before coming in to take a look. At one point it was only 30 feet away and had no fear of us.

Although this animal did not charge or seem aggressive, it was in no hurry to leave. We assumed the hanging game had attracted it. It took rifle shots and gunning truck engines to finally get it to move on.

The attack occurred on October 15th at about 9:30 A.M.

My father-in-law, Bud Scott, and I started our hunt for the day by leaving camp and walking down an old skidder trail we called the grass road. This trail is just wide enough for a full-sized truck if you don't mind having all your paint scraped off. It goes in for about a mile and then opens up into a fairly large grassy cut-block surrounded by timber.

Several days before, our neighbors had harvested a cow moose in this slash. They had returned there, as had other hunters, and hadn't seen any sign of animals except birds. In fact, birds were the only animals seen on any gut-piles of the few moose shot near the road.

As Bud and I walked in that morning, we saw a set of black bear tracks—these disappeared about 25 yards in and were replaced by numerous sets of moose tracks. As we arrived in the opening, we took up positions about 50 feet apart, and after scanning the area, we started using our moose calls. Even though we couldn't see each other because of the brush, we were close enough that we could've heard each other if talking in a normal voice.

About 30 minutes later, just as I finished a cow call, I heard the brush to my right come alive. The noise was coming from the other side of the skid trail. I immediately thought that we'd called in a moose from the timber across the slash. My heart began to pound as I looked to see what was coming. The crashing noise was moving quickly and seemed too loud for a moose. When I finally saw what came out of the brush onto the skid road, I knew I was in trouble.

Two large grizzly cubs appeared first, and as they ran into the opening, they split up. One headed into the slash as the other veered right towards the timber. I stood up from the stump I was sitting on and yelled, "Grizzly bear," so that Bud would be warned of what was coming. As I yelled, the sow came into sight on the edge of some willows. I moved slowly backwards yelling and waving my free arm, hoping that she would take off.

As she stood up on her hind legs, I could see that she was at least a third larger than her cubs. In an instant, she dropped to all fours and charged at me from 40 feet.

Everything seemed in slow motion as I saw this mass coming

*towards me. I remember thinking that this isn't happening. I point-
ed my rifle in her direction and fired from the hip. To my surprise,
she went down—but she wasn't dead.*

*I watched as the sow struggled to get up. She snarled and growled
as I tried to back up, but there was no place to go. I still wasn't sure
whether this was a dream or not. I was screaming for Bud to come
and help me, but I didn't hear anything in his direction. Again, everything was happening in slow motion.*

*When the bear finally got to her feet, I fired again, but somehow
ended up on my back. She had taken my leg out from under me in
a flash; I felt intense pressure, but no pain, as her mouth clamped
down. I was screaming for Bud and kicking her in the head with my
free leg. I still had my rifle, but for some reason I didn't think to shoot
her again. I then heard Bud shoot. The sow let go of my leg, turned,
and started moving back to where she had come from—swinging her
head from side to side. I remember saying out loud, "Thanks, partner."*

*I struggled to my feet and yelled for Bud. He asked if I was okay.
I told him that I had been bitten but could walk. I raced through the
willows towards Bud and started reloading my rifle as fast as I could;
I was afraid the sow was coming back. When I got to Bud I sat down,
and he inspected my leg. There was a deep gash exposing the
bone, but there was very little bleeding.*

*We moved out into an open area where we could see all around. I
used the radio-phone to call our partners and asked for help. All I
could think of was to get out of there—quickly.*

*In about ten minutes one of our party drove his truck up to the edge
of the slash, but I wasn't about to leave my spot until he pulled up to
within 50 feet. As I was unloading my gun, I began shaking and crying. The short distance to the pickup was one of the longest walks
I've ever made, and I didn't feel safe until I was inside the truck.*

*Bud and I were driven to the Prince George Hospital. The medical
staff were fantastic, and I was treated as if I were their only patient.
I had puncture wounds to my left shin, and one of the sow's teeth
had clipped the bone. After cleaning and stitching, I was released
with a prescription for antibiotics and pain killers.*

*We then went to the Conservation Officer Service office to report
the incident. Officer Mike Richardson was our interviewer. He listened intently as I described what had happened. I told him I felt
guilty about shooting the bear, but felt that my life was in danger.
Richardson said it appeared that I didn't have any other choice and
that he and other COs would investigate the site that afternoon. He
also told me that years before, when he was working for the Ministry
of Forests, he had been bluff-charged several times by a large male*

grizzly, so he knew what I'd gone through.

We arrived back at camp hours later, expecting to meet the officers. We were surprised to be greeted by hunters from all around the area—they wanted to shake my hand. It made me feel like some kind of hero. Everyone wanted to hear all the details of the attack.

I noticed a helicopter sitting in a nearby clearing, and we were told that the COs were down in the slash where the incident occurred. The pilot came up to me and asked if I wanted to fly over the site to pinpoint where the incident had happened. I agreed to; I had always wanted to ride in a helicopter.

As we flew, I began to feel uncomfortable, but not because of a fear of flying. We spotted the officers coming out of a stand of timber so the pilot dropped me back at my camp and then returned to pick them up at the slash.

I went over to greet the COs when they landed. I recognized Richardson as one of the three. One of them asked to speak to the guy with the limp—I assumed he meant me. He advised me that they'd tracked the sow for several hundred yards, eventually losing the blood trail. They believed she was dead, because the cubs had been seen alone in the logging slash. We were told not to go into that area for several days, and with that, they left.

That evening there was lots of discussion about what had happened, but I tried to minimize the incident. I didn't feel like talking about it. Bud and I discussed our hunting plans and decided not to stray too far from camp during the next few days.

Three days later we heard that the cubs were bothering a hunting camp a few miles away, so we drove over there and assisted the hunters in scaring off the cubs several times over a two-hour period. I called the CO service and advised them about the cubs. Both cubs were later killed for aggressive actions towards hunters. They were between 150 and 200 pounds in weight.

Mike Richardson had asked me to come back in to clear up a few details, so when our hunt was over, we went to the CO office when we passed through Prince George. Mike introduced me to an officer named Tony, and I was asked if I thought that maybe I wouldn't have been attacked if I hadn't yelled at the bears, and exactly where had I shot the sow, and was I aware that there had been a moose-kill in the slash. I felt that they were attaching blame on me for the attack—they made me feel it was my fault.

I told them that I'd followed the guidelines in the hunting regulations regarding yelling at an aggressive bear. I showed them the guidelines from their own copy and said that I thought that yelling would help the situation. They then acted apologetic for the information in the regulations that they obviously disagreed with. They also told me about a ring of grizzly hunters they had investigated and recently charged.

Richardson thanked me for coming in. As I left, other officers stepped out of their rooms, as if to look at me, and one said that I was lucky. I didn't appreciate his comment. Richardson's last statement was, "This is mauling season."

I had called my wife the day after the incident and gave her a brief account of what had happened. When Bud and I arrived home we told our story to all our family members. Again, I minimized the experience and was more concerned about my family's trauma than my own.

At work I was asked to repeat the story several times. I was referred to as Grizzly Adams, bear bait, and a host of other names. After 21 years as a policeman, I knew that people in my profession often used humor for dealing with traumatic experiences. Some of my co-workers treated me as a legend, others just wanted to see the scar.

My home life was normal, but my wife seemed detached. I hadn't heard from Bud since we got back and didn't feel like talking to him. I began to lose interest in my work and was starting to feel negative about things.

I began having nightmares where I would wake up saying, "It's only a dream." These dreams were usually about being bitten by a man I was trying to arrest or about trying to save my daughter from drowning in a river.

One day I received an e-mail from a peer who asked me to call him. I didn't want to respond, because I thought he wanted to hear the story. He eventually phoned and asked how I was doing. My emotions overcame me, and I began to sob. After our conversation, I contacted a counselor with our Human Resources Section.

The session with the psychologist was something I definitely needed. Dr. Aube listened as I described the attack. After the story I stated that it must have been my police and other special training that gave me the ability to survive the incident. Dr. Aube then asked me if the police department was teaching skills for surviving a sudden grizzly attack. I answered that they weren't. She then asked if they had taught me how to be a victim. Again my answer was negative. I began crying.

Dr. Aube explained the positive and negative symptoms of post traumatic stress syndrome. She said that there were secondary victims including Bud and my wife. I then released feelings that came from deep within. I told the doctor that I was angry at Bud for not rescuing me from the bear and angry at my other hunting partners for not getting to me sooner after the attack. Rationally, I knew they had all done everything they could, but the anger was still there. I also felt as though I was under a microscope with everyone watching me, and at the same time, I felt alone and misunderstood.

Dr. Aube explained that the nightmares were symptomatic of feeling helpless and being a victim. They would help me adjust to the fact that I wasn't a hero, but simply a man who'd had a bad encounter with a grizzly bear.

I decided to locate other people who had experienced bear encounters. I met and talked with several and discovered that I'm not alone. My brother-in-law, Jim Turner, introduced me to your two books. He is also a hunter and has encountered grizzlies over the years while elk hunting.

In reading your books, I've learned much about bear behavior and will be changing my habits. I will continue my research regarding bears, and I'm determined to continue enjoying the woods in my hobbies of hunting, fishing, and camping.

I waited for several months before calling Dave for a final interview as I wanted a later perspective. Dave said he'd recovered well but still had feelings of guilt about killing the sow. He had recently told this to a friend, who responded by saying, "Don't feel bad about it. Your wife still has a husband, and your children still have a father—that's all that matters."

———

I received an e-mail from Darin Brown in September 1999. He said he'd read my first book and wanted to contact me because he'd been attacked by a black bear on September 5, 1991, near Clearwater, B.C. I called Darin, and after he gave me an account of the incident, I asked if he'd write the story down. He said he would try to find time. I also suggested that he read my second book.

The following January I received Darin's account:

At the time of the attack, I worked for a forest consulting firm (Reid Collins and Associates) based in Vancouver. Our crew of four was just completing an inventory cruise for Slocan Forest Products. Our job was to establish strip lines with cruise plots to locate timber types and to estimate timber volumes.

My partner, Brooks Horne, dropped me off at the side of an old dirt road to start my strip line for the day. Brooks then took the truck and drove to the area where he was to start his strip line. For this project, we all worked alone in order to finish the contract on schedule.

I spent the day running the line and measuring tree heights and diameters in the many plots I established, and I saw considerable moose sign.

Late in the afternoon, I walked through a series of swamps connected by small pools of water. It was much easier to skirt the edges of these seepages rather than tripping through the dense brush in the forest.

I stopped to take a drink from my canteen and heard something moving through the bushes about 60 meters away. I knew it was the beginning of the moose rutting season, so I immediately thought that an angry moose was headed in my direction. I quickly removed my vest and other gear and started up the nearest tree.

Near the top, I stopped to listen and was shocked to hear the animal running at a fast pace directly towards me—I could also hear teeth popping. I was instantly horrified as I realized the sounds were coming from a bear, and I had no defense against it.

My gut wrenched as I saw a large black bear burst through the dense brush on the edge of the swamp and head for my tree at incredible speed. I said a prayer as I lost sight of it at the base of the tree, then heard the scraping of claws on the bark as the tree began to shake.

I looked down between my legs and saw the bear's head break through the limbs at my feet. In a flash it had my right foot in its jaws and began violently yanking me down the tree. I desperately grabbed from branch to branch to keep from falling as I kicked the bear in the face with my free leg. I was so terrified that I didn't even feel the pain of the teeth that were piercing my ankle.

I screamed at the animal, and to my surprise it released my foot, then climbed down to the ground. It began taking its rage out on my equipment—slapping it all over the place. I thought maybe the bear was through teaching me a lesson and would leave, but then I heard the claws on the bark again.

This time the bear bit into my right calf and pulled me down several meters as I relentlessly kicked it in the eyes with sharp caulks. It let go and once again retreated to the ground. The adrenaline rush and the fear of being killed had kept me focussed on surviving and I didn't even think about the injuries I was receiving.

I couldn't quite believe it, but the bear came up the tree a third time. It stopped just below me and hit my right leg with its paw. My original horror had changed into a focused fight for life, and now I became enraged at this animal that was tormenting me so. Without thinking, I grabbed onto two limbs and jumped upward and landed on the bear's face with both feet and all my body weight. The bear was knocked from the tree, but I was also falling and grabbing at passing branches. I managed to grasp the trunk just before landing on the ground, but still in a fit of rage, I jumped down and ran up to the bear—we stood two feet apart for a moment, in a stalemate. I pulled the small hatchet from my belt, picked up a piece of wood, and started swinging them at the surprised animal. I chased the bear around the tree we'd been in, determined to win this battle. It ran off about ten meters and stopped to watch me. We were both exhausted from the four-minute ordeal. I could see that it was cut-up around the eyes. I still didn't have a clue what my injuries were.

I banged the hatchet against my hard hat as I gathered up my vest and took off running away from the bear. I scrambled through brush for several minutes, then came to a large, partially dried-up swamp. I ran through the tall grass and reeds, avoiding small ponds here and there, to the middle of the swamp and sat down on an area of high ground. My heart was pounding a mile a minute. I stared in the direction I'd come from, hoping the bear wouldn't follow me. It was open all around me; I kept checking in all directions to make sure it wasn't sneaking up.

Eventually, I looked through the holes in my pant leg and boot to see how bad my injuries were. My boot was stained red, but the bleeding wasn't life-threatening. Panic started to set in as I realized I was lost in a swamp with an injured leg. I took off on a due-north bearing in hopes of hitting the road or finding anything I could recognize. As I left the swamp and scrambled through the timber, I was overcome with the terror of possibly running into another bear. Close to an hour later, I found a line of hip chain string that I'd put in during the morning and followed it back to the road.

I hobbled down the road until I found the truck. I yelled to see if Brooks was close enough to hear me. It was a pleasant surprise to hear him answer. I yelled that I'd been mauled by a bear and needed help. I was so exhausted but relieved when Brooks came into sight. My emotions were topsy-turvey; I was crying and throwing my equipment at the truck. Within an hour I was on my way to the Clearwater Hospital for medical attention.

I had canine puncture wounds to the top of my right foot and also to the outside of my right calf, which exposed the muscle. When the bear hit me with its paw, it caused a claw puncture wound across the back of my leg and down across the Achilles tendon. My right foot was badly bruised. I lost several months' work because the wounds were left open to drain.

The conservation officer who investigated the case told me that the attack occurred where they release their problem bears, and it might have been a relocated animal. He also told me that I was lucky to have survived and that fighting the bear made the difference in mak-

ing it out of the woods alive.

The immediate trauma associated with the attack is hard to describe. I didn't receive any formal counselling to deal with the mental anguish and suffered many years of recurring nightmares. These dreams were unbelievably vivid in detail, right down to the sounds of the claws ripping at the bark, the grunting of the bear, and the stare of those piercing dark eyes.

In the past eight years since the attack, the nightmares have subsided from nightly to weekly, and I now deal with about one a month. It's probably hard for my mind to put this incident away, because I still work in the woods and still fear going through the same ordeal again.

It took years before I could adjust to working alone again. When I know I'll be working in the field the following day, I have to be careful what I read the night before to make sure it doesn't trigger thoughts about bears. There have been times when I came across swamps that looked like the one where I was attacked, and I immediately became nervous and started listening for anything approaching. I've had squirrels drop cones near me that started my heart pounding violently.

Shortly after the attack, I obtained a permit to carry a 44 magnum handgun. I've had many bear encounters in recent years, including charges, and this important tool has given me the confidence to deal with an ever-increasing bear population. On two other occasions I have chased off persistent bears by running at them while swinging an axe.

I become enraged if a bear doesn't leave during an encounter, and this feeling is no doubt a carry-over from what happened to me. I'm still upset with the way the bear taunted and tormented me during the attack.

Every day starts off by seeing the scars when I get dressed. My leg gets very sore when I have to work on a steep sidehill; I still have a long-term physical injury as a constant reminder.

I suspect that some bear attack victims gain a new appreciation for life while others are left with anguish. Myself, I'm somewhere in between as I haven't been able to live life to the fullest—especially regarding my favorite activities of hiking, camping, and fishing—for fear of encountering another aggressive bear.

This whole affair has been a life-altering experience, but it would have been much worse if I hadn't had a supportive wife, family, and friends.

During the process of working on this story, I received a letter from Darin saying he'd read my second book and appreciated my comments about how bear attack victims, like himself, are often blamed for the incident because they were supposedly invading bear habitat. He said this is a weird concept considering that his work is part of the process for supplying some of the essentials of life for the very people who make such claims. When they buy wood or paper products, they are directly supporting his efforts on their behalf.

After sending the first draft to Darin for an accuracy check, I received another letter from him with the following comment: "I'm glad you asked me to write the attack down on paper because I believe it has helped me deal with the issue of being mauled."

Darin with his family.

Courtesy Darin Brown.

I arrived in Golden, B.C., at about noon of May 12, 1998. I was in the middle of a series of 11 bear safety courses that would put over 3,000 kilometers on my truck. I was there to participate in the second annual Bird and Bear Festival.

After checking into the Golden Rim Motel, I spent the afternoon preparing material for my evening presentation on Recreational Bear Safety. At about 3 P.M., I received a call from Jean Persson. She introduced herself as Gary Persson's sister. (Gary was the Rod and

Gun Club member who helped organize my part in the festival.)

Jean stated that there was a woman in Golden I needed to talk to. She gave me a brief description of the bear attack on Pat Howard and the ongoing consequences. Jean said she'd be willing to set up the interview if I had time to do it. I suggested the next morning at 10 A.M. in my room. A few minutes later she called back and confirmed the meeting.

As I continued working on my presentation, bells started going off in my head. I put the pencil down and stared out the window at the beautiful snow-peaked mountains to the west. I suddenly realized I'd heard about this attack before. A Ministry of Forests (MOF) employee, Melanie Milum, who I spent several years with on the Bella Coola Local Resource Use Planning Committee, had told me about this terrible event in 1992. She'd heard the story from Naima Schiesser, the woman who was with Pat during the attack.

I remembered thinking at the time how much I'd like to obtain the details of that story, but because of what I was told about the after-affects on Pat, I felt it would probably be a major intrusion if I tried to contact her.

My presentation that evening to a crowd of about 100 people went very well. Even the local boy scout troop was there to learn about avoiding bears and how to survive a bear attack. I toned down some of the details regarding particular bear attacks in my material because of the surprising number of kids in the audience.

10 A.M., May 13th: I waved at Pat from the second floor balcony as she stepped out of her car and then told her to come on up. Luckily, the room had a nice little table and two chairs where the interview could take place. We shook hands and sat down.

I asked Pat where she grew up. She stated that she was raised in North Vancouver in an average-sized family that was very outdoor-orientated. They enjoyed camping, skiing, sports, and many other activities. She speculated that was probably why she ended up living in a rural area like Golden with a career that primarily involved field work. Her husband also enjoyed working and recreating in the bush. Pat had always had a healthy respect for bears and their potential danger, but was not overly concerned about working in bear country because she knew that the risk of being attacked was low. (At the time of Pat's bear attack, 1988, bear sprays were not carried, and the prevailing view was to back away from a bear encounter and if attacked, to 'play dead'.)

The grizzly attack on Pat Howard took place on September 10, 1988.

Pat and Naima's work project for the day was to traverse several small logged areas for replanting. They drove out on the Big Bend Highway, northwest of Golden, and turned off at the 45-kilometer mark onto a logging mainline and then onto a secondary spur.

The road was badly grown in, and after a short ways, they came to a washout. When turning the truck around, they backed into the washout and got stuck. It took about 20 minutes to get the truck out. They would have to proceed to the first location on foot.

Pat was in the lead as they left the truck, and they started fighting their way through the brush and alder trees. They weren't thinking about bears because during the process of working the truck free, they'd made a lot of noise. It was only 50 meters later that Pat saw a sow grizzly and a cub through the alders. The bears were very close. "There's a bear," she said quietly, as she halted.

The two women started walking backwards, facing the bears. Very quickly Pat couldn't see the bears any more because of the trees. Naima was backing out of the other side of a washout as Pat started backing down into it. Naima could now see the sow as Pat fell down. Naima whispered, "Are you okay?"

As Pat got back onto her feet, she saw the bear coming through the brush; Pat hollered, and the sow stopped at eight meters. They lost sight of the bear as they backed around a curve in the road.

All of a sudden, Pat saw the sow moving along the top of a bank in front of her to the left. As the bear stopped, her two cubs piled up against her. Pat yelled again, but the three animals just stared at her. 'What do I do now? I don't want to be here,' raced through Pat's mind. Her last conscious thought was, 'Those cubs have round ears.'

Pat's mind slipped off into emptiness. She couldn't see or feel anything, but could hear someone screaming at the top of their lungs. Then she heard a voice say, 'If they don't stop screaming, they're dead.' Shortly thereafter, the detached voice came again, 'There goes a big chunk of meat.' Pat wondered who it was. Then darkness.

Suddenly, she heard the sound of gravel crunching; Pat's senses were coming back. She felt a vague physical sensation of having the wind knocked out of her and a mental sensation of, 'What was that?' But she was completely removed from what was taking place. Next there was silence, and then she sensed something right there, close to her head. As she struggled to her feet, she realized it was a truck bumper. Pat staggered around to the side of the truck; she saw a door open, and she got in. Now the truck was flying down the road, and she could hear Naima radioing the district office.

It was Pat's sister-in-law who took the call and heard the terrible news. Naima was told that people would be coming to meet them and help out. She was then asked if a helicopter was needed for evacuation. Naima replied, "Yes." Two ministry employees on the highway, Al Pollard and Ric Hardy, heard the desperate call and headed for the 45 kilometer turnoff.

Naima was concerned about Pat's statements that it felt like her feet were swelling inside her boots and that her right wrist was hurting. Naima could see that Pat's eye sockets were filling with blood. They pulled into a hunting camp they'd seen on the way in, but there was no one there to help. Now that they were away from the bears, Naima checked Pat's wounds and put pressure bandages on her neck, shoulder, and upper right arm, then down the road they hurried.

Lil Cacaci, a Ministry of Forests employee, had heard the calls and contacted Naima to keep a conversation going, which was very helpful for keeping up the spirit of both women.

It was a great relief for them when they saw Al and Ric's truck at the 45 km turnoff. The men rushed to the truck as it came to a halt and opened the passenger door. There was blood everywhere. The two men examined Pat first and then Naima. Al told Ric to call a nearby crew to come over and drive Naima's truck back to the office. Pat started insisting that she was okay and just needed to be driven to the hospital to be checked out. Naima insisted that Pat wasn't okay and needed immediate attention. Pat was getting annoyed about all the fuss being made over her; she was not aware of the damage the sow had inflicted, nor how bad she looked.

The chopper was there in short order, but the flight back to civilization seemed to take forever. Pat was lying on her back as shock started to set in. Ric kept his hand on her knee and was talking to her. The smell of the fuel in a nearby drip-torch was making Pat sick. Every so often Ric would shake her as her mind drifted in and out of a black fog. She desperately wanted this torture to be over.

The aircraft finally set down at the Ministry of Forests' heli-pad. Pat was lifted out of the back seat and immediately felt embarrassed as she saw all the people gathering around. She was half walked, half carried to the waiting truck; she felt weird and faint.

Pat was given a shot of Demerol as the doctor and nurses started cleaning and sewing. A newspaper reporter was trying to get into the emergency room but was quickly removed by a determined nurse. As the drug took affect, Pat starting feeling better, even humorous.

She had a deep laceration on her left shoulder, four on her right shoulder, and two across her right shoulder blade. She had two canine puncture wounds on her right breast and small lacerations on her hands, her right side, by her left eye, in front of her right ear, and on her forehead at the hairline. In addition, she had bruising to her arms and head, swelling on the right side of her head, and a badly sprained right wrist. But she'd been lucky—she could have lost a large part of her face and shoulder.

It was great when Pat's husband, Wayne, and other family members arrived and gave her the support she needed. Many messages came into the hospital that evening from friends and work mates wishing for a speedy recovery. But before going to sleep, Pat felt depression setting in as it finally hit her what could've happened.

Three days later, Pat was allowed to go home. She was off work for three months as her physical injuries healed. But there were no mental problems of nightmares, anxiety, or unreasonable fear; nor was there any memory of the actual event. The attack seemed to be deeply buried, with no conduit to her conscious or subconscious mind.

Pat went back to work for a short period and was then laid off for the winter. When she went to work the next spring, she made sure she always had a partner. Pat continued to work for the MOF for another eight years. In the beginning, even though she was sometimes very nervous working in the field, things went pretty well. Then as time went by, problems started surfacing. Some of the people she worked with noticed strange things about Pat's behavior. She would all of a sudden hesitate while walking in the bush and just stand there with a blank stare. If a work mate said something to her, she would start again, but would not remember that she had stopped and would later deny it. When she finally started working by herself, it was very difficult to be comfortable in the bush. By 1996, as the problems escalated, it became impossible.

Then Pat's nightmares about the attack began. The dreams revolved around absolute terror. But something else was happening, unrelated to her trauma. The bear population increased dramatically and she was now seeing more in the bush, along roads, and in her yard. When a bear unexpectedly appeared, she would freeze up.

The union that Pat belonged to paid for psychological counselling. The therapist helped her considerably by explaining that she wasn't losing her mind, and that what she was experiencing was the normal process of assimilating the terror of the attack. Pat decided to reopen her Workers' Compensation Board (WCB) claim in order to get more help.

After Pat was laid off by the MOF in the early fall of '96, she talked to the doctor who treated her after the attack and also to her regular doctor. The necessary forms were sent in during October, and several weeks later, Pat was requested to come to Cranbrook for a meeting with a WCB representative.

At the meeting, Pat explained what had happened to her regarding the attack and the aftereffects. She was given a questionnaire to fill out that contained over 100 multiple choice questions. Most were mundane, but about five were key, such as: Do you ever feel like life isn't worth living? Do you ever consider taking your own life? Do you ever have the urge to hurt other people?

A second discussion then took place where she was told that the WCB didn't have any money for her. Pat stated that she wasn't after money, she wanted to be retrained for a job that didn't include working outdoors. She then said that the WCB should talk with her past co-workers to obtain a clear picture of her problems.

When Pat and her husband drove back to Golden, she was very upset and felt that the whole thing had been a waste of time. She realized that someone who was after a disability settlement could easily get it by exaggerating or lying on the key questions of the questionnaire that were obvious indicators of a person's mental state.

About a month later, Pat received a letter from the WCB saying that her case wouldn't be reopened. Many of her friends told her to keep pushing and get the help she needed. Pat decided that it wasn't worth it; she would get the necessary training herself. She didn't have any further contact with the WCB, and later found out that they hadn't talked to any of her work partners.

The interview had taken almost two hours. I told Pat that I'd like to use her story in my next book; she said that would be fine. I then explained that I'd also like to interview Naima in order to acquire a perspective of what she experienced during the attack. I then gave Pat copies of my two books. We shook hands again, and we both left the motel as I had to attend a book signing.

The next day I concluded the second part of my commitment to the Bird and Bear Festival by participating in a panel of bear experts who answered questions from a large number of people regarding a wide range of bear-related topics. There were major sparks flying at one point between certain members of the audience and one of the biologists who stated he believed that there were only 6000 grizzly bears in B.C. After the panel exercise was over, I headed for Kamloops and more training sessions.

November 9, 1999. After I arrived home, it took a while to make contact with Naima Schiesser. When I was able to talk to her, she was very helpful and willing to explain what she saw the day of Pat's attack. She stated that they were working in the Clearwater Creek area that had burned many years before and had also been logged in parts of the burn. The planted trees they were to inspect were about 12 years old.

Naima said that after they got the truck unstuck and turned around, they started walking downhill on an old skid road. They were gone only a few minutes when they saw the bears. At first her mind wouldn't accept what she was seeing. She thought, 'Is that a moose, a horse, an elk?', but then reality finally set in. She was looking at a sow grizzly with one large cub on each side. Naima's next thought was different, 'How beautiful and graceful are the rhythmic movements of the sow's head swinging back and forth.'

Naima whispered, "Let's back up." The two women were close together as they started walking backwards. Pat fell down as they entered the washout. Naima spoke quietly, "Are you okay?", then looked back at the bears. She felt a powerful impulse to flee as she saw them coming. Instinct and terror took over as she turned and ran for the truck. She could hear Pat screaming and assumed she was being attacked, but her body was operating all on its own with no conscious thought. There was no way she could return.

By the time Naima reached the pickup, Pat was silent. Her first coherent thought was that Pat might be dead. She jumped into the truck and started it as a panicked thought was racing through her mind, 'I've got to get the bears off of Pat.'

She started ripping down the road backwards towards the washout, and then slowed down in fear of running over Pat. Finally, she could see her lying face down; Pat lifted her head and looked in the direction of the truck. Naima felt incredible relief and elation as she realized her friend was still alive.

She backed the truck as close as she dared, then opened the passenger door. She didn't get out because she couldn't see where the bears were. Pat looked stunned and awful as she climbed into the seat and closed the door. Naima gunned the motor as they made their escape.

Naima went on to tell me that she felt so sorry for Pat when she worked with her later, after the attack. "It was so difficult for Pat." Naima also told me she felt betrayed by the incident. "Those animals should've been able to sense that we weren't there to harm them. I was so disappointed by the whole thing."

Both women couldn't understand why the bears were still nearby after they'd made so much noise getting the truck unstuck. Why didn't the sow move her cubs away?

One of the most interesting aspects of this story is that neither Pat nor Naima actually saw what took place during the attack, but for very different reasons. Maybe it's better that they didn't.

Six months later, when Naima reviewed my written account of the attack, she called and said something important needed to be added.

For ten years, the attack had left her with bad feelings about bears and nature that were hard to shake. However, an incident took place in mid-June 1998, approximately 60 kilometers north of the location where Pat was attacked, that brought Naima's feelings back into balance. Naima and another woman were working on a boundary for a project to remove brush from a planted logging block. They had worked separately in the morning, then both came back to the pickup at lunchtime. Naima was sitting on the passenger side with the door open and was turned with her legs outside. As she began to eat, a slight noise at the back of the truck interrupted her thoughts, and then she heard another noise. Suddenly, something brushed her right pantleg—Naima was stunned to find a small grizzly standing next to her, with what appeared to be a smile on its face. The bear stepped back as she carefully reached out and closed the door. As the grizzly semi-circled the pickup, the other woman took a picture of it. The bear then walked off without even looking back.

The incident brought closure for Naima. She now clearly understands what is meant by 'bear behavior being unpredictable' and once again enjoys the great outdoors.

CONCLUSION

I hope this chapter will create a better understanding of what some bear attack victims go through. I often tell these people to relieve their stress by talking to family and friends who have similar experiences and knowledge—people with a serious interest in their well-being.

The most extreme case of bear attack trauma I've ever read is documented in Patricia Van Tighem's book, *The Bear's Embrace*, published by Greystone Books of Vancouver, B.C. ISBN 1-55054-807-7. The feelings written and shared in her book are unusual in our present cultural atmosphere.

Naima and Pat two years after the attack.

Courtesy Pat Howard.

11

DEFENSE STRATEGIES

Following is a revised chapter from my first book, *Bear Encounter Survival Guide.*

There are three general bear behavioral modes in relation to encounters with humans: wild, man-wise, and habituated. Wild bears don't have a learned fear of humans, but in some circumstances will retreat from what appears to be a dangerous competitive predator. Man-wise bears have learned fear of humans either from their mother, direct experience, or both. Habituated bears aren't fearful of people and come in a variety of types. Some are habituated to human presence, but not conditioned to human food or garbage; others are habituated and conditioned both. Some are not aggressive; some are very aggressive.

Coming up with simple strategies that will handle both species, all behavioral modes, and endless varying circumstances, is a supreme challenge. We'll never completely eliminate death and injury from bear attacks, but we can significantly improve on present concepts about bear encounter strategies. In general, there are three broad categories of bear attacks:

Defensive-aggressive: The bear feels that you are a threat and will try to bluff you away; if necessary, it will make contact, immobilize you, then retreat.

Predatory: The bear is stalking you as prey and will try to kill you for food.

Unknown behavior: This is the sticky wicket category. It has been increasing in frequency during recent years and in 1992 came forward as a major problem. I'm lumping many sub-categories into this class of attack, but they all have the same problem: Neither playing dead nor fighting back (bare-handed) will work well. In some of these sub-categories, the person involved can't determine species or behavior.

These sub-categories are not based on what the final outcome of an event was; rather, could the person involved have determined the attack category and therefore the appropriate response?

Unknown behavior sub-categories:
1. A bear is approaching people and they cannot determine which species it is.
2. A bear is approaching people and is showing some mild anger.
3. Extremely aggressive predatory black bears (probably starved).
4. Extremely aggressive predatory grizzly bears.
5. Sow grizzly encounters with second-year cubs that follow her lead (could be defensive-aggressive or predatory).
6. Progressive-predatory where the bear seems defensive-aggressive at first, then switches to a predatory mode.

These sub-categories are based on hundreds of accounts I've examined. Unfortunately, the aggressive behavior of both species is much too complex for simple strategies to work.

UNARMED DEFENSIVE STRATEGIES

Tree climbing: This can be an effective strategy in some cases, but there are also cases where bears have climbed up and yanked people down (see Darin Brown's story p. 153). Black bears are very effective at climbing trees. Even though grizzly bears lose their ability to hook-climb with their claws in the fourth year of their life, some adult grizzlies can climb trees quite well, particularly if the tree is medium size (30-60 cm, 12"-24") and has strong limbs. Don't climb a tree during a bear encounter if you have a spray for defense. Stand behind the tree and spray the bear at about four meters (12 feet).

I've heard several successful accounts of people surviving bear attacks by climbing trees. But in each case, the person broke off a limb or took off a jacket while in the tree, or took a limb up the tree with them and then beat the tree and yelled when the bear started up, or hit the bear when it got close. In one case, the black bear started up three times before backing off. If you kick the bear under these circumstances, hang on tight, aim for the nose, and retract your foot quickly.

Water: This can be a good defense under some circumstances. Several times I've stood on the edge of the Atnarko River, contemplating a quick dive if the sow got any closer. It must be a good-sized river or lake, and you must start swimming immediately to get enough distance for safety.

Backpacks: On many occasions backpacks have saved people from a more serious injury or death. If you can keep the backpack between you and the bear during an attack, do so. A dropped pack may distract some bears, but not all bears.

DEFENSIVE DEVICES

Airhorns: These and other loud noise-makers are important bear avoidance devices and should be deployed often when cover, noise, or wind conditions dictate. But they shouldn't be considered as a defense system because they sometimes do not work. Use deep, low-pitched horns only.

Flares: Flares have basically been proven to be an unreliable tool for deterring bears. They've been banned in some places because of their potential for starting fires. But I've heard several stories where flares deterred bears.

Bear bangers: These devices propel a projectile that explodes at a certain distance. Bear bangers work successfully about half the time. Sometimes the projectile goes past the bear, then explodes— driving the bear in the wrong direction. Knowing the exact distance that a banger goes off is important.

Many people who have experience with bangers shoot them straight up into the air. But if the bear doesn't know where you are, it may run in your direction. Also, some bears aren't afraid of bangers. Don't stake your life on bear bangers. They are worth carrying, but don't consider them as a defense system.

Pepper spray deterrence: In the mid-1970s, Charles Jonkel of the University of Montana and a Montana businessman, Bill Pounds, developed a bear spray that later became know as Counter Assault. They experimented with several types of chemicals, and it eventually became clear that oleoresin capsaicin, a derivative of cayenne pepper, was the best chemical for deterring bears.

Since that time, many other companies have developed and marketed sprays for bear, dog, and human deterrents. Some of these companies have come and gone. I've never sprayed a bear, but I've conducted wind and volume testing with Bear Guard, Counter Assault, and Phazer. Counter Assault and Bear Guard are the most popular brands in B.C., with Counter Assault probably the most widely distributed spray in Canada.

Retailers must keep records of purchasers of bear sprays, because it's a restricted product in Canada, and it is against the law to use it against anything other than what is stated on the label. Dog sprays are also available.

Pepper spray is not as effective as firearms for defense against bears, but it's the only alternative that has a high enough success rate to be considered a defense system. In the last 15 years, there have been many cases where people successfully deterred attacking bears by using spray. The following example illustrates this:

On the morning of April 22, 1992, Dan Baldwin started the day off badly when he fell in the river. Dan lived in Prince George, B.C., and worked for E. P. Runtz and Associates who were doing contract engineering for North Wood Pulp and Timber. They were working near Pass Lake, east of Prince George, at the time.

The river was about halfway to the bottom of the cut-block. After Dan drained his boots and wrung out his clothes, he and Gene, a coworker, proceeded the remaining three kilometers. At the bottom boundary, they split up. Gene started marking the boundary line and Dan ran a deflection line up the center of the block. It was close to noon when Dan reached the top boundary. He marked about 200 meters of the top line and decided to have lunch before starting his second deflection line back down the hill.

Both men were working on snowshoes as there was still over a meter of snow on the ground. Dan picked the base of a large spruce tree where the snow had melted back for a lunch spot; this gave him a nice view of the sidehill below and a tree to lean against. He was halfway through a sandwich when he noticed a grizzly emerge from the timber into a small opening 40 meters below him; it was right on his tracks. At first Dan thought the bear might go past him, but the bear stood up on its hind legs and started sniffing the air. All of a sudden Dan realized that the bear was down-wind and trying to locate him. Dan grabbed his pack to locate his bear bangers, but remembered he'd lost them in the river.

(Two days before this incident, Dan had an encounter with a large male grizzly; the two of them stood facing each other at ten meters for a couple of minutes before the bear left peaceably. This had frightened Dan, so he obtained some Counter Assault bear spray the next day. He'd stopped carrying a firearm about two years previously and didn't really have much confidence in the spray.)

Dan remembered the bear spray and removed it from his pack. When he looked back down the hill, things had worsened; there were now three bears—a sow and two large cubs—and they were starting up the incline towards him. Dan made a quick decision to yell at the sow, hoping she'd turn away, but this gave her his location, and she started lunging through the snow directly at him.

Dan readied the can of spray but had a gut-wrenching feeling come over him; he didn't know if the spray would work, and he now realized the sow and two cubs were hunting him as prey. The sow was on top of him in seconds, but she had to slow down at the last instant because Dan was sitting with his back against the tree. The two cubs were behind and off to the side as the sow attacked; her claws were just one foot from the tips of Dan's snowshoes when he pushed the lever on the spray (later confirmed by tracks in the snow).

Her front legs buckled, and she went down immediately. For an instant she was stunned, but just as quickly as she'd come, she spun around and galloped down the sidehill with the cubs right behind. Dan thought to himself that this was too easy; she'd probably come back. He waited about ten minutes, watching and listening, then dashed for the river.

The reason the sow went down wasn't just because of the blinding or burning effect of the spray, it was also because of the nerve shock to the respiratory tracts and the immediate asphyxiation caused by aspirated capsaicin.

While Dan's experience with pepper spray was successful, there are problems with spray deterrents that make it critical for users to know how to use it properly. In a 16 km cross-wind (10 miles per hour), the spray will go only about two-and-a-half meters (8 feet) before drifting sideways. If you're spraying down-wind, it will travel about six meters (19 feet) before dispersing too much to be effective. If you tried to spray a predatory black bear that was up-wind from you at about eight meters (25 feet) with 20 km (12 mile) gusts, the spray would turn right around at about three-and-a-half meters (11 feet) and come back on you. You'd immediately be asphyxiated, blinded, and burning all over. The bear would probably enjoy the pepper seasoning on its lunch.

The information on some cans suggests maneuvering the bear down-wind. This may sound ridiculous, but there are some predatory attacks where this may be possible. If you can move cross-wind and get behind a large rock, or tree, do so. It will help control the direction the bear will come from and possibly slow down its final approach.

There are, of course, some encounters, like Dan Baldwin's, where you'd have just enough time to get the can out of the holster and spray the bear at very close range.

Pepper spray is a close-range deterrent system, and you may get some spray on yourself, but if you can deliver a two- or three-second burst on a bear's face at three or four meters (nine to 12 feet), you will in most cases see an immediate reaction. However, recent research by one of the spray manufacturing companies indicates that the first meter (three feet) of a spray blast has most of the deterrent chemical locked up in the oil base; then after that distance, the air resistance starts to break up the blast into a fine mist with the chemical exposed. This may explain why the grizzly that attacked the canoeist in the Yukon River story (see p. 81) was not seriously affected by the spray. There are other accounts where bears have been sprayed at a meter or less with similarly poor results.

Any bear spray product should be considered a temporary deterrent. If you stopped the bear but didn't get a real good dose on its face, the bear may soon come back. Leave the area immediately. I have several accounts where people have sprayed predatory black bears, then had the bear return 15 minutes later after recovering from the effects of the chemical.

If you're serious about spray deterrents, you should buy three cans: One for testing during wind conditions so you'll clearly understand its limitations, and two for carrying on your belt. With a can in each hand, you have a significantly increased deterrent power. Every adult in a hiking party should have spray. Two or three people using spray together is a formidable defense. Sprays should always be in a holster or vest pocket for quick access. Practice getting the can out quickly, and familiarize yourself with pulling off the safety clip.

Pepper spray should be issued, stored, and handled as a weapon. Never leave it in a vehicle over winter or store it where it will be subjected to extreme cold. Take care of it, and it will take care of you.

Bear sprays are dangerous if you have an accidental discharge in a vehicle or aircraft. Spray should be transported in a sealed container. You can make a spray container out of three-inch ABS plastic drain pipe and fittings. Whenever flying, tell the pilot you're carrying bear spray.

I don't recommend a test spray burst from a can you're going to carry, as suggested on some labels. I have two reports of cans (that had test bursts) losing their pressure when tested again months later. Replace your spray after four years, and use the old cans for test spraying.

Pepper spray is not recommended for use by people with respiratory problems.

If you plan to bring pepper spray into Canada, contact Canadian Customs for information on the subject, as some products are illegal in Canada.

Final note about sprays: Bears, like dogs, are attracted to many types of scents and will roll on or rub against smells they find appealing. Once pepper spray is applied to an object and its fine misting properties are gone, it becomes an attractive scent to many animals, including bears. Don't use pepper spray for any purpose other than spraying an attacking bear in the face.

FIREARMS DEFENSE

In the last 35 years, I've killed many bears at close range; some were very large, and some were coming full-tilt. I've tested over 2,000 rounds of various types of rifle, shotgun, and handgun ammunition in wood and wallboard mediums. I've examined many wound channels in bears and recovered the bullets that made them. I've carefully studied what goes wrong with firearms and people when they are facing a dangerous animal.

In a normal bear defense situation, and excluding hunting of grizzlies at close-range, a person who is proficient with a large-calibre rifle or pump 12-gauge shotgun can reduce the risk of injury or death during a bear attack to about nil. Of course, the key point is firearms proficiency, and that means different things to different people. No matter how good you are, if you hunt grizzlies or guide grizzly bear hunters, you'll sooner or later have some close calls

Field workers and recreationists have a higher success rate than hunters in firearms defense against bears, because in most cases they are not deliberately getting close to bears or dealing with carcass defense behavior.

Any good-quality rifle that you're very familiar with and doesn't jam, that has 30-06 power and up, will do the job for black bears. A 338 Winchester Magnum and up is required for grizzly bears. High-quality ammunition with heavier thick-skinned bullets is needed, such as Federal Premium with Nosler partition bullets, or Remington ammunition with Swift a-frame bullets. If you load your own ammunition, Barnes X are good bullets that will smash large bones without disrupting too badly.

In the last ten years, I've seen thousands of rounds put through defense pump shotguns during range exercises. These shotguns are problematic, and if your operational techniques aren't just right, they will jam. I've met people who didn't believe this until I put them through one of my range exercises designed to simulate bear attack stress. If you're an experienced shotgun user and you get your techniques down pat, then a 12-gauge pump shotgun is a fast, powerful firearm.

Some people don't consider shotguns adequate for bear defense. The secret is in the ammunition. Never use buckshot; it might kill a grizzly at 12 meters, and it might not. Federal 1-1/4 oz. magnum slugs are what you need, plus a shoulder pad that fits under your clothing.

The only shotgun I'd recommend at this time is the Remington 870 police model with a three-inch chamber. It must have a 20" barrel with rifle sights, and it must be shot accurately, just like a rifle. Some of the Remington 870s that were manufactured in the early '90s have jamming problems, or they work well only with 3" ammunition. Make sure you thoroughly range-test any defense weapon. Get yourself a set of 12-gauge ammunition dummies and practice with them until you make no mistakes. NEVER PUT 3" AMMUNITION IN A 2-3/4" CHAMBER.

If you can legally carry a handgun and your work necessitates it, then a 44 magnum is minimum. A 357 magnum will not do the job on a frontal charging grizzly. Practice double-handed, single-action shooting at 25 meters for accuracy, and double-action shooting at ten meters. If you can't consistently put most of your rounds into a six-inch bull's-eye, then carry a rifle or a shotgun. Once you decide to pull the trigger on a bear, you must kill it quickly.

Always carry your spare ammunition in the same place and practice pulling it from that place when you do shooting practice.

It took me 20 years of trial and error to develop the advanced safety and weapons use procedures I use for firearms training. This method of training is completely different than other systems and is specialized for defense against bears. It has a fast-approaching target component that demonstrates what goes wrong with firearms and people in a defense situation.

The advanced safety aspect is based on the fact that most accidental firearm discharges happen near a camp, vehicle, or boat and usually when a person is loading or unloading a gun or carrying a firearm with a shell in the chamber. Another dangerous situation is during and shortly after a bear encounter.

My procedures are too complicated to explain here, but I'll give you some do's and don'ts:

1. You can't be safe with a firearm that you're not completely familiar with. Practice often.
2. Make sure there are no obstructions in the barrel by sliding a cleaning rod down it. Always put tape over the end of your barrel before going into the field.
3. Never cycle rounds through a chamber when unloading a firearm—this is the number-one cause of accidental shooting deaths. You can devise a system for almost any firearm for unloading without cycling rounds through the chamber.
4. NEVER CARRY A ROUND IN THE CHAMBER. Put one in only

when you're ready to fire or when danger is imminent. If the danger is temporarily over and you need to keep a round in the chamber, put your safety on, bring the barrel straight up, and keep your thumb or a finger on the safety. Dechamber as soon as the danger is over.

5. Never fire unless you are sure what your target is.
6. As soon as a bear incident is over, tell everyone with a firearm to immediately put barrels straight up and remove chambered rounds.
7. Always be careful of where your barrel is pointing.
8. Keep your finger out of the trigger cage until ready to fire.
9. Keep the action open when your gun is unloaded.
10. Always transport and store firearms in a protective guncase with a trigger lock or action lock in place.
11. Be properly licensed, and obey all laws.
12. 'A loaded firearm' in B.C. and many other jurisdictions means ammunition anywhere in the gun.

WHEN TO KILL A BEAR

The most difficult question that I've had to deal with over the years is, "Under what conditions is it appropriate to kill a bear in self-defense?"

When I first developed my bear safety program, I knew I'd have to answer that question decisively, or my program would fail. I also knew that no matter what defense guidelines I came up with, there would be some people who wouldn't like my strategies. But let me make one thing crystal clear: My bear hazard safety program is a safety program for people first and bears second.

If I'd developed my bear defense guidelines after the first 15 encounters I had, they would've been substantially different. If I'd developed them after the next ten encounters, they would've come out even more different. But many encounters later, I was subjected to what I call the five percent behavior. You have to have many bear encounters and study their behavior for years before you can recognize the types of encounters where there is high probability of the bear making contact.

After years of carefully analyzing bear encounters and attacks, I've come up with a group of encounter types where the probability of contact is high. This doesn't mean it's possible to determine that other, more normal types of encounters won't end in contact, or that these particular types will always end with contact. But we can recognize those types of encounters where the potential of a bear making contact is high.

There will be, of course, many encounters where the person involved can't read what is going on, but in many encounters, you'll have a pretty good idea why the bear is acting the way it is and what may happen next. The firearms defense guidelines that I propose are not perfect, and they are tipped in favor of humans, but they give both people and bears a reasonable chance of survival. In my opinion, if a large number of people followed these guidelines over a long period of time, for every three bears shot, two would've made contact, and one not. But many of those who have taken my course tell me now that they know most bear encounters don't end in contact and that they now understand bear aggressive behavior better, they feel they're less likely to shoot a bear unnecessarily.

Anyone who carries a firearm for defense against bears has the responsibility to practice good avoidance procedures and must try to avoid close contact with bears.

You have the lawful right to defend your life and property against wild animals. This, of course, must be tempered with not killing animals unnecessarily. But once it's clear in your mind that you are endangered, defend yourself vigorously.

These suggested guidelines are designed to give a person time for at least one good shot in a worst-case-scenario, but I don't guarantee a successful defense will always result.

75 meter guideline: At this range you must ready yourself for defense as some bears may choose fight over flight. I don't believe in giving bears warning shots unless there are two people with firearms. I will not use up any of my defense rounds, or take the chance of jamming the next round. With two firearms, one person can stay defense-ready while the other person can put warning shots ahead and slightly to the side of the bear.

25 metre guideline: At this range, you shoot the bear:
1. If you have a grizzly encounter where first-year cubs go up a tree, or second-year cubs charge with the sow, or a sow charges from a long distance without bluffing, or you think a carcass is nearby.
2. In any family encounter (black or grizzly) where the distance between you and the cubs cannot be increased, or where cubs accidentally run towards you.
3. If you have a surprise close-range encounter with any bear, and the bear immediately charges (may or may not be showing anger).
4. If you feel you're seeing predatory behavior by any bear.
5. If a bear comes at you in a low, crouched run.

If it is a straight frontal charge, shoot dead center of the body mass. If the bear is angling towards you and you can make a point-of-the-shoulder shot, do so. The first shot is to immobilize the bear by breaking shoulder and leg bones or hitting the skull or spinal column, then two quick follow-up shots to the center of chest (lungs) to bleed the bear to death.

It is your prerogative to increase this defense distance as you feel it's required. But if you shoot a sow at 50 meters when the cubs have already started away from you, you're not giving her much of a chance. I'm not going to give you an absolute rule that may get you killed. These are guidelines, and you must use your own discretion.

If you shoot at, wound, or kill a bear, call the nearest conservation officer as soon as possible. Follow his or her instructions regarding what to do. Do not remove anything from the bear before talking to a C.O. If you're out in the bush, and it will be days before you can contact authorities, try to warn anyone in the area about the location of the carcass, as another bear may soon be feeding on it. The carcass may have to be removed from the area.

ERN'S BEAR STORY

Ern Hegglun took my bear safety and firearms training back in the early '90s. You'll have to imagine Ern's heavy Aussie accent and his sense of humour as you read along:

Once upon a time (11th of September 1999), on the island of Chichagof, in the land of Southeast Alaska (about 80 miles west of Juneau), there was a forester (Keith Coulter) and a forest engineer (me—Ern Hegglun) walking to work. Keith had been dropped off earlier and had gotten bored with waiting, so he started to walk to the unit they were to lay out the boundary. I was dropped off later, and with much shooting and noise, we finally joined up in a hummock swamp. After walking awhile in the swamp, it was suggested we go through a small patch of pines and onto the muskeg at the other side for easier walking. That is when the day went to fecal by-product.

As close as I can recall, it was around 8:40 a.m. when we went through the trees. Keith shouted, "There's a bear," and he was right. She (big, tawny, beautiful, and really upset with me) was at the full gallop about 35 meters away with two cubs close behind. I was in front and knew I was going to wear her, so the only option was to choose the place. That was behind a small tree, on a hummock of moss, with my legs presented to the bear. She took the bait, letting Keith get his handgun out. All I can remember is being bit and lifted/shook twice on the left leg, the bear going away, coming back,

Keith shouting and shooting, and then the bear leaving. From first sight of her to the assault was probably 12 to 15 seconds; the whole thing took less than 30 seconds. At that stage, I knew that my toes could move and that I had no broken bones or badly damaged joints. There was discomfort but no pain and remarkably little blood around. I did let out a couple of good screams during the bites, which caused Keith to think I'd been more badly damaged than I had. As an aside, apparently the bear that Keith saw was a cub up a tree within 20 feet (six meters) of us, so the sow was going to attack anyway. There was also a lot of prayer going on during the incident, and I think it worked. I live, Keith lives, and so does the bear. One thing I did learn was that a shotgun in the pack is no use at all. Anyway, the helicopter came back, landed about 50 to 80 meters from me, and as Dallas (the boss) and Keith helped me to it, I was apparently singing 'The Teddy Bear's Picnic'.

The flight to Hoonah took ten minutes, where the paramedics did their thing, then to Juneau in a Cessna, and I was in Bartlett Memorial Hospital by 10 A.M. I have to tell you the staff of that hospital think I'm a bit touched in the head. Something to do with the CPR joke and a few others. The operation took three hours, and the gas passer (anaesthetist) told me he was impressed by the pile of empty suture packets. Anyway, they put three litres of fluid into me during the operation; I had one litre on the way from Hoonah, I was on a drip feed for a day or so, I drank water all the time, and did my kidneys work or what! Half a litre per hour for two or three days, I ended up with two pee bottles so the nurse could do other work. So here is commercial time: Bartlett Memorial Hospital has wonderful staff, and the food is great. The kitchen didn't quite make 100 percent of the food quality, but it was very close, and I'd go back just for the food. (Typical male, all he ever thinks about is his gut.)

Nine days after, I was in Dawson Creek. I could move freely, and the main problem now is to stretch my left calf so I can flex my left ankle properly. Most of the stitches come out tomorrow (hooray!). I should be walking properly within the month and at full fitness within two to three months. There is a one-centimeter hole in one of the shin bones from one of her incisors which should heal well. All told, while I could have done without this contretemps, I think the bear was very polite about the message she gave me: "Keep away from my cubs, you ratbag!"

One thing I should tell you, and one of the better lines of the day: One of the staff came in asking if anyone had seen the Beier Huggers (inflatable pants used to push blood from the legs to the torso) and I replied, "Nah, tried that, didn't work." My one dimly-flickering neuron must have been working.

ENCOUNTER STRATEGY GUIDELINES

It's not possible to devise a set of rules that will eliminate the chance of injury or death during bear attacks, but it's my opinion that the following guidelines create the best chance for survival:

GUIDELINE 1. Never expose yourself to the possibility of bear attacks without a defensive system (spray or firearm).

GUIDELINE 2. Never play dead with any bear; always defend yourself. (If your defense system fails, or if you're foolish enough to believe it's not necessary to defend yourself against bears, you have no choice but to play dead in a defensive-aggressive attack and fight back in a predatory attack—that is, if you're lucky enough to experience an attack that clearly falls into one of these two categories.)

GUIDELINE 3. If the bear is showing anger (defensive-aggressive), ready your defense system, and if possible, back away slowly.

GUIDELINE 4. If a bear is stalking you (predatory), ready your defense system, maintain eye contact, and quickly chase it off by yelling, throwing rocks, beating pans together, et cetera.

GUIDELINE 5. If you can't determine what's going on, or if you want to boil this all down to one guideline only, ready your defense system, stand your ground quietly, and defend yourself.

BEAR SAFETY VIDEOS

The Safety In Bear Country Society has just released (April 1, 2001) two videos entitled *Staying Safe In Bear Country* and *Working In Bear Country*.

The Society began development of the first drafts of the film scripts in 1998. In December of 1999, myself and 30 bear biologists were asked to review the scripts and provides suggestions for improving the material. The end result is that, for the first time, we have two very good human safety videos regarding bear attacks.

The films can be purchased from Magic Lantern Communications Ltd. In Western Canada call 1-800-263-1818; Eastern Canada at 1-800-263-1717; U.S. and International at 1-800-667-1500.

I congratulate society members John Hechtel, Steve Herrero, Grant MacHutchon, Andy McMullen, and Producer Phil Timpany for doing an excellent job on these videos.

Grizzly bears on the counting fence.

Section Three: Myth and Reality

12

BABINE RIVER SALMON COUNTING FENCE

The Upper Babine River is located in North Central B.C. and was completely isolated except by float plane until the middle 1970s, when a logging road was built into the area. The Department of Fisheries and Oceans (DFO) operates a salmon counting fence on the river two kilometers below the outlet of Babine Lake. A Carrier Native village is located on the lake just above the outlet. The fence is a concrete and steel structure that spans the river and has counting stations with metal grates in between that can be removed when counting is not being done. Just upstream from the fence on the north side of the river is a living compound for DFO employees.

In September 2000, I was asked by the DFO to develop a report entitled: *MANAGING HUMAN/BEAR CONFLICT AT THE DFO BABINE RIVER COUNTING FENCE AND LIVING COMPOUND.* The following report is self-explanatory.

INTRODUCTION

During the latter part of August this year, two separate grizzly bear attacks on DFO personnel in the Oweekeno Lake area created a concern in management staff regarding the safety of employees who are exposed to bears. I was asked by Biological Technician Steve Bachen to provide a Bear Encounter Survival Course for the crew at the Genesee Creek Camp, and I was also asked by Biological Technician David Southgate to do the same for the Babine River fence crew. In addition, David requested that I investigate the circumstances under which the DFO operates the counting fence and living compound. I was also asked to evaluate other aspects of human activity in the area that may influence human/bear interactions, including future park development, sports fishing, and bear viewing, then write a report that provides concepts for maintaining a high level of safety for DFO personnel. Following is that report.

The Babine River salmon counting fence and compound was originally constructed in 1946 and was slowly expanded during its 54-year history. There have been few problems with grizzly bears at the location until recently. Last year, there were many dangerous incidents that caused management personnel at the fence to question how they're going to maintain safety for their employees. The decision to build an electric fence around the compound and to install gun cabinets on the counting fence were excellent choices for dealing with safety issues.

We must ask ourselves: Why were there so few problems in the past? Why are there now serious problems? What's changed?

It is critical that Department of Fisheries and Oceans senior management understand we're entering into a new era in the way grizzly bears react to people. For a very long time, we had levels of mortality and types of mortality on grizzly bears that suppressed their numbers and made them fearful of humans. During the last 15 years, that influence has been reduced to the point that most bear populations are increasing, and many grizzlies no longer fear people. They are reasserting their position as a dominant species.

During the last two years of safety training, I've seen a new trend develop, which is the demand by many field workers in B.C. to have the right to carry firearms while working. This is taking place because of the increasing number of dangerous encounters with bears. This year I helped the Ministry of Forests (MOF) offices in Quesnel and Clearwater obtain the right to carry firearms; I also helped Weyerhaeuser in Powell River set up a firearms policy.

The B.C. Ministry of Environment, Lands and Parks (MELP) is now managing bears for maximum-phase populations everywhere in the province, and they are also managing people on the basis that if we properly handle unnatural attractants, bears will respect our space, and most human/bear conflict can be eliminated.

BASIC PREMISES

I carefully inspected the operation of the fence and compound. After hearing all the stories regarding interactions between DFO staff and grizzly bears at the fence and compound, then spending con-

Preceding page shows visitors on salmon counting fence. Above, is the DFO living compound and boat dock.

siderable time reflecting on the situation, I came to the conclusion that I could not possibly provide sensible, understandable suggestions for the task requested of me unless I first dispelled a series of myths about people and bears that are deeply embedded in biological literature and in our present cultural belief system.

Myth #1: Grizzly bears are shy nocturnal animals that will avoid humans whenever possible.

Grizzlies with that type of behavior have had significant mortality by humans, who first eliminated bears with higher levels of day activity and aggressive behaviors and modified the behavior of surviving bears that had family members killed, or have been wounded or dosed with shotgun pellets.

It takes 30 to 40 years of significant human influence before most females in a grizzly population are teaching their cubs to be nocturnal and to run when they see, hear, or smell a human. I saw many examples of sow grizzlies knocking their cubs down and making them run away from people or cars in the Bella Coola area in the late '60s when I first started encountering grizzly bears. But, once grizzlies are allowed to revert to their natural behavior, as is now taking place in most areas of B.C., it is difficult to retrain them to fear people. We will never again have a high-enough mortality on grizzly bears to modify their behavior to any significant degree, except in specific locations where rural residents feel threatened enough to initiate their own bear-control measures.

But if human-fear behavior is modified behavior, what is natural grizzly bear behavior? The criteria I am using for natural grizzly bear behavior are that behavior expressed by grizzlies (European Brown Bears) towards humans in Europe from 100,000 years ago until the end of the Stone Age (approx. 5,000 B.C.), and that behavior expressed towards Native North Americans (by North American Brown Bears) from approximately 10,000 years ago until European weaponry started to influence and reduce the type of aggressive behaviors that Lewis and Clark witnessed on the upper Missouri River in Montana in 1805.

But there is much more to natural grizzly behavior towards humans than just aggression. What do grizzly bears see when they look at humans? They see that our eyes are on the front of our heads, that we don't have large rotating ears seeking out every sound, that we're not continually jerking our heads around like deer searching for any movement, and that we move confidently and aggressively; we have the appearance and demeanor of a predator—because we are predators.

Grizzly bears treat humans with the same types of behaviors they use for interacting with and surviving other dangerous competitors. Within that behavioral system is the important ability to recognize, through repeated exposure, those competitors or classes of competitors that are not overly dangerous and do not require a fight-or-flight response. But we are also a group (pack) animal. This impresses grizzlies because of their age-old evolutionary war with wolves. A single wolf is an irritation, but five to ten wolves cannot be ignored and are dangerous to grizzly bears.

Humans entered into a symbiotic predatory/defense association with wolves (and eventually dogs) a very long time ago. During the last 20 to 30 thousand years, our use of wolves—now dogs—for hunting, defense, and alarm signaling has played a major role in our relationship with bears.

Grizzly bears class us as a competitive predator, and because they existed with and were subordinate to certain dangerous predators of the past (such as the American short-faced bear), they have evolved a cautionary behavior towards other dangerous predators that makes them teachable. That's right—we can train them to fear and avoid us under some circumstances, but the training must be done within their behavioral spectrum—like the training I've witnessed in the Bella Coola Valley for over 35 years. The basic premise of this training is that grizzlies can't enter buildings at any time, and they can't use certain areas in the daytime. This training is accomplished with hazing techniques, dogs, and the occasional killing of untrainable bears.

I must now make an important point: When a population of grizzly bears is losing its fear of humans, which takes about 15 years if mortality is low enough, these bears first revert to natural behavior then, in some circumstances, start to habituate to people (no fight-or-flight

Courtesy Brian Baldwin.

Courtesy Ian Bergsma.

response). An excellent example of this is what the fence staff observed with the sow and four cubs that were often seen in the Babine River area this year. The sow had reverted to the natural behavior of day activity and showing a cautionary fear of humans by leaving the river and going around people, but the cubs were habituating to people by showing little or no fear of them. That sow was no doubt raised by a mother that taught her to fear people. But the next generation, her cubs, weren't fearful of people and would, eventually, end up in conflict with humans.

Even though that sow may have tried to train her cubs to fear people, there is no way that she could have physically done so in the second year with that many cubs. What the fence crew didn't know was that they could have quite possibly saved those cubs from being killed by training (aggressive hazing) them to fear people.

Myth #2: Native North Americans lived in harmony with bears.

This is part of a larger mythology about Native people that originated in the writings of Cooper, Eastman, and Seton, was immortalized by Hollywood, and was eventually incorporated into modern left-wing environmental philosophy. Unfortunately, some Native people have embraced this myth in recent years for political reasons.

When I attended the Bear/People Conflict Workshop at Kamloops in January of 1996, a bear biologist became mad at me during a group discussion and stated the following: "For nine thousand five hundred years, Native Indians got along fine with bears, and if British Columbians don't stop killing their bears, American tourists should boycott the province." This particular biologist has had significant influence over the MELP's concepts about managing human/bear conflict in B.C.

When I moved to Bella Coola in 1965, I immediately went to work in the logging industry. I worked with and got to know many Native people. Some were Carriers from the West Chilcotin, but most were local Nuxalk people. My main hobby at that time was hunting and studying bears, so I asked many questions regarding the Native relationship with bears. Over the years, I've seen many incidents that demonstrated how Native people deal with bears. Also, during the time that I was involved in the guiding industry, I had many Native assistant guides and heard many of their stories about bears. I was able to obtain information about Native people/bear interactions before the present 'nature paradigm' was developed.

In order to confirm my knowledge on this subject and to obtain additional information, I hired archaeology graduate student Rick Budhwa of Simon Fraser University to research and reference a large sample of historical documents of all types regarding Native/bear conflict, bear attacks on Native people, Native bear hunting, Native dog use against bears, and Native bear snares and deadfalls.

The material was substantial and clear: Black bears were hunted for their meat and hides by most tribes and weren't considered very dangerous. However, the western tribes that interacted with grizzly bears were in continuous, dangerous conflict with this animal.

It is estimated that California had 10,000 grizzlies when the Spanish arrived, and this is where the worst conflict was taking place. Fray Pedro Font wrote in 1776: "They often attack and do damage to the Indians when they go to hunt, of which I saw many horrible examples." Jose Longinos Martinez, 1792: "The bears killed many Indians; within a short time I have seen two dead gentiles, victims of this ferocious animal." J. Quinn Thornton, 1885: "Grizzlies sometimes attack and devour the savages." J. S. Hittell,1863: "They break into the huts of the Indians and eat them." Chevers, 1870: "I saw many Indians bearing the scars of conflicts with grizzly bears."

One of the most interesting statements regarding Native/bear conflict in California came from Fray Francisco Palou and pertained to Spanish settlement. According to Palou, when the Spaniards moved into an area to build a mission and to establish cattle ranching, the first thing they did was unleash the army against the local bear population. Shortly thereafter, the bears were eliminated. Then, Natives from all around would come and camp near the new settlements, celebrating and giving gifts to the Spanish to thank them for destroying the enemy of mankind.

Accounts of Native/bear interactions in Oregon, Washington, British Columbia, and Alaska are different, because the farther north you go, the more successful Natives were in their war against the great bear. The primary reason for this difference was the use of northern type dog breeds and the use of snare and deadfall technologies. Many of the northern tribes hunted grizzlies, including the Carriers. Some tribes ate grizzly meat; some wouldn't touch it.

Dogs were often used to locate a grizzly den, then the bear was tormented until it tried to get past the waiting lances and arrows. Grizzlies were also hunted in the open with lances and arrows. But the important difference for northern Natives was the use of snares and deadfalls, which gave them the ability to suppress a bear population. Snares were set in bear trails and anchored to heavy logs. The deadfall structures required many people to build and consisted of a baited log pen with a bed log and a triggered drop-log in front.

There was a spiritual element related to killing grizzly bears, and many tribes saw them as a type of human that could understand spoken language.

Native people have a fear/respect relationship with grizzly bears that goes way back in time. We couldn't find a better circumstance and location for drawing parallels and analogies regarding the prehistoric Native relationship with grizzly bears and our modern relationship with grizzly bears than the Babine River counting fence. The compound is located on an ancient living site, and the people who lived there for at least a thousand years had weirs and fish traps in the river. Their presence and the DFO presence are similar, except that there would have been many more Native people at the site in the past.

The key to maintaining safety for people at the fence while conserving grizzly bears requires a realistic understanding of how Natives and grizzlies interacted on the upper Babine River corridor, because the DFO must mimic the same relationship that existed for a thousand years between Native people and grizzly bears.

The myth that Natives and bears lived in harmony implies that they stood side by side, sharing the fish resource and respecting each other's space without conflict. That is untrue. Like all Stone-Age people throughout the world, Native people lived in a fear/respect, stand-off relationship with grizzlies and other dangerous predators. This was accomplished by both species using aggression towards each other until an uneasy stalemate developed—but the stand-off had to be continually reinforced.

Both people and bears were occasionally injured or killed by each other, but northern Natives had the important advantage of dog defense, snares, and deadfalls. If a bear was getting into a fish trap and damaging it, five to ten people clacking rocks together, yelling, and throwing rocks, plus a dozen dogs barking, would unnerve most bears. On the other hand, individual people or small groups of people were vulnerable while away from the village during a close-range encounter with a sow grizzly and cubs or a bear defending a carcass.

If we could have been an invisible observer of this fear/respect stand-off relationship prior to European contact, we would have seen that after hundreds of years of interactions, the yearly conflict would have been minimal. In a given year, the villagers would have likely had to chase off several sub-adults and maybe a particularly aggressive sow. On many occasions, they would have had to repair fish traps in the morning that were damaged by bears during the night. Bears would have been killed each year through hunting, snares, and deadfalls.

But unlike the California Natives, bears were not a significant threat in their lives. They feared bears to a degree, but bears were one of many lessor dangers they had to live with. Many northern Native people lived for long periods in a condition of constant tribal conflict. Probably the greatest fear these people had to endure was that of being captured by a raiding party of another tribe and then living the rest of their lives as slaves.

Myth # 3: Grizzly bears are endangered and populations are declining.

During the last five years, I've heard many B.C. field workers state that the grizzly population in most areas is increasing and that many of these animals are losing their fear of people. When I provided training this past spring for the DFO stock assessment personnel who work on Quesnel and Chilko Lakes, they stated the same thing and expressed a concern about their safety as they have never carried firearms.

When I participated on a bear panel during the Bird and Bear Festival at Golden, B.C., in May of 1999, the Wildlife Branch's Wildlife Research Biologist, Tony Hamilton, stated that he agreed with me that the grizzly population in B.C. is increasing, with the exception of two areas in the southern part of the province. (There has also been a decline in the Oweekeno Lake area due to poor salmon returns since Tony made that statement.)

The companion report that I've enclosed with this report, *Grizzly Bears and Reality*, provides considerable information demonstrating that the historical decline of brown bears in both North America and Europe is over. I also explain in that document why the decline has stopped, so I will not belabor the point here. But it is important to have a realistic understanding regarding why the Babine River counting fence has existed for so long without grizzly problems, and why grizzly problems have only recently started to happen.

From the 1940s until about 1980, there was a level of hunting kills and unreported resident control kills on grizzly bears in the Babine Lake and River corridor areas that suppressed the population by at least 30 percent and possibly much more. Many of these kills, particularly in the '60s and early '70s—before compulsory reporting was initiated—would have involved members of family groups or complete family groups. The family of grizzlies killed upstream from the DFO fence this past August was not some isolated incident.

That level and type of killing over that period of time created a population of bears that were primarily nocturnal and fearful of people. That is exactly the type of behavior I witnessed in grizzlies when I moved to Bella Coola in 1965. The local grizzly population, including South Tweedsmuir Park, was suppressed by more than 50 percent. During the 1970s, I had the opportunity to encounter grizzly bears in the upper Kimsquit Valley, north of Bella Coola, that had no past experience with humans. Their behavior was completely different than the Bella Coola bears—they were not nocturnal, nor did they fear people. However, the grizzly bears in the lower Kimsquit had the same behavior as the Bella Coola bears because six guides with river boats had been hunting the area for a long time.

The Babine River area is now experiencing what took place in the upper Bella Coola Valley during the early '80s, when the grizzly population increased to near maximum for the first time in 70 years. Between September 1983 and September 1984, 15 grizzlies were killed because human tolerance for such high bear danger reached a breaking point. Since that time, hunting kills, control kills, and the continuous hazing of bears by local residents have created a fear/respect, stand-off relationship that must be maintained if both people and grizzlies are to share the same area. Unfortunately, we just lost most of our limited entry hunting (LEH) permits because the Wildlife Branch claims that the local control kill has been too high in recent years. This loss of LEH kills will upset the balance, and more unreported control kills will result.

The present condition in the Kimsquit Valley provides evidence of what happens when a grizzly population has 20 years of complete protection. People flying in helicopters over the lower 15 kilometers

192   BEAR ATTACKS II

of the Kimsquit River have counted over 30 bears active in the middle of the day. A new LEH season has just been initiated in the Kimsquit. I recently interviewed a member of a hunting party who hunted there this last spring. In the lower three kilometers of the riparian zone and in the estuary, they saw a minimum of 30 day-active grizzlies (possibly 35) and were shocked by the lack of fear these bears had of people. The grizzly bears in the lower Kimsquit have increased in population and reverted to the natural behavior of those in the upper part of the Kimsquit Valley.

Myth #4: The grizzly bear viewing activity at McNeil River Falls, Alaska, demonstrates how well people and bears can get along.
   This myth is believed by many employees of the MELP and could cause terrible problems in the DFO Babine River counting fence area.
   All animals have the ability, over time, to suspend the fight-or-flight response regarding certain other animals. This gives them the ability to conserve energy and to stay with an important food source or other type of use area.
   It took over ten years to develop the very special type of habituation to people that the McNeil River bears have, and wardens had to kill only two bears in the process. But very unique conditions exist there that cannot be duplicated on the Upper Babine: The human presence is small and predictable; the area is generally open ground where bears can see all around themselves; and the bears don't interact with fisherman, or hikers and campers, or a nearby town or village.
   The grizzlies at Brooks Camp, Alaska, have a somewhat different behavior—they are habituated but slightly aggressive. If fishermen didn't often travel in large groups and occasionally spray bears, and if the wardens hadn't developed a system of using radios to warn fishermen when bears are approaching and to get out of their way, the bears there would be much more than just slightly aggressive.

Myth #5: If unnatural attractants are eliminated, human/bear conflict will come to an end.
   There is an element of truth to this concept, but the principle is often extrapolated to situations where it doesn't work. I know of many cases in parks and other areas where a new policy for the proper storage of garbage has eliminated most of the problems taking place with bears in the area. But it is very difficult to make this work in rural areas unless the government enforces a law that forbids fruit trees, berry bushes, barbecues, outside dog dishes, and Native fish processing.

It is important that everybody do everything possible to eliminate bears' access to human food and garbage. But we must have a clear understanding of what the limitations of this mechanism are in relation to bear behavior.

If you look at what has taken place in Yosemite Park, in New Jersey, and in other areas of North America, you will see that bears can defeat almost any restrictions that are placed on people. For many years, the policy that park users must keep foods in stored in cars stopped Yosemite bears from obtaining access to foods—then bears learned how to rip open cars. The garbage handling restrictions placed on people in New Jersey worked for awhile, then bears started breaking into sheds and houses. During 1998, there were 16 home entries by bears in New Jersey, and in 1999, 26.

There are some people who believe that if DFO has no unnatural attractants in the compound area, bears would not try to enter the buildings. This view does not take into consideration a very important part of bear behavior: Bears have an exploratory search behavior for food that requires them to investigate every nook and cranny of their home-range area. This gives them the ability to discover food sources that weren't taught to them by their mothers.

If DFO personnel didn't employ significant resistance to grizzly bears that are trying to enter the compound during the phase that they are losing their fear of people, bears would enter and explore every building—and with aggression, if necessary.

All over North America, a new phenomenon is taking place where bears are moving into towns and cities. The people/bear conflict policies in all jurisdictions operate under the unfortunate fallacy that bears are coming to town because of garbage. But bears weren't trying to take up residence in urban areas prior to ten years ago, when garbage was handled far more carelessly. The real reason that this is taking place is not only unknown to bear managers, but also would not be accepted because it contradicts their present beliefs about bears and nature.

The real reason that bears are moving into some urban areas is because the bear population has increased dramatically in those areas, and young bears have no choice but to establish home-ranges in high human-density areas where the bear density is much lower. Also, many adult bears have expanded their home ranges into urban areas with lower bear density. And here's the kicker—the garbage that we're trying to deny them has become an absolute nutritional requirement for their survival during those years when there is a significant natural food shortage.

If we could eliminate all food and garbage sources where these town bears now live and stopped killing them through control action, would they move back out to wilder places? No, there are too many bears there for them to survive; they would have no choice but to start breaking into out-buildings and houses because their noses tell them there's food in those large containers.

Myth #6: The DFO presence on the river is causing the problems with grizzlies.

Would we claim that the Native people who lived on that site were causing the problems they had with grizzly bears? Of course not. They were living there because of the tremendous fish resource, and the DFO's presence there is to protect that same resource.

This myth implies that the DFO should remove the fence and compound and stop using the present enumeration system for managing the Babine River salmon stocks. Is it possible to do that without endangering the long-term survival of an important food source for Natives and bears alike?

I cannot emphasize the following principle enough: The DFO is the only entity that has the capability to train the local grizzly population into a fear/respect stand-off relationship with humans. This will reduce the potential of death and injury to all people in the area and also lower the number of bears that will have to be killed during the next 20 years. It will be impossible to create the type of habituation in the Babine River counting fence area that the McNeil River bears have, because of the large number of different types and the unpredictability of human user groups that bears will encounter.

Whether the DFO wants the responsibility or not, there is no choice but to play the main role in the long-term conservation of grizzly bears in the area because the very safety of DFO personnel will depend on developing a fear/respect, stand-off relationship with the local grizzly population.

However, if the MELP persists in maintaining the above-described mythologies that are part of their existing people/bear conflict policies, there will be a continuous process taking place that will undo this relationship.

SECURITY OF THE DFO PROPERTY

It is imperative that DFO does not allow any part of the Babine River counting fence property to become a tourist facility. If boat launching is allowed to continue from the parking lot until a proper launch is constructed, signs must be installed as soon as possible stating that no camping is allowed and that people are entering the area at their own risk.

There is a particular danger with grizzly bears that are in the process of reverting to natural behavior: a predatory attack on a person at nighttime. Most grizzlies do not place people within their prey-profile, but a bear can be triggered into this behavior when exploring a person sleeping on the ground, or exploring a tent that has a struggling creature inside emitting high-pitched distress calls. Under these circumstances, the bear wouldn't even know what it was about to eat. Once it has blood in its mouth, it won't stop.

There have been many attacks of this type in national parks, and there was a recent human death by a predatory grizzly near the bear viewing area at Hyder, Alaska. This type of attack could involve any category of grizzly in the area, but would most likely be by a sub-adult bear.

Unfortunately, now that I've made the DFO aware of this danger in writing, there would very likely be liability action taken against the DFO if someone was injured or killed by a bear on the property under this circumstance.

The primary reason that control over the DFO property must be maintained, and the reason that the DFO must do everything possible to convince the Parks Division of the MELP that the section of the river from the fence to the bridge be 'no-man's-land', is because most of the necessary training of grizzly bears will take place in this area.

During the next 15 years, the number of grizzlies that use the DFO's counting fence area could increase to over 50 bears unless some limiting factor develops. During this time, bears will become more day-active, will continue to lose their fear of people, and will become significantly more competitive for the fish resource. Eventually, bears will have to spread themselves out in both time and space. At some point, it will become difficult to remove some grizzlies from the fence when the day's work must begin. And some bears will start to approach the fence during the day when more powerful nocturnal bears are not present. In short, grizzlies will want control of all areas of the river, day and night.

These bears will have to be hazed away. But the most important bear hazing and training that DFO personnel will engage in over the long-term will be on two-, three-, and four-year-old bears. This is the age strata of bears that are the most receptive to learning about stand-off relationships with other competitive predators.

When the grizzly population reaches maximum-phase, you will see a sharp decline in the survival rate of cubs because of density-dependent cub killing by dominant males, and the total bear population will start to be influenced by the fish resource. If in any given year there is a low number of spawning fish in the river and also a berry failure, or if there is a multi-year decline in salmon stocks (as happened on the Oweekeno Lake system), bear problems could quickly escalate to a point where a condition of temporary retreat by all people in the area may be necessary, because individual bears will be fighting for survival. If this ever happens, 10 to 15 bears may have to be killed in one year at the Native village upstream on Babine Lake, because the residents will not be able to retreat. The 11 'known' grizzly bears killed at Oweekeno village by conservation officers and Natives in 1999 demonstrates this point.

If a campground is constructed in the area between the DFO property and the bridge, or if fishermen are allowed in that section of the river, it would be impossible to safely haze bears away from the fence, because bears will be retreating in a dangerous state of duress, and they must not run into people in the first 150 meters.

SAFETY FOR DFO PERSONNEL

The staff at the counting fence site have already responded to the new condition of more bears and bears with no fear. The most important safety reaction of the staff was the construction of the electric fence around the living compound. They have also learned that they cannot hike through the timbered hill behind the compound because bears bed in that area during the day. They have cleared an open area around the electric fence so that nearby bears can be spotted before staff get too close to the compound perimeter. They have installed gun cabinets at each end of the counting fence so that a defense weapon can be obtained quickly, if need be. The crew now pitches fish to the centre of the river so the carcasses will flush out, instead of building up at the edge of the river.

There are two general elements regarding staff safety: Site Safety and Personal Safety.

Site Safety: The compound area must be managed as a zero-tolerance area for bears. This need was made clear last year when a family of bears surrounded a cabin with someone in it, and then the sow charged the would-be rescuers, forcing them to retreat. There are two reasons why the electric fence might meet this requirement: 1. There is nothing in the compound to significantly attract bears. 2. It delivers a type of pain that bears understand, just like the pain they will deliver to those who enter their zero-tolerance zone.

It would be difficult, costly, and futile to try to keep bears off the counting fence during the nighttime—especially when the grizzly population reaches maximum and when fish are more readily available on the gates than in the river. Bears quickly learn that humans are day active only. This is a critical aspect of our relationship with them. Once they learn that certain areas are available at night but not during the day, most bears will follow the rules, except during periods of significant food shortages.

The fence crew estimates that there are presently about 20 bears using the counting fence at night, and four or five day-active bears using adjacent areas. The counting fence must be managed as a 'no bears in the daytime' area. This can be accomplished with hazing bears away, which I'll describe below.

If the bear population continues to increase, as is most likely unless there is a higher level of unreported kills than suspected, bears will eventually stay progressively longer on the fence in the morning and, at some point, will start challenging the crew for daytime control.

The areas above and below the fence need to be managed as bear hazing zones where people are not allowed to go. A loud buzzer device needs to be installed in the shed at the compound end of the fence. This buzzer should be activated each morning at the same time in a series of three 20-second intervals, two minutes prior to the staff leaving the compound area. This will eventually be deciphered by bears as an announcement alarm that humans are about to take control of the fence. The buzzer should also be deployed for a five-second interval to inform staff and bears when a hazing incident is about to begin.

If the bear situation worsens, a dog may have to be used when leaving the compound in the morning, and dogs could also be used to help keep control of the fence during the day. But the dog, or dogs, should not be allowed to interact with bears at night or under any circumstances that aren't necessary. The human and dog activity must be predictable to bears, and bears must be allowed to use as much of the area as possible, for as long as possible, if they are expected to follow the rules of separation.

Personal Safety: Each person who leaves the electric fence enclosure must have a can of bear spray in a holster on a belt at all times. Another gun cabinet needs to be installed at the centre of the fence for an additional shotgun. The defense guns should have rifle sights on them for accurate shooting capability. These guns are for crew safety only and should always have lead slugs in them. The shotguns are, of course, placed in the cabinets in the morning, then removed to a building at night. A system will have to be developed that insures multiple people on the fence will have keys for accessing the gun cabinets at all times.

DFO has a good firearms training policy. However, I would suggest that all fence crew members be required to have a Firearms Possession and Acquisition License and to qualify in safe handling and defense shooting techniques for shotguns (presently, half the crew meets this requirement). For personnel working in high-risk areas like the counting fence, a yearly refresher course is needed with at least four additional half-day practice exercises through the summer and fall.

HAZING AND TRAINING BEARS

The following concepts and methods are not intended to be absolutes, because the fence crew will—over time, through experimentation—discover what works best. And they may or may not have to use some of the following concepts, depending on whether the grizzly population continues to increase.

All bears that try to approach the fence or compound during the day should be hazed away. Boundary markers on each side of the river above and below the fence may be needed that mark the no-enter daytime zone. Sixteen-foot poles that are mounted on pivots, four feet back into the timber on the top of the bank, might work. These would have a pulley-and-rope system back to the fence for lowering the poles in the morning and raising them at night. The poles should be the same colour as the electric fence poles and have wire hanging down every 18 inches with ribbons attached, the same as the electric fence. These poles should have a stop system that prevents them from going to a vertical position, so that gravity will lower them when the rope is unhooked and let out, and then rehooked at a spot on the rope when the poles are horizontal. No more clearing than necessary should be done at the pole sites so that when they are in the raised position, they are unnoticeable. Three of these poles would be in the timber and one just inside the compound by the boat dock.

The distance to these markers should be 40 to 50 meters. But, experimentation should be done to determine the exact distance that a cracker shell goes off, and also how far staff can throw the main deterrence weapon.

I've seen bears turn around and clobber another family member when hit with a rubber bullet, and I've also seen bears hardly react when hit at 40 meters. Bears have to be able to identify the location of distant entities that are chasing them off in order for hazing to be effective within their behavioral limitations.

Bears use noise and large aggressive displays when removing other bears or competitive predators. We must do the same. At several locations on the fence and inside the compound, piles of starter wood should be piled for the main hazing weapon. Not kindling, not firewood, but starter wood. These are 18-inch long pieces that are approximately two inches by two inches—the kind of chunk that would hurt if you were hit in the head with it, but wouldn't do serious harm.

There are three particular sounds that get a bear's attention: Yelling a loud, deep "Hey," a hand clap, and banging river cobble together.

When a crew member sees a bear or family of bears approaching, that person should immediately activate the buzzer for a five-second interval. All fence staff should then assemble for hazing, and a defense shotgun should be brought out. When the bear or bears reach the boundary marker, yelling, banging rocks together, throwing starter wood, and using cracker shells with an additional shotgun should commence.

You want the bear to experience an instant, overwhelming fusillade of large spinning objects landing on it, loud noises, and shells exploding in front of it. But you don't want a grizzly to be able to identify any nearby target that it can vent anger against instead of retreating. Hazing should not be done at close ranges like ten meters. If a bear approached that close before detection, a dog could be released as the crew retreats. If a family of bears gets close to the compound electric fence before detection, crew members should immediately enter a building, because if a cub inadvertently contacted the wires and reacted with extreme duress, the sow could become enraged and attack any visible entity inside the compound. She wouldn't even feel the electric shock as she ripped through the fence in pursuit of her target.

However, at nighttime, there must be a continuous corridor available for bear travel on both sides of the river in relation to all permanent or temporary human structures, including the counting fence area. If you try to significantly restrict grizzly bear access to any part of the fish resource during the nighttime, you will reduce the ability to create a fear/respect stand-off relationship, because some bears will not get the nutritional requirements they desire.

Every so often, a bear will show up in the DFO area that has had no training and that could be difficult and dangerous to deal with. These will usually be sub-adult males that have just out-migrated from another area. The staff must never become complacent and assume that things are under control. The dynamics of the bear population will be constantly changing.

DEFENSE KILLING OF BEARS

Residents of B.C. have the right to kill animals that are threatening life or property. But there are also responsibilities regarding this right. There are two pertinent sections in the *Wildlife Act* that DFO personnel must be aware of: 1. Section 2 - 2 - 4 *"If a person by accident or for the protection of life or property kills wildlife, that wildlife, despite subsection (3), remains the property of the government."* 2. Section 75 *"A person commits an offense if the person (a) kills or wounds wildlife, other than prescribed wildlife, by accident or for the protection of life or property, and (b) does not report promptly to an officer the killing or wounding and the location of the wildlife."*

The *Wildlife Act* does not distinguish between the difference of protecting life and protecting property. However, I'm sure that all DFO personnel recognize that there is a difference in relation to grizzly bears. DFO staff should not invoke the right to kill a grizzly bear that is damaging property. Under this circumstance the Conservation Officer Service should be contacted and requested to mitigate the problem.

But anytime a DFO employee believes that a bear is about to make contact with him/herself or another crew member, that person should instantly kill the bear if possible. FIREARMS ARE ALWAYS THE FIRST LINE OF DEFENSE, WITH BEAR SPRAY THE SECOND LINE OF DEFENSE. Sprays are used only when a person cannot obtain a firearm fast enough.

There is another type of problem that will come up. You don't have the right to kill bears for preventative reasons. But if a particular bear is untrainable, and if it continues to be dangerous to people, the DFO and the Native Band should request that the CO Service eliminate the bear for human safety reasons.

Hopefully, a balance can be attained where the CO Service quickly responds to the concerns of local people regarding a particular bear, and local people will therefore tolerate bears that are not presently dangerous.

Looking back on the circumstances that have prevailed in South Tweedsmuir Park over the last 35 years, I would estimate that a grizzly bear will have to be killed in the Babine River counting fence area at least every two to three years to maintain the necessary condition for continued human safety.

OTHER HUMAN USE IN THE AREA

You couldn't have a more complex situation for managing people and grizzly bears than what will develop during the next 20 years on the Upper Babine River corridor.

If the Parks Division decides to build a campground and boat launch in the area, I hope they will recognize the need to be as far away from the DFO site as possible. Human activity centers on the river corridor need to be dispersed, with large bear-use areas in between. A campsite down and across the river by the creek would be a good location. The campsite should also have an electric fence around it that mimics the DFO electric fence.

What about bear viewing? The only way I can see that bear viewing could take place without danger to people and without intruding on the nutritional requirements for bears would be to build a foot bridge across the creek from a campground located as previously described, with a boardwalk and platform on the open sidehill at the

Grizzlies moving toward fishermen.   **Courtesy Ian Bergsma.**

river bend.   Viewers and photographers would require spotting scopes and long lenses, but that distance is necessary in this situation.

The DFO is lucky to have a Parks representative on-site with the experience and knowledge of Brian Baldwin. His presence will help immensely in the future.

And what about a sport fishery in the area? I believe it would be stretching grizzly bear behavior well beyond the breaking point to have a sport fishery as well as a campground in the vicinity of the DFO site. People and bears would end up being killed and injured— it just isn't possible.

I believe the existing logging bridge area below the counting fence should be restricted for any human use. This is where someone is likely to be mauled by a bear in the near future. It is also a safety hazard area regarding logging traffic. I also believe that bear viewing should be discouraged until a proper facility has been constructed.

The group that will be most affected by how bears are managed in the area when the bear population gets high is the Native people in the village upstream. At some point in the future, major conflict may arise between the locals and grizzly bears.

CONCLUSION

It is important that DFO management recognize that the relationship between field personnel and grizzly bears is changing and becoming more dangerous. This situation will not improve any time soon.

Present mythology regarding people and bears makes it impossible to reduce human/bear conflict. I believe the concepts I've presented here provide the best options for protecting people and bears alike.

The DFO must maintain security over its Babine River property to ensure safety of all personnel and other users. The property must not become a tourist facility.

There is a significant safety hazard for DFO personnel at the Babine River counting fence and compound area regarding grizzly bears. Whether we like it or not, hazing techniques, an electric enclosure, and the elimination of some bears will be required to develop the fear/respect, stand-off relationship with bears that is necessary for human safety.

DFO personnel have the right to defend themselves against injury or death from bears, and they should do so. A more vigorous attitude towards firearms use and training is required to maintain a high level of safety for the crew.

Other human use in the area will significantly influence the relationship between DFO personnel and grizzly bears. Hopefully, all future development in the area will be complimentary to the DFO mechanism for training bears.

What is badly needed is an overall plan for the Upper Babine River corridor that is co-prepared by the MELP, DFO, the Native Band, and other stakeholders. If this isn't possible, then the DFO will have to go it alone and concentrate on staff safety.

13

BEAR HABITAT
REQUIREMENTS

In recent years, our community and the whole Central Coast has been drawn into the world-wide war taking place between environmental groups and the resource industries. B.C. is a major battlefield in this war because our pristine landscapes contain very valuable resources. We don't have the wealth of Alaska's tourist industry; we still depend on natural resources to a large degree.

The present NDP Government, with its sympathy for environmental activism, has created dozens of new parks and other types of protected areas. They've reduced the allowable timber harvest, developed new environmental restrictions on industry, new waste management guidelines, new stumpage fees for logging, and new taxes of all kinds. They've also created policies to reduce bear hunting and other types of bear mortality.

The worst thing that has happened to the Central Coast economy has been the successful ongoing campaign by environmental groups to get U.S. and European building supply companies to boycott wood products from our area. Their success has been based on the claim that logging is eliminating the remaining old-growth timber and also decimating grizzly bear populations. Their claims are untrue and are based on selective science.

The scientific literature regarding all aspects of wildlife and nature is so huge, so diverse, and so contradictory that any advocacy group can develop a lopsided body of information by selecting only the research material that meets its needs.

We all know that we're well into the information age. But we are also well into the misinformation age. Those individuals and groups who have learned how to effectively use selective science, the media, and the Internet, and who believe that any means justifies the ends, have a hundred-fold advantage over those of us who are compelled by our own ethical standards to use conflicting scientific material in a fair and objective way.

The last ten years of research by mainstream bear biologists have clearly demonstrated that logging, mining, and other land altering industrial activities, when done to modern standards, have little negative impact on bears.

But this scientific information is not well known by the general public or by many politicians because good biologists don't jump up and down calling attention to their work when it's published, and also because of successful propaganda campaigns by extremist groups.

The concept that all human activity in nature is detrimental to all aspects of nature comes not from the science of biology, but from the purveyors of environmental doom.

The following is intended to provide an even-handed look at what bears need to survive into the future.

BEAR HABITAT REQUIREMENTS

Even though black and grizzly bears depend primarily on plants in most ecosystems, they are not ruminants like moose, deer, and caribou. Unlike those animals that have been plant eaters for millions of years, bears can't break down cellulose and extract nutrition from many types of plant species . Their digestive system is that of a carnivore, with some modifications for better utilizing plants.

In the springtime, bears feed on immature plants that are succulent and digestible, such as grasses, sedge, horsetail, and clover. In the summer and early fall, fruit crops such as wild berries become their mainstay and are extremely important for building up fat reserves. Salmon provide an important food source for coastal bears in the fall. Bears also kill other animals throughout the year for food whenever the opportunity arises.

Many of the plants that bears digest well are regeneration plants that grow profusely in altered disturbance areas such as flood riparian zones, snow slide areas, avalanche chutes, and burns. These plants also grow profusely in human-disturbed areas like logging slashes, agricultural clearings, roadsides, hydro and gas right-of-ways, and even in people's yards.

During the last 1.5 million years of the Pleistocene Epoch, both black and grizzly bears evolved in areas of the world that were subjected to continuous alteration by at least four different glaciations.

One of the primary reasons that existing bear species survived the extinction episode at the end of the last ice-age is because they are generalists that are very adaptable to changing environments.

To quote a paragraph under *Nutritional Requirements* in the *Grizzly Bear Compendium* (1987):

Bears are the youngest family within the order Carnivora. Over the course of evolutionary history, the Ursis line has followed a broad trend towards increased body size, longer claws, reduction in cheek teeth and replacement of carnassial shearing teeth with blunt bunodont molars. Bears also have the unspecialized digestive system of a carnivore, although somewhat lengthened. The Ursidae have a cecum, not a ruman, that passes food through the digestive system relatively quickly. Few nutrients are extracted, but bears compensate for this by a higher rate of passage. These physical characteristics are clearly an adaptation to an herbivorous diet without sacrificing the ability to digest animal matter. This flexibility has allowed Ursidae to exploit a wide variety of foods in numerous habitats.

Bruce McLellan, president of the International Bear Association, has done a significant amount of research regarding grizzly bears, primarily in the Flathead Valley of British Columbia. He and a group of other biologists published a study paper in the spring of 1999 in the *Journal of Wildlife Management* entitled *"Rates And Causes Of Grizzly Bear Mortality In The Interior Mountains Of British Columbia, Alberta, Montana, Washington, and Idaho."*

The abstract of the paper starts off by stating: *"Trends of grizzly bear populations are most sensitive to female survival; thus, understanding rates and causes of grizzly bear mortality is critical for their conservation."*

Data were used from seven bear research areas that included parks and protected areas and adjacent lands, and also six bear study areas that were primarily nonprotected with varying amounts of logging, mining, gas and oil exploration, and hunting. The 13 research projects were done between 1975 and 1997 in areas with a wide variation in climate, ecotype, and human activity.

There were 388 radio-collared grizzly bears involved, with a total of 704 radio-tracking years. A total of 90 bears, or 23 percent, died during these various studies over 22 years, and another nine bears were suspected to have died. Causes of death were analyzed, and survival rates were determined for different age and sex classes.

It was determined that a survival rate of above 90 percent for adult females is needed to sustain a population. In the South Fork Flathead study in Montana, grizzlies were determined to be decreasing, while in the North Fork Flathead study in B.C., conducted by

Bruce McLellan, grizzlies were increasing rapidly. Both areas are multiple-use, with logging, mining, and gas exploration. But the big difference is that about 40,000 more people live in the Montana area.

The most important conclusion of this study is that adult female grizzlies survive equally well or better in areas of industrial activity as compared to protected areas—unless there is considerable human settlement. Following is a portion of the study conclusion:

The lack of difference or perhaps even higher survival rates of adult females in some multiple-use landscapes compared to areas dominated by protected areas is an important consideration in developing conservation strategies. Although few radio-collared grizzly bears died when inside park boundaries, grizzly bears had high mortality rates on the periphery. The high mortality rate along park boundaries is likely an indirect result of nearly 1 million people (Calgary metropolitan area) within a 1 - 2 - hour drive, and 43,000 residents and 28,000 hotel beds in occupied grizzly bear habitat of the Mountain Park study areas. Similarly, within the SF Flathead study area, Mace and Walker (1998) found that grizzly bears with home ranges entirely within multiple-use areas [with logging, mining, oil drilling, hunting, and etc.] had higher survival rates than grizzly bears that also used rural settlements or designated wilderness areas. We suggest that the long-term conservation value of protected areas is not only related to the amount and quality of habitat they contain and their grizzly bear management programs, but also to the number and activities of people using the protected area and adjacent lands. Multiple-use lands remote from human population centers may be critical to the long-term conservation of grizzly bears, provided that they are managed for low-density human-use.

This conclusion does not surprise me, because I've been telling people this for over 15 years. Bears are very effective at adapting to altered landscapes because much of their genetic heritage has designed them to do exactly that.

Because recent research has, to a large degree, negated the concern regarding the impact of logging on bears, preservationist biologists have jumped onto a new bandwagon. That is the claim that logging road construction and the resulting vehicle traffic excludes female grizzly bears from important habitat.

A research project entitled *Landscape Evaluation of Grizzly Bear Habitat in Western Montana*, authored by Richard Mace, John Waller, Timothy Manly, Katherine Ake, and William Wittinger, was published in Volume 13 of *Conservation Biology* in April of 1999.

This paper is the primary study being used as the basis for the claim that roads can have a negative effect on bear populations. But to make that claim requires a very unscientific approach by ignoring many aspects of the material and ignoring many other research projects.

The Montana study area in this project is that part of the Rocky Mountains lying east of the Flathead Valley and the city of Kalispell. It is directly south of Glacier National Park and is mainly surrounded by isolated or protected wilderness areas.

The area is a heavily-timbered, mountainous region with a mix of natural burns, avalanche chutes, rock lands, and grasslands. Fifteen percent of the area has a past history of logging. A network of roads was established in the 1940s for accessing timber and for constructing Hungry Horse Dam. Most private lands in the area are developed for permanent homes, farms, and service facilities.

Habitat types were broken into ten classes of greenness; the highest greenness classes were preferred by bears because of the high-quality deciduous plant foods. Roads, trails, campsites, and human residences were plotted as potential disturbance sources and also rated by their nearness to high-quality bear habitat. Roads per square kilometer were calculated, and individual roads were monitored by magnetic counters and were rated as light (one vehicle per day), moderate (one to ten vehicles per day), and high (ten+ vehicles per day). Eight radio-collared adult female grizzlies were continuously monitored between 1987 and 1996. These bears preferred low elevation areas with succulent green plants during spring, then generally shifted to mid elevations for summer and spent the fall in mid to high elevations.

The main conclusion of this study was: *"Across all levels of greenness, the greatest mean reductions from potential [bear use] were due to high-impact human activities and increasing densities of high-use roads at low-temperate and temperate elevation zones."*

There are two more interesting statements in the conclusion of this paper:

1 - *Although closed-canopy timber was often used by grizzly bears, vegetal foods sought by grizzly bears were generally less abundant in the dry forest types of the Bob Marshall Wilderness than elsewhere. Further, much of the documented grizzly bear use of closed timber habitats in the [study area] was adjacent to open canopy sites with abundant succulent vegetation, such as avalanche chutes, meadows, rock lands, and timber harvest units.*

2 - *In fact, the high greenness values in the TSA [telemetry study area] were due in part to past timber harvest activities that removed overstory conifers. In the TSA, some timber harvest units provide*

important seasonal foraging areas. Timber harvest units may not be valuable to bears in all areas.

This study indicates that in that area of Montana, female grizzlies may be excluded from good habitat adjacent to roads with high levels of vehicle traffic which could eventually result in a lower population because of less available nutrition. It also shows that past timber harvesting has created high quality bear foods in many areas.

Let's now take a look at another bear study with information regarding roads and grizzlies in the Kimsquit Valley just north of Bella Coola, B.C.

This work was done by Donald A. Blood and Associates of Nanaimo, B.C., for Western Forest Products. Following are a series of statements from the research project:

[The] major objectives were to describe green forage and berry production in 2—15-year-old seral, stages and adjacent old-growth, to make observations of grizzly bear use of logged sites and other habitats near logging-related activities, and to observe their reactions to potentially disturbing activity.

In 1997, the Kimsquit Camp was manned from late March to November 14th, with most logging activity occurring from late April to October 25th. Up to 80 people resided at the camp during peak periods. Active logging and road-building activity was almost entirely at the head of the valley (km 40—56). Heli-logging was active in the lower valley for about 1 month; those logs were trucked via East Main to Kimsquit Main. The log sort and booming grounds were active daily through the summer. About 13 loads of logs were brought to the log sort each day (26 return trips), and there were an estimated 20 trips per day by other vehicles carrying fallers, yarder operators and road-builders. Most vehicles left camp around 5 A.M. and returned at 5:30 to 6:00 P.M. Average use of the airstrip involved 1 fixed-wing flight per day, but 2 or 3 flights per day occasionally, plus landing and take-off by helicopters involved in heli-logging, stream cleaning, tree planting, or survey operations.

Despite the above activity, many grizzly bears utilized habitats in close proximity to the Kimsquit Main Road, active logging operations, the camp and log sort. Of the 38 grizzlies seen on the ground by study personnel, 9 were on the Kimsquit Main Road when first seen, 6 were in adjacent cut-blocks (within 300 m of Kimsquit Main), 17 were in or along the Kimsquit River (mostly within 200 m of the Kimsquit Main, but up to 1 k away) and 6 were in the estuary (about 200—1,000 m from the airstrip and log sort). Of the 176 grizzly sightings made by loggers and plotted on maps, at least 95% were within 300 m of Kimsquit Main, the camp or log sort. Over half of those grizzlies (62%) were on the road when first observed, and 20% were in recent clearcuts along the road. Many of these sightings were probably of the same bears on different days, and we do not know how many different individuals were frequenting the area observed by loggers. Likewise, we do not know how many grizzlies were present in habitats not readily observed from the road, i.e. what proportion of the Kimsquit Valley population was frequenting the road corridor and logged blocks along it.

Nevertheless, it is obvious that numerous grizzlies made daily use of habitats along the valley bottom, in close proximity to logging activity, in 1997.

With respect to responses at the population level, some researchers have noted that yearling grizzlies and females with cubs use habitat near roads more than other bears (McLellan and Shackleton, 1988). This is apparently because fewer adult males, which often kill cubs and yearlings, utilize habitats near roads or other areas of activity. We cannot prove whether this pattern occurs in the Kimsquit area, however, our 1997 sightings, all made relatively close to roads and other logging activity, contained a high proportion of sows with cubs. Of 83 individuals seen by study personnel and 270 by loggers, 52% and 54% respectively were sows and cubs. This is a higher proportion than would be expected in a random population, suggesting that differential avoidance may occur.

Some people may be suspicious of this study because it was funded by a logging company, but the validity of the above statements have been verified by independent observers who are familiar with the Kimsquit, such as Department of Fisheries and Ocean personnel, Ministry of Environment personnel, Ministry of Forests personnel, and local aircraft pilots.

What preservationists don't know is that some of the best protected bear areas in the Lower Kimsquit Valley were logged during the First World War and have subsequently regenerated into excellent habitat. As a matter of fact, considering that almost 20 years of logging have just taken place in the Kimsquit, and considering the amazing number of grizzlies observed recently by a variety of people while flying over the Kimsquit River, you couldn't find better proof that logging has little impact on grizzly bears.

But why aren't there dozens of biologists lined up applying for research grants to study the Kimsquit phenomenon? This is especially interesting considering that it defies the logic of proposed forest management policies in B.C. for protecting grizzly bears that will severely damage our economy in the near future.

This is a clear example of how biological evidence that defies prevailing myths is completely ignored, even when hundreds of millions
of dollars worth of timber and our communities are at stake.

It's very likely that the majority of people in the U.S. and Canada
believe that logging causes a decline in bear populations. How did
such a misconception ever get started? Donald A. Blood addresses
that very question in the Kimsquit Study:

*Numerous reports have stated or implied that logging is a serious
threat to grizzly bears in coastal British Columbia. The authors have
often been rather uncritical concerning specific causes and effects,
and about their geographic applicability. The provincial grizzly bear
conservation strategy (Ministry of Environment, Lands and Parks,
1995: p. 19) rated the present impacts of 11 land-use activities on
grizzly bear habitat. For coastal B.C., (the Coast and Mountains
Ecoprovince), only forestry was given a rating of High for the region
as a whole (the other 10 land uses received lower ratings). Although
the term 'impact' is not defined, and could theoretically be positive or
negative, the context implied by that tabulation certainly suggests a
negative impact. The uncritical reader would therefore logically con-
clude that if forestry is presently having a high impact on coastal
grizzly habitats, that it is also having an impact, probably a high
impact, on grizzly survivorship and population status. To the best of
our knowledge, this has not been demonstrated with respect to log-
ging-mediated habitat change.*

*In Coastal B.C., Archibald and others (1987) refer to '. . . a pattern
of logging followed by declines in grizzly bear populations . . .,' and
states unequivocally that 'Extraction of timber from coastal forests
has reduced certain grizzly bear populations and, in some cases,
extirpated the local population.' Those authors attribute this statement to Archibald (1983), without further substantiation. However
the Archibald (1983) report provides absolutely no evidence that
coastal logging has caused grizzly population declines, and in fact
states that '. . . a clear cause and effect relationship between coastal
logging and grizzly population declines does not exist.' Archibald
(op. cit.) does state that 'Grizzly bears have been extirpated from . .
. many of the south-coastal watersheds of the province,' but provides no supporting data. This statement may be true for a few (not
many) watersheds like the Fraser Valley and Squamish, but human
settlement rather than logging is the fundamental reason. Such
statements are misleading in a grizzly bear problem analysis 'with
particular reference to intensive forestry.' Further, statements such
as '. . . forestry access roads provide legal hunters with the capability to hunt unexploited populations,' without elaboration, are misleading in a document dealing with grizzly bears and coastal logging*

because so few coastal valleys have road connections to the outside world. Various conservation societies, possibly encouraged by the above kinds of uncritical or misleading reports made by government scientists, have tended to make even stronger statements about impacts of logging on grizzly bears. With reference to the coastal rainforest valleys of B.C., the Raincoast Conservation Society (1996) concluded that grizzlies have declined greatly in numbers and that 'The main reason for the population declines has been the accelerated logging over the last fifteen to twenty years . . .' They also state that 'These industrial zones are permanently inhospitable to the grizzly bear.'

Our observations at Kimsquit do not support the above statements.

Why would a ministry of the B.C. Government imply in its Grizzly Bear Conservation Strategy document that logging has a high impact on coastal grizzlies when there is no scientific evidence to support this claim? Where are the four or five high-quality research studies that clearly show logging is detrimental to coastal bear populations—studies required by any responsible government before enacting policies with such serious economic consequences?

There's a big difference between preserving an adequate amount of old-growth forest because of its uniqueness and beauty, as we are currently doing, versus the notion that we must preserve vast amounts of old-growth forest to insure the grizzly bear's survival. Are we really going to lock up billions of dollars worth of timber and destroy a large part of the B.C. economy and damage people's lives based on erroneous beliefs held by environmental extremists?

For the first time in modern history, the Native people in this area, who make up the majority of the population, are beginning to have a share in the forest resource. How do the people of the Central Coast survive economically and win against international environmental corporations when our own government works against us by using the same unfounded information?

The Grizzly Bear Compendium, published in 1987 and sponsored by the Interagency Grizzly Bear Committee, is the authoritative compilation of grizzly bear research by first-rate bear biologists. Following is the Compendium's conclusive statement regarding logging:

While many studies document reduced grizzly bear use of logged areas, others report no evidence that logging impacts grizzlies. Aerial surveys over a 6-year period in the northwestern U.S. and southern Canada showed no changes in grizzly bear populations and little reduction in the number of cubs produced per year as log-

ging pressure increased, however, bear home ranges were substantially reduced during this period. These conflicting results suggest that while bear numbers may not be immediately affected by logging activities, their behavior is almost certainly modified.

CONCLUSION

For over 30 years, I've carefully examined how bears utilize human disturbance areas, including logging slashes. It absolutely amazes me how some organizations have been so successful in convincing the general public that logging, in itself, reduces bear populations. In many types of forest systems, like the wet coastal forests, there are vast areas of closed-canopy timber with little bear food. After logging, there is often a surge of plants and berry crops that bears can utilize for 15 to 20 years. It doesn't matter to a bear whether it's standing in a logging slash, if that's where the best berry crop is. And if the bear happens to dislike being in the open during the daytime, it will feed there at night.

There are factors related to logging that can have negative influences on bears and other species—primarily, easy road access by people. But that isn't a problem in the remote Central Coast. And, of course, logging slashes eventually grow into closed-canopy stands that will produce very little bear food for a long time. But even in that case, bear habitat in most coastal watersheds will be comparable to what existed prior to logging because of the natural mosaic of fragmentation in coastal forests. Most of the best herbaceous forage sites are nontimbered and protected from logging—sites such a estuaries, freshwater wet lands, riparian zones, avalanche tracks, and seepage areas.

There will be an increase in bear populations resulting from the bonanza of plant foods created by logging, and then as the forest canopy closes there will be a population decrease in 30 to 40 years, back to previous levels. But if logging slashes are continuously available for bears in an area, the bear population will be higher than in areas with no logging.

We are engaged in an environmental war on the Central Coast that has gained world-wide attention. The belief that logging causes grizzly populations to decline is a major part of that battle. But there is much more at stake than just our economic future. The new millennium will be predominated by globalism. If preservationists obtain what they want on the B.C. Central Coast, they will gain the power to assault free-enterprise activities anywhere in the world by using the undemocratic means of boycotts instead of existing processes.

14

BEAR POPULATIONS

During the next 20 years, politicians and biologists will have great difficulty devising workable solutions for managing bears—not because of the prevailing view continually shown on TV that bears are endangered, but because the ever-increasing bear population will cause serious havoc.

BEAR POPULATION HISTORY

Humans and bears have been interacting throughout different parts of the world for at least 100,000 years. In Europe and Asia, bear populations started suffering declines thousands of years ago as a result of human expansion and agricultural activities.

Bear populations in North America started to decline in the first century of European settlement, with a significant decrease taking place between 1840 and 1940, then continued to slowly decline until the late 1970s.

Bear population changes in the distant past and in more recent times were primarily a result of bears being killed for food, killed as prime competitors for game species, killed as predators of domestic stock, and killed for being potentially dangerous to humans.

In all past cultures and in many modern cultures where agriculture is still the main economic activity, bears and other predators can have significant impacts on the well-being of small rural communities. The decline of bear populations during the last 150 years has resulted primarily because of agricultural expansion in cultures that barely rendered a living for their inhabitants. Bears were eliminated primarily for economic reasons.

During the last 30 years, North American, European, and other cul-

213

tures have developed economies that no longer have large numbers of their human population working in food production. And, because wild predators have been eliminated from core agricultural production areas, the impact of predators on the total economy has been reduced to minuscule proportions.

The modern conservation of bears in these more advanced cultures couldn't have taken place until our economies developed to a point that it became affordable. In most areas, we no longer have to kill bears for economical reasons, and as a result, THE HISTORICAL DECLINE OF BEAR POPULATIONS IN NORTH AMERICA AND EUROPE IS OVER.

BROWN BEARS AND GRIZZLY BEARS

Before I go any further in this chapter, I must clarify an important point about the relationship between European brown bears and grizzly bears.

After crossing the land bridge from Siberia at the beginning of the last ice-age, European brown bears moved from the ice-free portion of Alaska into Canada after the ice sheets receded. These migrants are now known as North American brown bears (commonly called Alaska brown bears, Kodiak bears, and grizzly bears). The European brown bear population and the North American brown bear population are now separated by the Bering Strait and have been isolated from each other for approximately 10,000 years. No significant evolutionary divergence in genetic makeup between the two could have occurred in that short time-span. For comparison, European human races and the Australian Aborigine race were genetically isolated from each other for a time-span four times greater than the two brown bear populations have been separated.

Whether you call them European brown bears and North American brown bears, or all brown bears, or all grizzly bears, they are the same animal with some minor differences. But there are no survival-threatening differences in habitat requirements between the brown bears in the Carpathian Mountains of Romania and the brown bears in the Cassiar Mountains of British Columbia. Either population of bears could function well in the other's habitat.

There are many preservationist biologists who overemphasize the differences between European and North American brown bears while underemphasizing their similarities. They do this so that a parallel cannot be drawn from the fact that European brown bears have been increasing in numbers for over 20 years in many areas of Europe that have significant human alteration to the environment.

EUROPEAN BROWN BEARS

The International Bear Association (IBA) is an organization of bear biologists who promote research and publication of scientific work and provide information for the conservation and management of bear species throughout the world. The nucleus of this organization is a group of excellent scientists who have contributed significantly to our knowledge of bears.

The *International Bear News* (IBN) is the official quarterly publication of the IBA. Over the years, there have been many articles regarding research on human/bear conflict. Most European and many Alaskan biologists believe that past research clearly indicates that hunting and control action create populations of bears that are wary of humans, thus reducing the potential of property damage and attacks on people. In contrast, preservationist biologists in Canada and the Lower 48 states disagree strongly with this interpretation and claim that all hunting of bears must stop, or bears will suffer extinction in many areas.

In the February 1999 issue of the IBN, several articles back up my claim that the historic decline of bear populations in Europe and North America is no longer taking place. Bruce McLellan, IBA president, included a letter he wrote to the head of the Nature Protection Section of the European Commission. Mr. McLellan asked the commission not to ban brown bear exports from Romania to other European countries.

Bruce McLellan stated the reason for the IBA Executive Council's support of hunting brown bears in Romania *Due to hunting, and in particular exporting trophy bears to other EU countries, brown bears are an economically valuable resource in Romania. This economic value promotes tolerance of bears by Romanians and the bear management needed to provide sufficient populations for hunting. Eliminating or reducing the economic value of brown bears will seriously erode government and public support for bears in Romania. We believe that reducing the economic value of bears may also lead to increased proportion [of] unrecorded deaths of brown bears and thus greater uncertainty of management.*

A year later, after the 12th International Bear Conference was held in Brasov, Romania, new information regarding the Romanian bear situation was reported in IBN issue of February 2000. The brown bear population in Romania increased from about 800 in 1953 to almost 8,000 by 1990. Bears were completely protected in 1960 and a supplemental spring feeding program was started in 1970. Through hunting, the population is now being deliberately reduced to about 4,800 bears in order to reduce human deaths and injuries, livestock depredation, and property damage. Since 1990, 18 people have been killed by bears (mainly shepherds) and 101 injured. Also killed by bears were 3,232 sheep, 1,003 cattle, donkeys and horses, 183 pigs, and 140 goats.

Brown bears in Romania have a higher reproductive rate than grizzly bears in B.C., and the supplemental feeding stations (where they are now more significantly hunted) have increased their survival rate. But those two factors alone cannot account for the fact that Romanian bears are doing very well in a highly agricultural country one-quarter the size of British Columbia with 22 million people. British Columbia, by comparison, has about four million people, and vast wild areas. Preservationists (including some biologists) are claiming that we have less than 6,000 grizzlies. Consider also that Alaska, which is only slightly more than one-third larger than B.C., has a grizzly population count of a minimum of 32,000 bears and possibly as many as 45,000.

The events in Romania provide compelling evidence that claims by preservationists regarding the decline of bears and their reasons for that supposed decline—human population growth, logging, mining, and agriculture—are unfounded.

Another article in the February 1999 issue of IBN from the Department of Zoology of the Norwegian University of Science and Technology explains research that compares brown bear management in Sweden and Norway. In Sweden, brown bears recovered from about 100 to 1,000 between 1930 and the present, and there has been a carefully regulated quota hunt since 1947. In Norway, brown bears were given complete protection in 1973 (40 years after their extinction in that country). Between 25 and 55 bears have now dispersed into Norway from Sweden. The Norwegian Directorate for Nature Management allows a certain number of bears to be killed each year based on the recent level of livestock predation. There are also some bears killed in self-defense.

This article outlines a research project that followed radio-collared brown bears in both countries and states, *The Kaplan-Meier method gives estimates of annual mortality due to human causes of 5.8 and 20.4 percent in Sweden and Norway, respectively. This is very interesting, considering that the brown bear is a game species in Sweden and is totally protected in Norway.* In other words, there is a higher mortality in Norway, where bears are protected, than in Sweden, where they are hunted.

The situation in Norway and Sweden parallels a phenomenon that has resulted in areas like California, where cougar control kills now exceed previous hunter kills, before cougar hunting was banned.

Brown bear populations are increasing in other areas of Europe as well. And even though there is concern over recent hunting activities in Russia, a system for managing brown bears in that jurisdiction is slowly developing. Russia has a huge brown bear population.

NORTH AMERICAN BEARS

New Jersey has the highest human density of any U.S. state at 1,000 people per square mile. The recent events regarding black bears in that jurisdiction are a classic example of what is in store for many areas of North America in the near future—and what already exists in B.C.

Black bear hunting was halted in New Jersey in 1971 when the population fell to about 100 bears. Since 1980, bear populations have been slowly increasing, but they rapidly increased during the last five years. There are now approximately 1,000 bears in the northwestern part of the state mixing with 700,000 people.

In 1995, the Division of Fish and Wildlife handled 250 bear complaints, which jumped each year to reach 1,659 in 1999. During 1998, more than $50,000 was spent to educate people on how to live side by side with bears. Also, government personnel were employing an array of aversion conditioning techniques to teach bears to stay away from residential areas.

By early October 1999, there were 157 reports of property damage, 21 livestock killed, 13 beehives destroyed, 10 rabbits killed, 7 dogs attacked, 30 vehicles damaged, and 26 home entries by bears. Bears were being killed for livestock depredation and property damage; one that was hanging around a schoolground was killed, and another that chased a woman into her neighbor's garage was also killed.

In the spring of 2000, the New Jersey Fish and Game Council proposed the first black bear hunt in 30 years for that fall. The plan was to target 350 bears for the first year, with hunts in the two following years intended to bring the total state population down to about 300 bears.

Animal rights groups, the state senate, and a large number of city residents rallied together in an effort to stop the hunt. After public and political pressure began to build against the hunt, the Council reduced the number of bears to be killed in the first hunt to 175. A public hearing was held at Lawrenceville on the evening of June 6, 2000.

As the two sides squared off, a veteran ranger from Yellowstone Park stated, "We have a greater chance of being hit by lightning than being attacked by a bear." A representative of the U.S. Humane Society said that contraceptive shots should be used to limit the bear population. A doctor suggested that bears could be spayed and neutered. Hunting advocates argued that hunting was the only sensible way to reduce bear populations and that hunters have paid for the cost of wildlife management in New Jersey.

Contrary to Governor Christine Whitman's belief that the hunt was necessary, the state senate passed a bill in late June to ban the hunt which she, at first, threatened to veto. The bill also included $95,000 to be spent on alternative methods of bear control. However, animal rights groups were shocked when the same bill authorized a deer management program that includes increased hunting.

A coalition of anti-hunters kept up the pressure through late summer, and in September, just ten days before the hunt opening, Governor Whitman asked the Fish and Game Council to call it off. She implemented a new policy that municipal police officers would be trained to shoot bears that break into houses, kill livestock, attack pets, or threaten people. The governor stated that the new policy would provide a higher degree of overall safety than a general hunt.

It's hard to imagine how Governor Whitman was persuaded into believing that having police officers shoot bears in and around subdivision homes would be safer than hunters killing bears out in the woods. By choosing control action only, politicians in New Jersey have opted for treating the symptom rather than the cause. Control action is necessary to remove bears that are causing significant property damage and pose a threat to human safety. But control action by itself cannot stop a burgeoning bear population from increasing.

Hunting mortality is the only economically-efficient mechanism that can reduce a bear population and then hold it in check at a level where human/bear conflict and property damage is minimal. And this system utilizes volunteers with no huge amount of taxpayer dollars involved for control action, aversion conditioning, contraceptive measures, and replacing destroyed property. Even more importantly, when a bear is finally killed through control action, it is often killed too late to prevent potential attacks on people. On the other hand, hunting can target day-active bears that have no fear of people— exactly the type of bear responsible for most attacks on humans.

One of the most unfortunate aspects of the existing and upcoming battles regarding bear population management is that it often pits city people (who have far more voter influence) against rural people who have to put up with all the damage, the loss of freedom, and the danger that bears present.

Black bear populations are also growing in New Hampshire, Massachusetts, Maine, Tennessee, Kentucky, Wisconsin, Colorado,

Utah, Idaho, Nevada, Washington, California, and probably many other states. And, of course, conflict and damage is escalating in those areas as well.

Also, the forest resources in Northern California, Oregon, Washington, and Southern British Columbia, are being damaged at an ever-increasing rate by black bears killing trees when feeding on cambium bark (the underlying live growth between the dead wood and the outer bark) in the springtime.

With the booming economy that we've had for the last ten years, most of these areas can afford to waste the millions of dollars in damage that bears are causing. But if we should experience a serious recession any time soon, it will become very apparent how costly bears are when managed for maximum-phase populations.

Human population growth is often blamed for the recent increase of human/bear conflict, and even though it is a factor in some areas, the rapid increase in bear populations is the most influential factor to the present dilemma including the threat to human safety.

I can remember in the late '70s and early '80s when biologist after biologist predicted that the Yellowstone grizzlies would be extinct by the year 2000. Well, they're not only not extinct, they're increasing steadily and causing significant problems for rural residents in Wyoming and surrounding states.

Food sources for bears vary from year to year, and on cycles of four to five years, there are significant shortages. In northern ecosystems the lack of food usually pertains to berry crops; in the south and east, it's acorns, and in the mountain states, White Bark Pine nuts. These are the types of plant foods that bears can convert into much needed hibernation fat.

In the year 2000, there was a White Bark Pine nut shortage in the Greater Yellowstone Ecosystem. As a result, there were 31 grizzlies killed in conflict with people from a population estimated at between 400 and 600. Hopefully, the grizzly bear will be delisted as an endangered species in that area so that hunting can be reinstated to keep the population in check to maintain safety for people.

CANADIAN AND B. C. BEAR POPULATIONS

Black and grizzly bear populations are healthy in Canada and increasing in most areas. The recent banning of the spring black bear hunt in Ontario has created more problems and difficulties for rural residents who must live with bears. The reason for this ban was to eliminate the orphaning of cubs when hunters kill female bears by mistake, even though the vast majority of bears killed in the spring are males.

Unfortunately, animal protection groups and politicians who are responsible for the ban don't know enough about bear biology to realize that by stopping the spring kill of male bears, there will be far more cubs killed and eaten by males during breeding time than will ever be saved by eliminating the small amount of orphaning that is taking place. And believe me, the cannibalizing of a cub by a large male is not quick or nice to watch. (I am one of the few people in North America to have witnessed this type of event.) This is an example of how people can increase the suffering of baby animals when common sense is abandoned.

Some biologists are claiming that grizzlies on the east slope of the Rocky Mountains in Alberta are decreasing. But I've received many letters from ranchers and hunters in that area who claim the opposite.

Similarly, in British Columbia, the vast majority of rural residents know that the black bear population has increased dramatically in the last ten years. The main reason for this increase is directly related to an abundance of plant foods created by logging. There are now approximately 150,000 black bears in B.C., and the total human-caused mortality is less than 7,000 annually. At this latitude, black bears have an annual recruitment rate of about 12 percent; we would have to kill 18,000 bears yearly to hold the population in check. However, there will eventually be a reduction in population 20 years hence because of the present rapid declines in logging activity. I'm predicting that predatory attacks by black bears during that time will become a major problem because of starving bears.

Also, according to field workers all over the province, grizzly bear populations are increasing in most areas. The hunting mortality of grizzly bears in B.C. has been reduced from over 400 to approximately 250 annually.

The Wildlife Branch's grizzly bear estimate at 10,000 to 13,000 is low; in reality, we have at least 16,000. The grizzly population will go over 20,000 in the next 15 years, and it's not going to be fun for rural residents, field workers, hikers, campers, and many other people.

Black bears are now moving right into cities and towns; in 1998, B.C. conservation officers killed over 1,600 black bears through control action. If preservationism continues on course, within a few years there will be half as many grizzlies and black bears killed through control action as are killed through hunting, and within 15 years we will very likely be killing more bears through control action and defense of life and property than hunting. By that time, the bear attack rate will be high enough that most people will see the relationship between bear management policies and danger to humans.

CONCLUSION

One of the unfortunate concepts incorporated into the new cause-science of the 1970s was the principle that bears cannot survive in human-altered habitats. In the last ten years, many bear biologists have been caught off guard when they discovered that their success in protecting black bears is now leading to serious human/bear conflict problems because bears are capable of living right amongst people. And guess what? There is no system yet developed for mitigating these problems except severely regulating people and control action killing of bears, because hunting, the primary regulating tool of the past, is no longer socially acceptable in many areas.

The concept that many people don't understand is that it's possible to manage a suppressed black bear population in a given area by imposing an annual hunting mortality slightly higher than the recruitment rate, which would result in less property damage caused by bears and fewer being killed through control action.

On the other hand, the same bear population could be managed by banning hunting, which would result in a continuous increase in the number of bears. Property damage and livestock depredation would then become severe. There would be an increase in the potential of bear attacks on people, and the necessary control kill of bears by conservation officers would eventually exceed the previous hunter kill. Not only that, there would be far more cubs killed each year, by cannibalizing males in the protected population, than there would be cubs orphaned in the hunted population by hunters who mistakenly kill lactating females.

The same principle holds true for grizzly bears as well, except that the annual hunter kill and the rate of population increase would be lower than with black bears.

The first management method is based on conservation, the second on preservation.

While it's uncommon for wolves or cougars to get into your garbage can, or damage your fruit trees, or rip into your outbuildings, it's common for bears. Unfortunately, our survival requirements overlap too much with bears for us to get along well. Humans are predatory omnivores, and bears are omnivoristic predators. We arrived at our similar evolutionary status from opposite directions. It's extremely important that people do everything sensible and economically feasible to eliminate access to human foods and garbage by bears, but the only realistic solution for reducing significant human/bear conflict and to reduce the frequency of bear attacks, is to keep bear populations in check with hunting mortality.

Author's son, Tyler, with 150-pound male cougar, killed in back yard.

Section Four: Epilogue

15

COUGAR ATTACKS

Many people in the Bella Coola Valley were happy to learn in the fall of '99 that Conservation Officer Keith Rande was returning to this district. He and his family had lived in the Valley during the middle 1980s and had left in 1988 for a two-and-a-half-year posting at Squamish, then on to Dawson Creek for almost eight years.

Keith is well-liked because of his policy to administer game regulations by the spirit of the law and common sense. He knows there are times to be tough regarding deliberate offenses and times to back off a little when someone has made an honest mistake. He's also an active member of the community and takes the conservation side of his job seriously.

Keith arrived in early January 2000. Within a few days of being here, he was informed that the cougar population was extremely high, that many had been seen near homes in the area where he now lived, and that some of these cats weren't afraid of people. Keith needed to use up some holiday leave before starting work, so he decided to do some cougar hunting in order to appraise the situation.

In the early hours of January 15th, Keith and his 11-year-old son, Brycen, jumped into their pickup truck and headed out the driveway for a day of cougar hunting. Right where the driveway joins the main road, they saw what appeared to be a stain in the snow; it was still dark, so Keith grabbed the flashlight and went out to inspect it. He and Brycen soon found a blood stain on the main road, and a trail leading across their yard looking as if something had dragged itself through the snow. He immediately assumed a dog had been hit by a car and had crawled off to die.

They followed the mark through the front yard and into the timber about 25 meters where they found a dog's body. Keith moved the dog's leg with his foot and found rigor mortis hadn't set in, so he figured it must have recently died. A decision was made to check the dog further during daylight hours, and also to contact neighbors to see if any were missing a dog.

When they returned from their hunt early in the afternoon, Keith called several neighbors. The Obornes informed him their dog had been missing since the previous evening. Soon, Renata Oborne arrived and accompanied Brycen to identify the dog, but within a few minutes, the two ran back to tell Keith the dog was no longer there. They'd found a bloodstain and some strange tracks in the snow and decided the best thing to do was get out of there.

With rifle in hand and Brycen in tow, Keith followed what he could clearly see were cougar tracks. The dog hadn't been killed by a car; it was killed on the road by a cougar and dragged to where they'd found it. He'd heard about all the sightings, but hadn't expected something like this to occur right in his own front yard. Now he realized that potential danger to Brycen and other neighborhood kids could be lurking nearby.

They discovered the dog had been moved about 150 meters from where they'd last seen it. The head had been fed upon, a patch of hair had been licked off the side, and the upper body had ben partially covered with leaves. The father and son team found a safe, location nearby and watched for the cat until dark, but it didn't return.

That evening, Keith called David Hall and asked if he'd bring his dogs over to track the cougar.

At first light, Keith walked out to check on the dead dog. It had been moved again; the cougar had eaten more of the head and had licked the hair off one side of the dog's body, exposing the skin that now resembled tanned leather.

Shortly after Keith returned to the house, David Hall arrived with his hunting dogs. David's dad, Clarence, his son-in-law, Ben Smart, and John Willis were accompanying him.

The five hounds were kept on leashes until nearing the site. After being released, the dogs cautiously milled around the dog's body searching out every scent, then the lead hound let out a bay and the chase was on.

Ten minutes and one mile later, the cougar was treed near rock bluffs at the edge of the mountain. After Keith shot, the cat hit the ground on the run, but was mortally wounded. Within 100 yards the cat collapsed and died.

Upon inspection, it was found that both upper canine teeth of the 100-pound female cougar were broken off at the gum line. This lack of important weaponry may explain why the cat attacked easy prey such as a dog.

COUGAR ATTACK

On the evening of January 31, 2000, I sat down with Barry Mack at his home on the Bella Coola townsite. I had entered the townsite by turning right, off Highway 20, onto a road with a north/south heading that separates the Native reserve on the right from the white community on the left. The reserve is an approximate 11-square-mile area in lower Bella Coola Valley and is home to the Nuxalk People. The two communities have existed side by side since 1929 when the original Native village was moved from the other side of the Bella Coola River to higher ground after a great flood. There is also a newer, second Native community at the east end of the reserve four miles up the Valley.

The town of Bella Coola has about 120 tightly-bunched homes and a dozen commercial buildings and government offices. Being in a coastal wet climate, the town is surrounded by brush and trees. And

Barry's house is in lower center behind dark tree.

because the area is a true wilderness, there is no shortage of bears, wolves, and cougars adjacent to all the people. It's common for bears to be killed close to, or sometimes right in, the town. Usually, there are few problems with wolves and cougars, although they are occasionally sighted nearby. However, one week earlier, on January 24th, a local cougar hunter, 74-year-old Clarence Hall, was attacked by a cougar just behind Barry's house.

When Barry greeted me in his front yard, he said there was a cougar scare currently taking place. He explained that two different cougars were seen during the day in the reserve section of town. As we entered the house, Barry pointed at a pickup driving by and said, "That's Chris King now, he's in one of three trucks with people cruising the village looking for those cats."

Shortly after Barry and I sat down in his front room, we were joined by his girlfriend, Melanie Tallio. I asked Barry to start at the beginning:

The family dog, Kiko, had been doing a lot of barking at night for about two weeks. Kiko was a small, mixed-breed, Lassie-type dog. Even though she was five years old, everyone assumed she was just a little puppy because she was so small and cute. Barry had noticed that in the two days before the attack on Clarence, Kiko had often given her 'scared' bark. At 1:30 in the morning of January 24th, Barry was awakened by Kiko yelping. He could tell she was running from the back yard to the front, and he could hear what sounded like the running footsteps of a large dog in pursuit.

Barry jumped up, threw on some clothes, ran downstairs, and burst through the front door. There was a street light off to the right that backlit the dark shapes of Kiko and a large dog on top of her. Barry charged forward and was half way into a soccer kick when he saw that the intended recipient was not a dog, but a cougar. The cougar had the dog's head in its mouth, its front claws locked into Kiko's shoulders, and was now glaring up at Barry.

In a split second, Barry retracted his foot, spun around, and headed into the house for his .22 Hornet rifle. By now the rest of the family was up to see what all the ruckus was about. Barry explained what was going on as he retrieved the gun from the closet. He knew that the cat would drag Kiko around back, so Barry headed for the back door as he was ramming shells into the magazine clip. Barry's mom, Cecelia, and his brother, Dorian, both grabbed flashlights and shortly had the cougar illuminated. It was lying on top of Kiko at the edge of the back yard. The cat's eyes reflected like bright headlights. Barry asked his brother if he should shoot it, then he asked a second time, "Should I shoot it?" Barry started firing when he heard the word, "Yes," but the cougar didn't move until the fifth shot.

The animal lunged to the edge of a ditch, then disappeared into the darkness. They couldn't tell if it had been hit. Barry asked his mom to call his friend Chris King to come over and to also call the conservation officer. When Chris arrived, the young men spent two hours searching for the cougar. Cecelia had tried to contact the RCMP and the Conservation Officer Service, but had only managed to leave a message at the C.O. office. Finally, at about 3:30 A.M. Barry dragged poor little Kiko's dead body into the house so she wouldn't be eaten, and everyone went back to bed to get some sleep.

Barry was still trying to catch up on lost sleep when he heard Clarence Hall knock on the door at 10 A.M. After getting dressed, Barry went outside and explained the night's events to Clarence and located the spot where he shot at the cougar. Clarence explained that he was waiting for the rest of the tracking crew and his dogs to arrive.

It was quite cold, so Barry went back inside to put more clothes on. When he returned, he couldn't see Clarence in the back yard, or in the front yard, either. Barry figured he must be further back towards Tatsquan Creek looking for blood or tracks.

Clarence was just beyond the tree at the edge of the yard when the cougar attacked.

All of a sudden, Barry heard Clarence screaming at the top of his lungs, "Help, help, help!" As he ran into the back yard, Barry saw Clarence on his back with his knees pulled up. Barry's first thought was that Clarence was having a heart attack, but when he got up to him, he saw the cougar lying perpendicular on the other side of Clarence. The two of them were locked in a struggling embrace, and the cougar was obviously trying to choke its victim to death. Barry could see deep gashes on Clarence's neck and head.

It was now another race for the gun. Barry was yelling at the house, "The cougar has Clarence! The cougar has Clarence!" Cecelia rushed to the door and opened it as her son sped by. She could hear Clarence screaming but felt completely helpless as she stood there. It took Barry more than half a minute to find the rifle, as he had asked Melanie to put it away for him the night before and wasn't sure exactly where it was. Luckily, he still had ammunition in his pocket. By the time Barry reached the back yard, once again loading the rifle on the run, he didn't think Clarence would still be alive. But he heard another cry for help, much fainter than before. Barry had the rifle shouldered and ready to go as he approached; the cat now had a grip on Clarence's head and was using its hind legs to spin its body around, trying to increase its leverage. It seemed to be twisting Clarence's head sideways, trying to break his neck. Barry was aiming the gun, but wasn't sure where to shoot; the cat's head was too close to Clarence's head for a head shot. Then, to Barry's surprise, Clarence yelled, "Get close, get real close!" Barry stepped forward and crouched down, placing the barrel across Clarence with the muzzle pointed in a way he couldn't possibly hit Clarence, and pulled the trigger. Barry worked the action and fired the gun three more times at point-blank range. With the last shot, the cougar, struck in the spine, relaxed its deadly grip. Clarence said, "That's enough, that's enough" as he pulled the cougar's fangs out of his scalp and pushed it away. Clarence was on his feet instantly, but it took him a few seconds to get his bearings. The two men walked into the front yard. Chris King had arrived by that time, so Clarence jumped into Chris's pickup and they sped off to the hospital.

I went over some points of the story again with Barry and asked why he was hesitant to shoot the cougar the first time—why had he asked his brother if he should shoot it? Barry said he wasn't sure if he should kill it or leave it up to the conservation officer. If Kiko had still been alive, he wouldn't have hesitated.

I then asked him and Melanie how the Nuxalk people were dealing with the present threat of more cougars on their doorsteps. They

Barry with his trusty 22 Hornet.
Above and following picture courtesy Barry Mack.

Because cougars are a semi-specialized predator, they begin starving first before wolves and bears when deer are in short supply.

said people are walking in groups, no one goes out late at night, kids are escorted to and from school bus stops, and the guns are ready.

Five days later, on Saturday, Clarence welcomed me into his home. I'd decided to wait for awhile before interviewing him because he'd been deluged by the news media during his three-day stay in the hospital and also after he returned home. He'd even received a message from the Premier of the province, wishing him a speedy recovery.

I sat down at the table, and Clarence remained standing. After talking for a while about the predator problems in the Valley, I asked, "Do you realize this is one of the first cougar or bear attacks where preservationists have had difficulty spinning the incident into a 'humans-are-at-fault' scenario?" Clarence laughed, then said, "Yeah, but during a radio interview the previous week, a caller had stated the cougar attacked him because it knew Clarence was a cougar hunter. And another caller had said that hunters had killed all the mother cougars in the Valley, so the young cougars hadn't been taught properly what they're supposed to be eating."

I had a good laugh, then told Clarence I'd heard one person had claimed that all the deer in the Valley had been killed by hunters, so that was the reason for the attack. We chuckled because we both knew that the deer population was declining because of to many predators, not hunters. After about 15 more minutes of similar conversation I said, "All right Clarence, let's get down to it.":

Clarence received a call from Conservation Officer Keith Rande at 9:00 A.M. Keith explained about the cougar attacking Barry Mack's dog and said that he, John Willis, and Ben Smart would be there in an hour, and the four of them could proceed to the reserve with the dogs. About 30 minutes later, Clarence decided to go down to Barry's place by himself, to scout the area and let the others bring down the dogs.

After knocking on the door, Barry escorted Clarence into the basement to look at the dog. He could see that Kiko had canine teeth puncture wounds to her head—she looked to be about 25 pounds in weight. As the two men went out into the yard, Barry explained the night's events, then went back in the house for a jacket.

Clarence knew the track was nine hours old, and he didn't want to release the dogs near the houses when they arrived. He decided not to get the rifle out of his car, because it didn't seem appropriate with all the houses around, and he wasn't sure about the legalities of carrying a gun on reserve. He walked through the back yard and continued south towards Tatsquan Creek, which crosses under the main

highway from the south, then turns east and runs along the back of
the houses on Barry's street. The area has short brush and small
trees, but is relatively open in the wintertime when all the leaves are
gone. When Clarence got to the boulder rip-rap at the bank, he
could see that there was a buildup of ice on each side of the creek,
with a fast current flowing in the middle; there were some spots
where the ice completely crossed the water.

Clarence immediately realized he didn't want the dogs near
Tatsquan Creek—or they might drown trying to cross. He assumed
that the cat had walked over one of the ice-bridges and was on the
sidehill beyond the highway. If that was the case, they could release
the dogs over there, off reserve. He began scouting for tracks to
confirm his suspicions.

Very soon thereafter, and to his complete surprise, he saw a
cougar a short ways away, lying under a small spruce tree, no more
than 100 feet from the house. It looked like it was sleeping, but he
saw the body move. Clarence instantly crouched and stayed still; he
didn't think the cat had seen him. He carefully turned and headed
for Barry's back yard, thinking about whether he should get his gun
and shoot it or wait for the rest of the team.

Clarence had just decided it would be best to wait for the others
and was about 50 feet from the back door when he was struck on the
left side of his neck with what felt like a 40-pound baseball bat. In
the next instant, he was flat on his back. The cougar had come over
his left shoulder, bit into his neck, and forced him down backwards.
For a split second, Clarence couldn't fathom what had happened,
then in the peripheral vision of his left eye, he recognized the shape
of the cat's head, which was parallel to his.

Two upper canines were sunk into his scalp above the ear, one
lower right canine was in the side of his neck, and the other was
piercing his throat near the jugular vein. The cougar's body was at
a 45-degree angle to his.

The cougar made another bite in the same area for a better grip as
they fought each other. Clarence started yelling for help as he had
a horrible image raced through his mind: 'This cougar's going to kill
you.' His brain dredged up an old remembrance from the past: 'If
you're ever attacked by a dog, grab the lower jaw behind the
canines, and you can control the animal's head.'

After jamming his right hand into the cougar's mouth, Clarence
pushed down to release the lower fangs, then pushed up to remove
the uppers as the cat tried to resist. At this point, he feared the front
claws would now start ripping his chest and belly to pieces, so he
pulled his chewed-up hand out of its mouth, got his left arm on the
other side of its chest, then, and with both of his arms, pinned the

cougar's upper body to his chest with its paws in between. Then Clarence had another thought: 'This is a struggle for life and death and only one will survive—I'm going to survive.'

When Clarence pinned the cat, it was left with freedom to move its head and instantly latched onto the top left side of Clarence's head—he felt the canines sliding along his skull as they locked into the scalp. Clarence sensed the cat was starting to realize it had tackled something very difficult to deal with.

Clarence had been yelling for help from the beginning of his ordeal, but wasn't sure if anyone could hear him. He was thinking about Plan B: to spin the cat into a face-down position and roll on top to smother it. Then he saw the movement of someone running from the scene, and he knew that Barry was going for a gun.

It didn't seem like more than a few seconds before Clarence saw Barry approaching with the gun aimed. Clarence yelled at him to get close, and as he held the cougar with his upper arms, he indicated with his hands a distance of 12 inches. Then the gun went off four times in rapid succession, and the cougar went limp. As Clarence stood up, he had to release a canine tooth from his scalp—for a moment, he held the cat's head in his hands, then became filled with anger and threw it into a heap.

I asked Clarence if he thought the cat was weaker than normal because of its condition. He said, "Yes, Keith estimated its weight at 70 to 80 pounds—underweight by about 35 pounds. It was real skinny. If it had been in top condition, or if it had been a large male, I wouldn't be sitting here talking to you now."

We discussed many other things, and at one point in the conversation, Clarence referred to Barry's gun as a semi-automatic. I told him it was a bolt-action rifle, not a semi-automatic. He couldn't believe that Barry had fired that fast with a bolt-action. Clarence stated he was very thankful Barry had the guts, determination, and ability to kill the cougar. And he was real glad he didn't have to try Plan B.

Some readers may find it difficult to believe a 74-year-old man could defend himself with such gusto, but anyone who has been around Clarence knows that his body condition and attitude are those of a man in his fifties. Clarence is a very religious man and believes he received divine guidance and help during the attack.

Keith Rande was willing to come to my house on the evening of February 10th to be interviewed about the attack. He brought his wife Shannon and son Brycen with him. Following are the details of the interview:

Fellow Conservation Officer Paul McGhie received a phone call about the dog killing at 8:30 A.M. Because he was off duty, he called Keith and informed him about the cougar incident. Keith headed for town to verify the event and stopped at Clarence's house to alert him that the hounds may be required to track the cougar. Clarence's son, David, has a contract agreement to supply dogs to the CO Service when needed, but the dogs are kept at Clarence's home.

While at Clarence's, Keith decided to call Chris King and do his verification by phone in order to speed up the process of response. After getting details from Chris, Keith told Clarence what had happened and said he was going back home to change his clothes and would ask Ben Smart and John Willis to help. He would also pick up the dog pens. Keith told Clarence that he'd be back in about an hour, and they could all go together.

When Keith, Ben, and John arrived at Clarence's, they started loading dogs and wondered where Clarence was. After talking to Clarence's wife, Beatrice, and looking around, they noticed the car was gone. They then assumed he must have gone ahead to Barry's by himself, which concerned them. The three men and dogs proceeded to the townsite in two trucks.

Keith went into the Nuxalk Band office to inform them he was going to start a hunt for the cougar on the reserve. The secretary stated that a man had been mauled by the cougar. "What man?" Keith asked with concern. "The guy that has the dogs; he's been taken to the hospital," was the answer.

Keith was upset and disturbed as he walked out to the truck and told the others what he'd heard. They zipped over to Barry's house to make sure the cougar was dead. A large crowd of people was circled around the dead cougar. After talking to Barry, the three hunters walked out back to inspect the area where the incident had happened. They found Clarence's blood in the snow at the attack scene, then walked farther and found the big spruce tree where the cat had spent the night. They were unable to detect the exact route the cougar had taken when stalking its victim because of all the fresh human and dog tracks.

When they arrived at the hospital, it was a relief to find that Clarence was doing well, even though it had taken over 100 stitches to close him up. He was already vigorously telling the story to all who were present.

At the end of the interview, Keith explained that the cougar was badly under weight and loaded with porcupine quills in its gums, paws, forearms, and chest. We discussed the fact that cougars kill

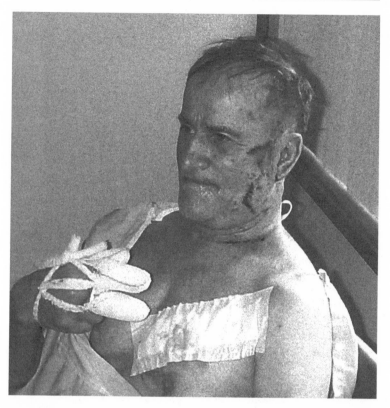

Clarence in hospital.

Courtesy Peter Rhem.

and eat porcupines all the time and that their systems can usually handle a fair amount of quills, but this cat had more than I'd ever seen or heard about.

It was obvious to both of us that a cougar in this kind of condition is more likely to attack a person. But it's common for cougars to go through phases of starvation when deer numbers decline. This starvation condition now exists in many areas of B.C.

Keith's final statement was that the cougar had been struck twice by bullets, both in the spinal area. Apparently, the cougar hadn't been hit when Barry shot at it the night before the attack.

In order to understand what Clarence was up against, an explanation of how cougars kill animals is necessary. Cougars kill small- and medium-sized animals with a bite to the back of the neck or head. But they kill large animals by asphyxiation. A cougar prefers to take large prey from behind by leaping onto the animal and biting into the neck, then pinning the animal to the ground with its body as it controls the shoulder area with its front paws. It tries to keep its body angled away from the potentially dangerous feet of its victim. As the prey fights for survival, the cat waits for the perfect opportunity to go for a better bite across the throat to close off the windpipe. Then the cougar holds on, controlling the struggle, as the victim suffocates—cougars are in no hurry; they wear their prey down.

Cougar attacks are actually more difficult to survive than most bear attacks, and coming up with defense strategies, other than the use of a firearm, is not easy. Cougars are often not afraid of a single dog, even when it's right next to a person. Two large, very aggressive dogs have a good chance of keeping a cougar at bay.

I've been waiting for a long time to be able to answer a question I'm often asked in my training courses: How well do bear sprays work against cougars? I have always answered by saying that theoretically, sprays should work against cougars, but I have no accounts of this type to know for sure.

I was glad to receive an e-mail regarding a spray-use incident involving a cougar that was prepared by a Weyerhaeuser Logging employee and brought to my attention by Derek Molter. One spray-use account is too small a sample for drawing sweeping conclusions, but there a is a lot to be learned from the following report:

Cougar Incident - Weyerhaeuser, Vavenby, B.C.
This event took place near Clearwater, B.C., on Oct. 1, 2000

There were no signs or smells leading up to the incident.
There were trails within the bush, but they could have been caused by anything.

Two employees were engaged in road layout, about 10 - 15 metres apart, cutting a line with machete, making a lot of noise. Ryan was in front, Ron was behind. The wind was blowing crosswise.
Ron and Ryan were working up a hill (North to South) around Block 12 area (AJ Tie). The cougar was spotted, and they immediately thought it was a dog because it was so close (3 - 4 metres away). Then the cougar turned, and Ryan saw it clearly and started yelling at the cougar and also to Ron. The cougar then circled above Ryan and charged at Ron. Ron started yelling at the cougar and for Ryan to come over to him. Ryan ran over and the cougar backed off. Ryan and Ron were then together and backed away through the thick alder (they backed away one at a time to keep an eye on the cougar).

Ron called the Weyerhaeuser Office with his radio and asked for help; first call (2:40 p.m.). The cougar then started sneaking around below them, creeping through the grass and alder. The cougar stalked to within two to three metres and stopped, because Ron and Ryan were yelling. Ryan sprayed the cougar with bear spray. The spray hit the brush and the cougar. The cougar backed up and shook its head, then started moving forward again. Ryan and Ron moved backwards toward a tree. Ryan got stuck for a moment in alder, then freed himself and headed for a tree (15 - 20 metres from seeing the cougar to the tree). Both Ryan and Ron turned and started climbing the tree as fast as they could. When Ryan was three or four metres up the tree, he looked down at the cougar that was at the bottom of the tree. Ryan was not sure what the cougar was doing, but it was there. The two continued up the tree to about 15 metres and could still see the cougar at the bottom. The tree was about 17 metres tall, and very limby which made it hard for the cougar to climb.

Ryan radioed again for help.

The two men remained in the top of the tree and broke off branches to be able to see the cougar and to be able to spray it if necessary. They tried clipping their waist belts to the tree to help hold them up, but they weren't long enough to go around them and the tree. (3:00 p.m.)

Yellowhead Helicopter arrived at about 3:30 p.m. and hovered around the tree with the siren going to scare off the cougar. After the helicopter arrived, Ryan accidentally dropped his radio from the tree, but Ron still had his so they were able to communicate. The cougar remained at the bottom of the tree until the helicopter scared it away. The cougar appeared to be very healthy.

About the same time, Curtis, Brett, and Gord arrived in a truck and headed through the bush toward Ron and Ryan. It took the rescuers about 20 - 30 minutes to travel the 500 - 700 metres to the bottom of the tree. The helicopter was getting low on fuel so it landed on Barriere Mountain Road. Ron and Ryan then started down the tree and were finally safe when they reached the ground and walked out to the truck.

Back at the Weyerhaeuser Office:

Rich Willan received the call at 2:40 p.m.

Rich was not sure what to do. He told them to make themselves big and get a stick.

Rich then called Clearwater Answering to get ahold of a helicopter.

Kurt Dodd headed home to get his rifle.

Brett Gunn phoned Gord R.

Curtis Monroe, Brett Gunn, and Gord R. headed up the hill (3:00 p.m.).

Ambulance and Police were on standby at the bottom of the road.

Learnings and Recommendations:

Could have used a gun. The cougar was not scared and did not back off.

Bear spray helped; it deterred the cougar for a few seconds.

A dog may have helped, but might have complicated things.

Only a gun would have helped, more people would have complicated things.

Ensure radios charged and both carrying radios. Radios should be secured to vest.

Firearm and experienced hunters; should make contacts in valley. End of report.

According to a 1992 National Geographic story, between 1890 and 1990, there were 53 documented cougar attacks in North America—30 of them occurring in British Columbia.

These accounts wouldn't include most cases where people killed cougars in defense, because reports are not usually initiated unless there is injury or death to a person. Since 1990, a rash of cougar attacks has occurred in B.C., the worst taking place on August 19, 1996 when a mother and three children were attacked while horseback riding. The mother gave up her life to save her family.

There are some cougar attacks, like the one on Clarence Hall, or the one that killed a young woman near Banff, Alberta a year later, where a desperate fight for life takes place. One moment a person is moving along, and the next moment they're flat on the ground, stunned, with something latched onto them. But there are also many cases where a person sees a cougar approaching that hasn't quite made up its mind yet whether or not the person is 'takable'. Under this circumstance, move children directly behind you, stay facing the cat, look for any nearby weapon (limb, rock, daypack, etc.), and back away slowly. If the cougar charges, move forward and fight for your life. If you have bear spray, or if several people have spray, line up side by side and spray the cat when it's about four meters (12 feet), and hope that it works.

In the Weyerhaeuser cougar incident, the two men climbed a tree and the cat didn't pursue them, so that strategy might work. Cougars, of course, are excellent climbers, but their attack method is usually ground-launched. If a cougar came up a tree after you, you could lock both arms around the tree and start kicking it in the face area.

If a cougar attacks from behind without warning, the only weapon that could be effective, besides a handgun, is a good knife. Even if you were carrying a rifle, you could lose it on initial impact.

I highly recommend a eight-inch, fixed-blade knife in a good scabbard for defense against cougars. It should have a large hilt so your hand won't slip forward, and a rubberized, notched grip that will not be slippery when covered with blood.

Once you realize that you have been taken down by a cougar, use one arm to hold the cat away to keep it from biting across your throat. Then pull the knife out of its scabbard and repeatedly stab the cat in the chest.

When I go into the bush without a gun, I carry two cans of bear spray and a very good defense knife on a belt. I have a spray on each hip and the knife dead center in front. With this configuration I can obtain a can of spray or the knife no matter what position I may end up on the ground.

To put it very simply, if you want to survive a cougar attack, you must use extreme violent aggression.

16

DEFENDING REALITY

Man prefers to believe what he prefers to be true.
—Francis Bacon

For more than 20 years, I've been engaged in a struggle against proponents of preservationist philosophy. Their numbers are legion, and they have made significant inroads into B.C. during the last two decades. British Columbians will pay a high economic price during the next ten years for allowing preservationism to rule our province.

The material in the *The Natural History Of Grizzly Bears*, the *Bear Habitat Requirements*, and the *Bear Populations* chapters were originally part of a report I prepared for the Central Coast Land and Coastal Resource Management Plan Forum. This group is presently developing a land-use plan for the area where I live that will significantly influence our economy for the next 20 years. The *Grizzly Bears and Reality* report I submitted to the Forum was intended to counter the large number of unsubstantiated claims made by representatives of environmental groups involved—claims such as, grizzly bears are an old-growth dependent species and therefore logging is reducing bear populations.

The report to the Canadian Department of Fisheries and Oceans (DFO) in the *Babine River Salmon Counting Fence* chapter resulted because of a conflict between DFO employees and provincial government Ministry of Environment employees regarding how grizzly bears should be dealt with in the vicinity of the counting fence. The DFO hired me as a consultant to provide the best possible standards for personnel safety at the Babine River counting fence and compound, but I couldn't do that unless I first debunked a series of myths that would make it impossible to create a realistic plan for human safety.

In my training business I have to continuously dispel the growing misinformation regarding predators. It's one thing for city people who rarely venture into the wilds to harbor fallacies about animals and nature, but a completely different situation for B.C. field workers who are often exposed to bears and cougars.

Even though preservationists are winning on many fronts, there is now growing alarm regarding its damage to our economy. Also, there is a rapidly growing demand for reality—as the myths pile up, those who are endangered by them are vigorously looking for alternative information.

The three following events demonstrate what defending bear reality is about.

WYOMING STATISTICS

In late 1999, Gary Goldberg of Palmer, Alaska, sent me a copy of the Nov/Dec 1999 issue of the U.S. Fish and Wildlife Service News and drew my attention to a particular article regarding the development of a bear safety course in Wyoming. The article explained what sounds like an excellent program for educating guides and hunters how to reduce conflict with grizzly bears and is a collaboration between the Wyoming Outfitters and Guides, the Professional Guide Institute, and the Division of Law Enforcement of the U.S. Fish and Wildlife Service in Region 6.

After reading the article, I knew a major problem would soon result due to the following statistical information in the material:

Based on the investigation of bear attacks since 1992 by Service law enforcement agents, who help teach the course, people encountering grizzlies and defending themselves with firearms suffer injury about 50 percent of the time. During the same period, those defending themselves with pepper spray escaped injury over 90 percent of the time, and the remaining 5 to 10 percent experienced shorter duration attacks and less severe injuries.

Although there's nothing wrong with this statement regarding its validity for Wyoming during that time period, the big problem is this: Certain individuals within government ministries and agencies and other individuals within environmental groups quickly started using this statement as if it was based on a continent-wide research project, with the conclusion applying to all areas of North America. In addition, these statistics contradict my research, but only in a certain way.

In the spring of 2000, the B.C. Ministry of Environment, Lands and Parks released a set of Safety Guidelines for People Travelling in Bear Country, adapted from the Center for Wildlife Information and Parks Canada material. The first paragraph in the Bear Attacks section states:

If you surprise a bear and it defends itself: If you have pepper spray, use it. If contact has occurred or is imminent, PLAY DEAD! Lie on your stomach with legs apart. Protect your face, the back of your head and neck with your arms. Remain still until the bear leaves the area. These attacks seldom last more than a few minutes. While fighting back usually increases the intensity of such an attack, in some cases it has caused the bear to leave. If the attack continues for more than several minutes, consider fighting back. Use of a firearm during this type of encounter may aggravate the situation.

Portions of the above statement seem contradictory as to whether you should 'play dead' or not, and the last sentence is there because of the Wyoming statistics. The second paragraph (which isn't shown here) dealing with predatory attacks is quite good. The third paragraph regards bear pepper spray and states the following:

No deterrent is 100% effective, but compared to all others, including firearms, bear pepper spray has demonstrated the most success in fending off threatening and attacking bears and preventing injury to the person and animal involved.

The above statement also resulted from the Wyoming statistics, and, once again, you would assume that it's based on continent-wide research.

I was suspicious that the people in Wyoming who investigated the attacks weren't separating firearms use against grizzly bears involving carcass defense into a distinct category.

I use the following statistics in my training program regarding potential success (no injury or death) against bear attacks: Firearms 95 percent; spray 70 percent; and play dead/fight back 45 percent. But the 95 percent firearms defense success rate is based on B.C. field workers only and doesn't include B.C. hunter defense against grizzly bears. This latter category pertaining to carcass defense is by far the most dangerous type of bear aggression and if I include B.C. hunters in the firearms defense category, then the success rate goes down to about the same as spray defense.

In other words, when a hunter tangles with a grizzly defending an animal carcass or a grizzly coming into camp searching for meat, the danger in this type of attack is significantly greater than the average type of encounter that a backpacker carrying spray would be involved in.

This is an important subject, because there are many individuals and groups who would like to see all firearms use against bears stopped. I deal with this issue on a continuous basis because there are many field workers who are presently denied the right to use guns for their own defense, and they ask me to act on their behalf.

If I really believed that pepper spray was superior to firearms in all or even most defenses against bear attacks, I wouldn't hesitate to advocate sprays over guns. But my research doesn't indicate this, and I feel we need both methods of defense available for people to choose from. I strongly advocate the use of pepper sprays against attacking bears in my training program, because the vast majority of participants don't have the ability to use firearms, or don't want to use firearms, or are not allowed to carry firearms. I personally would always choose a firearm over spray, not because I enjoy killing bears, but because in my case it provides the best possible method for reducing the potential of injury or death during a bear attack. This wouldn't necessarily be true for someone who has no experience in killing bears with firearms.

I decided I needed to interview the people in Wyoming involved with the safety course in order to learn more about their material and to compare it with my own research.

It took several calls to different U.S. Fish and Wildlife Service offices throughout the Western US to find the people who had developed the training program and statistics. On November 28, 2000, I was able to reach Senior Resident Agent Dom Domenici, with the Division of Law Enforcement, U.S. Fish and Wildlife Service, Region 6, in Casper, Wyoming.

Dom was very willing to explain the research material and answer any questions I had. I first asked if a large number of the firearms failures involved hunter encounters with grizzly bears. He answered yes. I then asked if they had separated the firearms failure attacks involving a grizzly after an animal carcass into a distinct class. He said no, they were classed as surprise encounters, (the same as someone carrying a spray and surprising a grizzly at close range).

Dom then explained that in the year 2000, they saw a significant change in the success rate of firearms use against grizzlies. It was a bad year for bears because of the White Bark Pine nut crop failure. As a result, grizzly/human conflict was worse than any previous year. There were 31 grizzly bears killed in the Greater Yellowstone

Ecosystem (Northwest Wyoming and parts of Montana and Idaho), out of a population estimated to be somewhere between 400 and 600 animals. Twelve of these kills were hunters defending themselves, defending a camp, or defending meat. The other grizzly bear kills related to depredation on livestock, conflict near homes, and illegal kills.

I told Dom I would send him copies of my two books and would call him back after he read my material to discuss their information again. He suggested that I also talk to Guide Outfitter Duaine Hagen, who helped develop the training program.

I talked to Duaine Hagen several times in December 2000 and in January 2001. He explained that he had owned and operated a guiding territory ten miles from the east boundary of Yellowstone Park between 1984 and 1998. During that time, the grizzly bear population was increasing and hunter conflict with bears also increased. He had worked hard to employ strategies to reduce the problems with grizzlies and was quite successful. Many of the things he and others learned were incorporated into the training program they developed.

I called Dom again on January 24, 2001, to continue the interview. Dom said he was aware that their statistics were being used in ways never intended by them. Dom stated that many of the hunters in that area didn't really have the knowledge or firepower for effective defense against grizzly bears. The defense portion of their program provided firearms and spray defense training, but left it up to each participant to decide where and when these two different systems were appropriate.

The conflict events in 2000 indicated a significant shift in firearms success, but Dom felt some hunters were lucky to have come through without injury. Of the 12 cases where hunters defended themselves against grizzlies, only one hunter was injured.

Dom said the Wyoming State Game and Fish Department had considered making it mandatory for hunters to carry bear spray, but found it difficult to do for legal reasons. Dom made it clear that in their training, they didn't advocate spray over firearms. Both systems of defense were important and necessary. He also stated that the reason for advocating spray was not to save bears, but to save people's lives. If an additional result of that strategy was fewer bears killed, that was great.

I went over the information Dom faxed me that was prepared by Bear Biologist Chris Servheen in a paper entitled *Brief Comments on the Relationship Between Hunting Mortalities, Total Human-Caused Mortalities, and the Increasing Grizzly Population in the Yellowstone Ecosystem*.

The paper stated that of the 14 grizzlies killed by hunters in 2000, 2 were mistaken identity (thought they were shooting black bears), 7 were chance encounters while hunting, 3 were bears coming into camps, and 2 were conflict over game carcasses.

The percentage of hunter-defense kills had gone up in recent years and was now 60 percent of all human-related grizzly mortalities, even though there had been no increase in hunter numbers. Interestingly, the paper stated that although hunter-defense kills increased, the total human-caused mortality hadn't risen significantly because other types of mortality had decreased. It was suggested that this resulted from better management of garbage and other types of conflicts.

Another interesting point was the estimate that annual hunting activities in the area created 495 tons of carrion for bears and other scavengers, and bear movement data indicated that bears were now moving into hunter use areas to search for carrion and gut-piles.

Following is the conclusive statement of the paper:

In summary, in the Yellowstone ecosystem, hunter encounter grizzly mortalities are increasing faster than mortalities from other human causes. This is due to a combination of factors, including:

*Increasing grizzly bear use of areas where successful hunters are killing big game and subsequently providing food for bears. This results in seasonal density increases of grizzly bears in the areas where hunter success is high, thus increasing encounter frequency. Such bears are apparently receiving food rewards related to hunting and are apparently becoming increasingly interested in seeking such hunter-related foods. Bears that receive food rewards in association with human activities are more likely to be in conflicts. It is unclear what percentage of bears are exhibiting such behavior, but the number of such bears may be increasing.

*Possible increased competition between bears for food as the bear density increases. This competition is exacerbated in poor food years when all bear conflicts usually increase.

*There are more hunter encounters with bears, and some hunters use lethal force during these encounters, resulting in more hunter-encounter bear deaths. Pepper spray can be a valuable tool, but as one law enforcement official said, "Any bear that can be sprayed is also close enough to use lethal means and claim self-defense."

What this all means is that grizzlies are leaving Yellowstone Park in early fall to engage in 'gut-pile search behavior' in the surrounding areas, which already have numerous bears, and they are competing against hunters and other bears for an important food source—a food source that is very likely partially responsible for the increase of the bear population in the first place.

I now want to repeat a statement from the *Carcass Defense Chapter* in this book:

> *There's a very good reason why carcass defense behavior is so dangerous in bears. Bears evolved from a true predatory ancestor to become omnivores that primarily depend on plant foods. But they have retained much of their original carnivore digestive system and supplement their usual diet with animal tissue they've killed or taken from other predators. Their predatory behavior is opportunistic in practice.*
>
> *During years when plant foods that bears can extract fats from (berries, acorns, beech nuts, pine nuts, etc.) are in short supply, which happens on four- or five-year cycles, obtaining and holding onto large carcasses can mean the difference between life or death during the following hibernating and spring den-emergence period. For this reason, bears have evolved a high level of aggression for defending an important fat source.*

The three bears killed entering camps and the two killed in conflict over carcasses with hunters reported in the paper Dom sent me obviously fall into what I call carcass defense behavior. But what about the seven grizzlies killed in chance encounters? This number appears far too high statistically for these to have happened as random events. There are three points I want to make about those seven bear kills:

1. Some hunters are probably walking near the carrion of previous kills that they are unaware of.
2. Grizzlies are very likely doing deliberate searches right around hunting camps they have discovered, which would increase the number of encounters.
3. When grizzly bears are engaged in gut-pile search behavior, they are in a state of anxiety and are extremely aggressive towards anything they perceive as a competitive predator.

In other words, I'm suggesting that many of these chance-encounter hunter-defense kills also pertain to the 'complex' of behaviors related to carcass defense. I called Dom again and asked if any of the chance encounters included other factors like walking near a gut-pile from an earlier kill. He said yes, some of them did.

The bottom line is this: No matter what certain individuals claim, the truth is, firearms and pepper spray are both needed for defense against bears, but for many people, firearms provide the best system for reducing injury and death inflicted by bears. It would be very unfortunate to have people killed just because some individuals, groups, and governments want to eliminate firearms use against bears.

BLACK BEAR RE-INTRODUCTION

On February 4, 2000, I received an e-mail from Susan and Brad Neff of Jamestown, Tennessee. They first thanked me for writing my books, then asked if I'd help them try to stop the re-introduction of black bears into the Big South Fork National River and Recreation Area (BSFNR&RA). The project is a joint effort by the National Park Service and the Tennessee Wildlife Resource Agency. The area of planned re-introduction is approximately 100 miles northwest of the Great Smoky Mountains National Park.

Susan and Brad stated the BSFNR&RA is used significantly for recreation, and they were concerned about the bear conflict and bear danger that would result from the re-introduction for both recreationists and people in the surrounding rural communities. In particular, they asked permission to reprint two stories from my second book in local newspapers, and they also requested any additional information I may have on predatory black bear attacks.

I agreed to help them with this battle, even though I knew I'd take many hits from certain members of the biological community and preservationist groups as a result. I provided Susan and Brad with the following warning that was published in their local newspapers, along with the two predatory black bear death stories:

Bears are now being managed for higher populations in many areas of North America, and the push to stop bear hunting is just getting started. The end result will be less freedom and more danger for people who live in rural areas. The first regulation will be bear-proof garbage cans, then restrictions on fruit trees and berry patches; next will come limitations on barbecues and dog dishes. Your favorite recreation area will become so restricted that you won't enjoy yourself while out there camping. And finally, when a person kills what he believes is a dangerous bear or a bear doing serious damage to his property, a healthy fine will be the reward.

Even though the frequency of predatory attacks by black bears in the Lower 48 states has been traditionally low, this type of attack will no doubt increase as more people encounter bears and as more bears lose their fear of people. In the last eight-and-a-half years, there have been between 70 and 80 serious injuries and 19 deaths inflicted by bears in British Columbia, Alberta, Alaska, and the

Yukon. Of the deaths, 13 were by grizzlies and six by black bears. All of the black bear-caused deaths were by predatory bears. During the last 20 years in British Columbia, bear inflicted deaths have been about equal between grizzlies and black bears.

The battle was fought at a packed courthouse during a two-and-one-half hour Fentress County Commissioners meeting on February 10, 2000. Eight out of ten commissioners voted against the re-introduction until the National Parks Service addressed certain issues in their management plan. One of the commissioners, Rodney Jones, spearheaded the opposition drive and stated: *There is widespread opposition to bears that is not being listened to by the Park Service. I have heard from county residents who fear the bears will not stay in the Big South Fork. In my efforts to give the people all the information they should know about these dangerous animals, I have obtained permission from Mr. James Gary Shelton, author of Bear Attacks - The Deadly Truth, to republish two of the true stories in his book written in 1998.*

Shortly after the meeting, I received an e-mail from Susan and Brad thanking me for helping them. The war wasn't over, but the re-introduction was derailed for now.

The issue remained unchanged through the spring and then something bizarre and very tragic happened on May 21st.

Glenda Ann Bradley, 50, a school teacher, was killed and partially eaten by a female black bear and a cub in the Great Smoky Mountains National Park. Other park users tried to chase the bears away by screaming and throwing rocks at them, but the animals stayed, guarding the body until they were killed.

The attack story made headlines all over the Eastern US and was, of course, very big news in Fentress County.

Even though this was the first black bear fatality in the park's history, you can imagine how vindicated the people felt who fought hard to stop re-introduction in the nearby Big South Fork, and also, how disappointed the biologists must have felt who claimed it couldn't happen.

In reality, the two events—the fight against the re-introduction and the predatory attack death—are a statistical aberration. There is no direct link between the two. However, there is an indirect link. During the last four years, four predatory black bear attacks in the Lower 48 states have occurred in areas where they've never happened before. A slow increase in this type of attack is taking place, and statistically, someone would probably have been attacked in the Lower 48 states in the year 2000. But it was a strange twist of fate that it happened when and where it did.

To my knowledge, this is the first time a bear re-introduction plan has been temporarily stopped.

Another interesting fact regarding this case is that hunter groups in Tennessee were in favor of having bears in the Big South Fork. Some people may find it strange that I'd be on the opposite side of an issue from other hunters. The main reason I got involved was to defend my main interest—rural culture. In most circumstances, defending this interest includes hunters as well, but not always. In this particular case, I feel those hunters are mistaken in their belief they'll eventually get the opportunity to hunt those bears. What will most likely occur after the re-introduction is that the bear population will grow unchecked until it becomes a terrible burden on local rural residents, who will suffer significant property damage, loss of freedom, and increased danger from bear attacks. I say this based on experience, not theory.

GRIZZLY HUNTING BAN

During the 1970s, I spent a lot of time with my friend Darryl Hodson hunting, fishing, and exploring. Darryl owned a steelhead fishing lodge on the famous Dean River just north of Bella Coola. He also operated a guiding business with the specialty of taking trophy class grizzly bears.

Darryl was raised on the outer B.C. coast in the isolated town of Ocean Falls and had spent every waking moment of his youth engaged in outdoor activities. He had tremendous knowledge regarding every aspect of nature and became a bear expert at a very young age. Fortunately, he was willing to share what he'd learned with me and other people.

For many years, Darryl and I lived, breathed, and thought mainly about grizzly bears. There was no limit to where we would go or what we would do to unlock the mysteries of these animals. When Darryl bought a Piper Supercub airplane on floats in 1971, we then had the means to step back in time by landing on small, remote rivers where no person had walked for a half-century.

We spent many pleasure-filled evenings around campfires or in small, leaky cabins, often accompanied by Darryl's younger brother Randy, and the topic of conversation was often the same—grizzly bears. By 1980, we'd come to a joint conclusion that at some point in the future, grizzly bear hunting in B.C. would come to an end, not because of a shortage of bears, but because sooner or later grizzlies would be elevated onto the same pedestal as wolves, and anti-hunting forces would use their new status to stop what they perceived as a sin against nature. We both felt that when that day finally came,

Darryl Hodson preparing the Supercub for take-off on the Kechikan River in Northern British Columbia.

our era would be over.

In 1991, Darryl was killed in a tragic helicopter accident. He didn't live to see what we both dreaded—a world too futuristic for our kind.

After a four-year battle in B.C. between advocates for and against grizzly bear hunting, an important demarcation line took place in my life. On February 9, 2001, I received a fax from my daughter, Julie Scheven, with a note in the margin: "It's beginning!"

The fax was a B.C. Government press release announcing a three-year moratorium on grizzly hunting. The press release stated that the closure was due to the widely differing opinions between bear experts as to how many grizzly bears there are in the province and whether the hunt is sustainable.

Very quickly the moratorium turned into a political battle. One of Premier Ujjal Dosanjh's cabinet members, Highways Minister Harry Lali, resigned in protest against the unilateral decision made by the Premier to end the hunt. With the provincial election only months away, the opposition party leader, Gordon Campbell, quickly took advantage of the situation. He stated that his party, upon being elected to form the next government, would reinstate the hunt but would create a panel of experts to make sure the bear population is not threatened.

Preservationists groups were successful in convincing the Premier to stop the hunt primarily because of the efforts of certain bear biologists. These biologists claim that there are approximately 4,000 grizzlies in the province, and their numbers are declining. They advocated the moratorium so that research work could confirm what the grizzly population actually is. I know these biologists well and have participated with them in arduous debates on several different occasions at public forums. Their stated agenda for wanting the moratorium is not quite accurate. In reality, they want all grizzly bear hunting of any kind taking place anywhere in the world to stop, period. And, of course, the only jurisdiction in the world foolish enough to grant their wish is the B.C. New Democratic Party Government.

If someone in the government had spent a day calling safety officers with the different ministries and agencies, and also conservation officers, they would have found, based on direct observation by hundreds of people, that the grizzly population is doing well and increasing in most areas. This type of information is every bit as valuable as hit-and-miss population research. The cost to actually count the B.C. grizzly population would be prohibitively expensive.

The struggle for this particular aspect of reality has been temporarily lost, but will continue.

There is presently, in North America, a major assault taking place against people who live in the less inhabited regions. A legion of environment groups and politicians are working on and enacting policies that damage or eliminate logging, mining, ranching, trapping, guiding, hunting, and a host of other rural activities. This is a war between preservationists and those who still live and work on the land and have a more direct relationship with nature. Unfortunately, preservationists are often winning the support of those city people with middle-of-the-road values.

17

CONCLUSION

I've done my best in this book to shed more light on why bears attack people and how best to survive an attack, how the politics of the day influence bear management, and unfortunately, how the preservationist movement has cast a dark shadow over science.

But in truth, my efforts are more like demolition and reconstruction than research and writing. In order to provide realistic information about bears and nature, I must first demolish the deceptive edifice of mythology ingrained in the North American nature paradigm, then start again with a foundation based on reality.

Those who need the myth and dogma of neo-pantheism seem to have forsaken mankind and find justice only in a nature devoid of humanity. They would deny the importance of our existence, and also deny that justice is a human invention. Unfortunately, there is no justice in nature. A large asteroid could strike the earth at any time and many life forms, including ourselves, could end up nothing more than dust of the past. A hundred times more species have suffered extinction in the past than now exist. Nature cares little about those creatures we desperately want to protect. We must look for the foundations of human belief in ourselves and others, whether religious or not, rather than molding nature into a mythological form and then using it to deny the stark realities of this planet.

The most important and obvious attribute of *Homo sapiens* is the ability to alter and reorganize natural resources for our survival and comfort of life. Our species has employed that strategy for at least a million years. During the last three centuries, humankind took up science because it's the best mechanism available for unlocking the mysteries that bewilder us. It's also the best instrument for finding the balance between our need to survive and our need to leave nature as undisturbed as possible.

Many times I've stood on mountaintops adjacent to Bella Coola and examined the striated gouges left in solid rock by glaciers from a mere 16,000 thousand years ago, when the Valley was covered with 6,000 feet of ice. It was a time when the huge Douglas fir trees and grizzly bears did not exist here. This glimpse of the massive power of an advancing ice sheet that once was, has helped me to understand the temporariness of what exists around us.

Is there beauty in nature? Absolutely, and we can see it more clearly when our view is unobstructed by the preservationist lens. We must accept ourselves as an intrinsic part of the constantly evolving forces that shape nature, and whether we like it or not, we are now the primary participants and caretakers of that domain. Let's accept our stewardship with the positive knowledge that good science and common sense are far better than mythology for protecting both the wonders of nature and ourselves.

I want to thank the hundreds of people who have written and made comments about my books, and also those who have sent me their stories. Your positive responses have made the long hours on the road and the long hours at the computer all worth it.

Gary Shelton

www.bearattacksurvival.com/cabc/

Appendix

One of the difficulties I've faced when finalizing my books, particularly this one, is to determine where this book ends and the next one begins. Because I'm conducting research on a continuous basis regarding a broad spectrum of subjects, I always have a large body of material referenced in files ready for use that may or may not fall within the scope of a particular work in progress.

One of the most important principles I've tried to follow in my books is to present information about bears, nature, and environmental issues in an objective way so that my material is acceptable to the majority of people who have middle-ground opinions, and do not necessarily share all my views. It's easy to write books for like-minded people, but extremely difficult to write books on controversial subjects that will appeal to a broader spectrum of the general public.

The following information actually falls in between this book and my next, but I decided to include it here because during my travels in recent years while providing training, doing speaking engagements, and conducting research, I've had many people, particularly young people, ask me why certain events are taking place in our culture that they strongly disagree with and don't understand.

Firstly, I will take one of the important aspects of this book, bear biology, and place it within the history of science and demonstrate the cultural influences that have altered that discipline. Secondly, I will take another important aspect of this book, preservationist philosophy, and place it within the broader context as a sub-philosophy of the Postmodern cultural/political paradigm that has been drastically reshaping our society during the last 15 years.

If you are satisfied with the direction our culture is presently headed and are not particularly interested in science or political philosophy, then you may want to close this book now and consider it finished.

BEAR BIOLOGY AS A SCIENCE

Did you ever wonder why a study can be released to the public claiming that coffee or aspirin or some other product is good for you, then a year later another study comes out claiming the opposite? This happens all the time.

Do you believe the conclusions from past research sponsored by tobacco companies regarding whether cigarettes are hazardous to human health?   What about bear population status studies by preservationist biologists who receive research grants from funding bodies who believe that bears are endangered and may be headed for extinction?

The first question regarding contradictions in science has to do with problems in methodology—usually not having all the necessary information for a valid conclusion, and sometimes, it's a serious error. The last two questions have to do with biases in science.

Many people make the mistake of thinking that the spectacular advances in technology—such as computers, with the precise and powerful science required to produce them—is representative of how most scientific research is conducted. Unfortunately, that's not the case, and when we step into the realm of biological and environmental sciences loaded with contemporary issues regarding nature, wildlife, and man's role in nature, it's a wonder there are still many biologists and technicians producing high-quality work.

However, there is an increasingly negative influence on the nature sciences that can be understood only by having a clear perception of the history of science, including its philosophical underpinnings, and the origins of present-day environmental philosophy.

THE HISTORY OF SCIENCE

Sir Francis Bacon (1561 - 1626) is credited as being the father of modern science. He criticized the Thomas Aquinas/Aristotelian science he was taught that claimed truth was first discovered in the mind, then confirmed by observation. The 'Aristotelian syllogism' was purely deductive logic without controlled experimentation—conclusion from a set of 'empirically untested' premises. This previous philosophy for acquiring and increasing knowledge had dominated western thought since the middle of the 13th century and was maintained by religious scholars.

Bacon insisted that truth came only from the careful observation of nature—truth flowed into the human mind, not out of it. He developed the methodology of observation, classification, generalization, and experimentation. His method of inquiry, generalization from observation, was 'induction'—reasoning from particular cases to general conclusions. Also, Francis Bacon understood that the gathering of knowledge must be insulated from the supervision of theologians. He initiated the modern concept of separating knowledge from belief.

Bacon envisioned science as a unified discipline that would significantly improve the conditions of mankind. His conceptual advance ushered in the period of Enlightenment that still provides the basic underpinnings for western culture. Bacon wasn't a great scientist or mathematician; he was a brilliant thinker who vastly improved the philosophy of science.

The first true modern scientific figure was Rene Descartes, who expanded Bacon's enterprise by developing algebraic geometry and the use of 'deduction'—reasoning from general principles to particular cases—in order to dissect and analyze component features of natural phenomenon. He reversed Bacon's methodology by first identifying a set of general principles (generalization), which were then applied to particular cases (observation), in order to arrive at a conclusion—Descartes introduced reductionism and analytical mathematical modeling. Most important, was his concept of systematic doubt as the first principle of learning. All conclusions and knowledge must withstand the continuous assault of vigorous research. Even though the 'Cartesian system' looks strikingly modernistic, and even though many of his principles were incorporated into the scientific process, Descartes' deductive methodology languished as Baconian induction reigned king in most branches of science for the following two centuries.

During those 200 years, Bacon's and Descartes' legacy was added to by Galileo's mathematics and astronomy, Newton's physics, Linnaeus's classification of plants and animals, Lyell's geology, Owen's paleontology, and Cuvier's zoology. During that period, philosophy and science slowly split into separate disciplines, but they were still strongly linked. The great empirical philosophers—Locke, Hume, and Kant—pushed science towards a clearer and more precise vision of good reasoning, but also reinforced the use of induction by refuting the causal link needed in deduction. In that same time span, western science found its home in the universities of Europe.

By the time of Charles Darwin, science had evolved into various disciplines of inquiry regarding many aspects of nature. However, most of these branches of learning used different types of methodology based on induction. Also, these bodies of knowledge existed within the Judaeo-Christian framework which incorporated the principle of God's laws of design and purpose.

The theory of evolution had existed for almost a century before Darwin provided the mechanism—natural selection—that made the theory plausible. Darwin's model eventually amalgamated many branches of science into a larger whole and removed the necessity of Godly design. But equally important was Darwin's system of using both inductive observation and a vastly improved form of deductive logic. In his early career, he claimed to be an Inductionist, but after Liebig published his convincing repudiation of inductive science in

1863, Darwin admitted to using deductive logic. Liebig's criticism that inductive investigation alone could never generate the theories needed for significant advancements—coupled with the power of Darwin's methodology—brought the era of pure inductionism to a close. Darwin's methods influenced other scientists towards a more unified system for developing theories and hypotheses and then conducting the necessary research for verification.

The last half of the 19th century was a unique period for science, because it was the only time when science was truly free from religious, political, economic, and institutional influences. Between 1855 and 1910, the bright stars of science advanced knowledge of the natural world to an amazing degree. Darwin and his contemporaries laid the groundwork for the new science of hypothetical-deductive methodology. Most of these people were not atheists, but they clearly recognized the extreme importance of unobstructed scientific enterprise.

However, by the time the First World War ended, a new era for science began as governments started to realize that scientific technology could win wars and drive industry.

The older branch of learning, the humanities (creative literature, poetry, art, etc.), had existed parallel to Aristotelian science and Bacon's modern science for centuries. A third branch of learning, the social sciences (sociology, psychology, anthropology, economics, etc.), was developed and established during the Darwinian period and eventually became an important influence on cultural advancement.

By the 1920s and 1930s, science was becoming heavily governmentalized in agencies, more significantly institutionalized in universities, and industrialized in companies. Soon after these developments, funding became the main selective force directing many branches of science. Great strides were made in technological engineering and manufacturing, in pharmaceutical research and the development of medicines, and in the improvement of agricultural crops and animal husbandry.

The 1930s and 1940s saw the development of the new biology resulting from the synthesis of Darwin's theory of natural selection and Mendel's population genetics. But a more ominous trend came to light during that period as the Second World War clearly demonstrated that the future survival of nation states would depend on technological science. As the war began, leading scientists in aeronautical engineering and nuclear physics became direct employees of governments around the world. To this day, branches of science that provide important advancements in war machinery are under the control of governments, and their activities are jealously guarded.

During the1940s and 1950s, the branches of science dealing with animals and nature were under the domain of university studies and governmental policies and were guided at the implementation level by wildlife biologists, forest technicians, and other types of specialists. By this time, a very sophisticated system of conservation biology had been developed in North America that was premised, firstly, on man's right to manipulate and use natural resources for human benefit and wealth creation, and secondly, on the belief that a principle of stewardship must be used for protecting nature.

At the world level, an intellectual debate was taking place between the followers of Marxist doctrine and the followers of capitalist doctrine. For over 40 years, Marxist ideology had significantly influenced the sciences of economics, politics, and sociology, and the stage was set for the first class struggle in North America that would alter and influence nature sciences forever.

The tumultuous '60s were truly a revolution against the Industrial Military Complex that President Eisenhower had warned about, and against the capitalist system as well. It was, however, also a revolution against the very foundations of the scientific tenants of man's role in nature. Marxist principles had finally been extended to a broader range of human interests.

The original spirit of the Enlightenment, that all scientific disciplines could operate within one general system, had been fading for half a century. The social sciences had evolved different methodologies as they slowly split from the natural sciences. And then, as the 1960s antithesis pervaded psychology, sociology, anthropology, economics, and political science, a drastic left turn was taken by our culture regarding science. The 'postmodernist movement' had existed for more than a decade, but it expanded with increased momentum as the new visionaries claimed that the Enlightenment was nothing more than a contrived 'White European Male' science. They insisted that the existing science was one of many possible systems for understanding the world and humanity. Soon after, the foundations were laid for 'feel-good' education, multiculturalism, victim group classification, and affirmative action.

During the 1970s, the postmodernist paradigm was incorporated into the ecological and wildlife sciences. A new nature philosophy evolved that denied capitalistic man's place at the top of the heap and relegated modern-living humans to the category of an intrusive life-form that is threatening the world's beauty, energy, and essence. This philosophy now underlies the research structure of many branches of science and is still the reigning nature philosophy of our culture.

As the Soviet Empire collapsed, neo-socialists in Europe and North America redirected their dislike for the free-enterprise system, and 'deep ecology' was established. In the late 1980s, this powerful new force was welcomed into the major environmental groups, and the preservationist movement was born. We've been in the age of neo-pantheism every since. This period has been dominated by those who see nature as created by itself—a special entity existing separate from mankind and having an organized, balanced web of life with purpose and natural justice. The conservationist principles of stewardship and sustainable resource use were replaced with the concept that nature is its own steward, that mankind must live in a condition of limited materialism, and that the continuing assault on nature by corporations and governments must be stopped.

Let's now step back in time again and re-examine the foundations of modern wildlife biology, with additional information and with an emphasis on methodology.

MODERN WILDLIFE SCIENCE

During the first half of the 20th century, three brilliant theorists—Max Planck, Albert Einstein, and Niels Bohr—demonstrated the amazing power of hypothetical-deductive methodology—showing how strange concepts born of the mind regarding space, time, and matter could, decades later, be proven correct by experimentation and observation. It is a precise and powerful system for unlocking the mysteries of the hard sciences such as astronomy, nuclear physics, chemistry, electronics, and computer technology—the mathematical laboratory sciences. Theory and deduction became our canons of the day, logical empiricism our church of reason.

This rigid scientific methodology served us well during the industrial age and will continue to do so in many branches of science. But there are problems with this orthodoxy—it is heavily biased against the importance of inductive observation independent of theory that is needed for some types of research, such as teasing out the subtleties of human and animal behavior.

Jane Goodall's research with chimpanzees at Gombe Reserve in Tanganyika, that started in 1960, has radically changed our views about animal and human behavior. Her work has clearly shown that unbiased inductive research is far superior to hypothetico-deductive research for discerning animal behavior. As a matter of fact, when she was working at Olduvai Gorge in Kenya with the famous paleoanthropologist Louis Leaky, he chose her for the chimpanzee project because she didn't have a formal education in animal behavior.

He knew that a university education would bias her views against the kind of long-term inductive research that was necessary for unlocking the mysteries of chimpanzee society. Also, it was extremely important that she did not harbor any preconceived notions regarding what makes chimpanzees different from humans. The acceptance of Jane Goodall's work has improved wildlife science by demonstrating that good research is an interweaving of inductive and deductive methodologies.

During the last 20 years, a system using a relaxed form of hypothetical-deductive methodology has developed for wildlife research. Some projects inductively gather general information using telemetry (tracking radio-collars), observation, and other types of data gathering. Other projects attempt to test a particular hypothesis, or multiple hypotheses, deductively. These research projects must then pass a peer-review process by other experts in the field before final acceptance of the work takes place through publication in a respected journal. As these projects build on one another and increase our knowledge regarding individual species, like grizzly bears, better projects are conceived for obtaining more and more specific and accurate information.

The structure for this type of science is: identifying a problem or area of interest, gathering existing data, hypothesis formulation, experimentation and observation through research projects, interpreting resulting data, and drawing conclusions. Underlying this process is the important principle of modern science that all concepts, hypotheses, theories, and information must be falsifiable— that is, all aspects of scientific knowledge must exist in a form that can be tested for verification by future research.

Wildlife biologists like to use models. This method is based on a hypothesis or a series of hypotheses that tries to incorporate all or most existing research material for exploring certain phenomenon. Some research projects result in conclusions that favor certain models over others, but the door is left open on all competing models until a significant amount of material accumulates that eliminates a particular model.

PRESENT INFLUENCES ON SCIENCE

In my lifetime, I've seen a significant increase in negative influences on some types of science—what I call the bending of science. I'm not referring to the normal biases that individual scientists may have, or the usual favoritism for certain competing hypotheses that better fit with our cultural beliefs. I'm talking about the institutionalized preference for postmodernist science by governments and universities that is eliminating 'systematic logico-deductive thought'. We've entered a new era that's similar to what existed prior to the Darwinian revolution.

During the 1970s, as the new nature philosophy was forming, many university biology courses were changed and a series of assumptions were incorporated that were not scientifically based, but rather originated from environmental ideology, such as:
• Industrial activities like logging and mining reduce bear populations.
• Grizzly bears need pristine environments for survival.
• Bear populations are in decline, and in many areas extinction will result.
• Bears have a natural fear of humans and will avoid people whenever possible.
• Bears will not choose to live near people if they have alternatives.
• Bears attack people only when threatened.

These hypotheses, and many more like them, are incorrect, and hopefully my research and other writings will expose many of these misconceptions for what they are. But it will take decades before objective bear biologists throw off the remaining shackles of the underlying preservationist nature philosophy. They have the same task as Darwin.

With the exception of that brief period after Darwin's zenith, there have always been significant influences which may bias how scientific enterprise is conducted, and there probably always will be.

An extremely important part of modern science is its relationship to fund-raising and institutional purpose. A funding agency is rarely interested in spending precious research dollars for the general inquiry of random knowledge. Research proposals must state the nature and purpose of a project as well as the cost. A scientist is not going to obtain research funding unless he or she provides an expectation of results that the funding agency is interested in.

Most funding during the last 35 years for bear research has been based on the concern that bears are declining and may face extinction in many areas of the world. An industry of preservationist research and alarmist activism has been created by this funding and concern. If it became widely known that bear populations are no longer declining, much of the present funding would dry up. Preservationist biologists are not about to give up their outdated beliefs; they must maintain the illusion that bears are severely threatened. Even though these biologists constitute a minority of the biological community, they are extremely vocal and are the ones who continually use the news media to draw attention to their selective science agendas.

I've read many scientific papers created by preservationist biologists. They use the cause-science techniques of selective science, the mixing of substantiated and unsubstantiated concepts, and authority by reference. Firstly, they select the needed material from the massive body of research papers (many of them contradictory); secondly, they use small segments of good research mixed with dubious statements; thirdly, they include a huge appendix of referenced research papers that supposedly provides the authority for their claims. The authors of these papers are careful not to make statements that can be easily disproved. These preservationist works usually flourish in a relatively unchallenged atmosphere.

These deep ecology papers often end up as sanctioned documents for government ministries and agencies and are used extensively by the United Nations because many preservationist groups have consulting status with the U.N. as Non-governmental Organizations (NGOs).

Many preservationist biologists have gravitated to job positions where their biases are valued because of the politics of their employers. And in many federal, state, and provincial jurisdictions, they now have significant influence over government policies or over propaganda released to environmental extremists.

They have another influence on bear biology that has to do with the public relations campaign for bears. If a biologist does anything to make bears look bad, such as explaining to the general public that the large male grizzly in the movie *The Bear* would have actually killed and eaten the baby bear, that biologist is subjected to harassment from preservationist biologists (such as receiving a letter claiming that severe damage has been done to the public's interest in protecting bears). This bear public relations campaign has created a condition where many of our best bear biologists are hesitant to make any effort to correct the weekly TV fare of doom and gloom for bears—they're unwilling to stand up and defend science.

After 40 years of watching TV programs about wolves and bears, it's obvious to me that sequences showing these two species killing and eating other animals are carefully edited so their image is not damaged. The public relations campaign for wolves and bears exerts an unspoken pressure on filmmakers to eliminate certain scenes, even though similar material showing African predators ripping and tearing baby animals apart is okay.

And this brings us to the worst form of science bending. Almost every organization with the ability and funding to produce TV programs about bears has bought into preservationist doctrine lock, stock, and barrel. After these organizations develop a script for a particular program, researchers interview many bear biologists but use only those who will project the underlying script philosophy, rather than using various biologists who would present a balanced picture of all scientific work on the subject. Unfortunately, in our modern culture, people basically believe what they see and hear on TV.

The final type of negative influence on bear biology relates to my line of research. For many years, there has been a concerted effort by preservationist bear biologists to downplay bear attacks and to attribute human causes to these events. Many people are shocked when they read my books and discover accurate details regarding particular attacks they've read about before. These people often call or write and make comments about how they mistakenly believed the original interpretation of the event in the news media.

CONCLUSION

In recent years, I've read many articles and papers by scientists who are concerned about the present bending of science. In a paper entitled *In War, Truth Is the First Casualty* (May 1999), by Brian W. Bowen and Stephen A. Karl of the Department of Fisheries and Aquatic Sciences at the University of Florida, the authors expose the efforts of other biologists to manipulate scientific data so that certain sub-species of animals can be classed as a *"unique evolutionary unit"* in order to qualify as an endangered species. Following is the most important statement in their paper: *"Our original paper, however, is not about the rules of taxonomy but about the misuse of scientific findings to promote conservation goals, and ultimately about the deeper tension between science and advocacy in conservation. It has been argued that conservation is a war, and in wartime it is acceptable to tell lies to deceive the enemy. Should legitimate scientific results then be withheld, modified, or spun to serve conservation goals? Emphatically, we say no. Conservation goals will change with time, but scientific principles should not."*

The above scientists use the term conservation where I would use preservation, because the tenants of the former are based on science and the tenants of the latter on cause-science. To be more accurate, preservationist biologists are postmodernists who are actually anti-science—that is, they don't trust pure empirical science without humanistic interpretation. The justification for bending biological science seems to be based on the spiritual concept of 'higher truths' that transcend mere science.

Based on the recent rash of book publications, articles, and letters by concerned academic scholars, it appears that most of our colleges and universities are badly infected with the insidious disease of politically correct higher truths. Even though hard science departments and many other aspects of educational life are not yet censored, the basis for intellectual debate, rationality and evidence, seems to be severely corrupted by the agendas of victim group politics and preservationism in many social science, humanities, and nature science departments. Professors give biased lectures and students are graded on the willingness to accept conformity. Whole topics of potential discussion are forbidden in many classrooms.

Also, on many campuses, students are subjected to staff or student body judicial systems that enforce speech codes, political re-education, and in general, an obligatory acceptance of political, historical, and nature revisionism. Our universities no longer require philosophy, literature, and history as the basis for serious human learning. Many of our young people consider the past as irrelevant and the future as unimportant; they live only in the present, unable to use the yardstick of important past knowledge for measuring what's going on around them.

All of this is extremely important because the virus responsible for causing the disease of higher truths is infecting our young, idealistic future scientists. This mind-set is already responsible for eliminating common sense and sound biology from bear management policies all over North America. Bears are now classified as the latest victim group that deserves special status and protection.

Instead of picking certain icon species and placing them on the pedestal of mythology, we need to protect all of nature—including humans.

It's literally impossible for a biologist to be an advocate of some cause and, at the same time, be an objective scientist, whether the cause is for preservationism or for industrial interests. There have been times in the past when right-wing interests had significant negative influences over branches of science and in some cases still do. I've focused on negative left-wing influences on science in my books because, at this time in history, promoters of that ideology are responsible for most of the misinformation regarding bears and nature that I must deal with when teaching people how to survive bear attacks.

Bear biology is presently under the influence of preservationist pseudo-science in many areas of North America and this branch of wildlife science may soon be swallowed up by postmodernism. However, there are many excellent bear biologists doing superb research who are mustering strong resistance against anti-science forces in our culture. I take my hat off to these people and look forward to reading their future works.

POSTMODERNISM

I remember the 1950s very well. I came from a poor family living in Utah, but we were rich in spirit and freedom. My parents actively supported me and my sibling's endless search for knowledge about the natural world around us. We went camping, hunting, fishing, prospecting, and exploring. I collected rocks, artifacts, plant specimens, coins, stamps, and a host of other interesting items. I was encouraged to read books, and that activity became a life-long passion. It was a great period of time for many people, but not for all people.

Then came the 1960s. This was a difficult era for most of my generation—our culture and belief system was turned upside down and systematically stripped of its importance and vigour. It was an age of rebellion and confusion.

During the '70s and the early '80s, a 15-year synthesis process took place that created a new society in North America. Many of us from the old culture hated the changes, such as the break down of the family unit, feel-good education, intrusive government, and so on. But there were also important positive changes that resulted from the 1960s: freedom for woman, civil rights for minorities, less intrusive religion, and many other benefits that most of us now cherish.

The present manifestation of postmodernism is a cultural/political paradigm that originated from marxism, but was modified during the 1960s and then slowly grew during the 1970s and early 1980s, then took flight as a political force in about 1985. It is a powerfully seductive paradigm that is difficult to identify, because it is well hidden under the twin banners of political correctness and higher truths.

The origin and outcome of postmodernism has been recently documented in a publication authored by Alan Charles Kors and Harvey A. Silverglate. They inform us in *The Shadow University*, 1998, that the underlying logic for the present speech codes, and behavior tribunals in our universities and other similar doctrines in our culture, can be found in the writings of little-known Marxist/socialist philosopher Herbert Marcuse. During the 1960s, Marcuse added to the works of Rousseau and Marx to create an alternative concept for liberty: Liberty is not individual freedom, but rather, equality—that is, government enforced equality.

The Marcusean doctrine requires that the North American European races (the oppressor class) must have their free speech, free access to jobs, free access to firearms, and many other liberties temporarily suspended so that minority races (the oppressed groups) can be elevated to a higher level of income, status, and power in our culture. As a consequence, verbal assaults by individuals of a minority group against individuals of the oppressor group are justified and cannot be construed as prejudicial or racist. However, verbal assaults by members of the oppressor group against members of a minority group are prejudicial, racist, and subject to being classed as hate crimes. Marcuse states that deep pervasive censorship of the power class is required, and if necessary, violence against the oppressors as well. Liberty and freedom of speech becomes subordinate to redressing past historical wrongs inflicted on minorities groups.

Postmodernists believe that in order to proceed to humankind's destiny—the pinnacle of civilization—we must use social democracy, including undemocratic means if necessary, to guarantee absolute equality between all citizens. Also, more recently, we must create equality between humans and animals (preservationism).

Most of the conflicts that erupted between the 1950s and 1960s generations have now been resolved, but the core beliefs about family, spirituality, and liberty between modernism and postmodernism are not synthesizing and are becoming more polarized all the time.

Bill Clinton was the first U.S. postmodernist president. His value system is completely different from all those who proceeded him, whether Democrat or Republican. That post has now been taken back by a modernist president who appears to have middle-of-the-road views. The ugly battle that took place during the last presidential race demonstrates the polarizing of the core beliefs between the two paradigms presently fighting it out in our culture. Judging by that election, the U.S. appears to have reached the half-and-half stage in power between the two rival ideologies.

The political situation in Canada is significantly different. Canada was quickly ushered into the postmodern era during the reign of Pierre Trudeau. The federal government of Canada and some provincial governments embrace the Marcusean philosophy that the oppressor class must be heavily taxed in order to pay victim groups for crimes committed against them in the past.

The two beliefs systems can't be simply defined by placing individual people into one box or the other. There are many politicians, groups, and individual advocates in both camps who are easily recognizable, but the majority of North Americans hold values coming from both viewpoints. The general public moves back and forth depending on the issues of the day.

The reason the preservationist philosophy and all other sub-philosophies of the postmodernist paradigm are so difficult to stop has to do with 'political spiritual energy'. This motivating force behind all past historical political movements is the belief in a set of principles or a divinity that exists at a higher level than humankind. Postmodernists have the spiritual energy and higher truths of Marxist/Marcusean socialism that is going to finally right all the wrongs of the past and create equality for humans and animals alike. The only real defenders of the modernist era with spiritual energy is the 'religious right'. But there's a big problem: Some of the views held by the religious right are unacceptable to the majority of middle-ground people.

This majority is now slightly conservative but basically neutral on abortion and homosexuality, and even though most are religious, they're indifferent toward promoting creationism. I believe that most people would be against postmodernism if they clearly understood where it's heading, but there is no significant political spiritual energy for the present majority position.

The new Alliance Party in Canada tried to capture the backing of the center-of-right majority, but failed because of accusations the party would legislate laws and policies based on the religious right viewpoint of the party's leaders.

One of the statements I receive from my editors is this: Okay, you've identified the problems, so what's the solution? What are the marching orders? I'm a center-of-right skeptical-conservative holding a particular philosophy that is weak politically. Why? Because I don't have the slightest ambition to control the way other people act. I definitely want to provide people with what I believe to be a more accurate view regarding bears and nature, and I also want to defend what freedoms I have left, but I offer my material on the marketplace of ideas.

The biologists I mentioned at the end of the *Defending Reality* chapter, regarding the grizzly hunting ban, who are now reveling in their success in stopping the grizzly hunt, are very different from me. They have spiritual energy and believe in a set of neo-pantheistic principles that transcends mere humans. It's not that they don't want to hunt grizzly bears, they want to stop others from hunting grizzly bears, and the status of the bear population really has nothing to do with it. And what's so unfortunate about all of this is that cause-science can quite easily win over true objective science in many situations like the grizzly hunting ban.

Those biologists and all postmodernists have a very powerful advantage over those of us who are truly scientific and willing to admit that some or all of our views could be wrong. They have the power of 'spiritual rightness' and the 'intellectual enforcement mechanism' of political correctness. Almost all movie and TV production companies are controlled by postmodernist true believers who have conveyed their views so effectively, they've won by default. If every kid in North America sees and hears a hundred times in movies and on TV that logging and hunting is reducing grizzly populations, then it simply becomes true—scientific evidence becomes irrelevant. The concept is politically correct, because it expresses the postmodern socialist antithesis to our free-enterprise system and obtains credibility by no other means than repetitious presentation—it gains the superficial appearance of being right. Consequently, anyone who claims the opposite is suspected of harboring nature-destroying motives. Try telling any sixth-grader in Canada that David Suzuki may be drastically wrong in his dooms-day claims and see what response you get. It's a closed case, and unfortunately, the case was won with anti-science.

So, what can people do who don't like the direction our society is headed?

One of the main purposes of this material is to clearly define the distinct differences between some of the sub-philosophies of the modern and postmodern value systems so that reasonable middle-of-the-road people can better understand what issues deserve their attention.

The election of George W. Bush will derail postmodernism in the U.S. and at the U.N. for at least four years and possibly much longer. The recent Liberal Party victory in Canada with an even larger federal majority government will put the postmodernist movement in this country on the fast-track, but it will be hindered to a degree by the U.S. situation. If Al Gore had been elected, postmodernism would already be a speeding freight train.

The many organizations throughout North America fighting against intrusive liberty-destroying governmental policies have done a good job, but must do even better at explaining to the general public the horrific costs and lack of real benefits from the postmodernist drive towards utopia. There may be significant help coming in the near future for this task.

Our economy is presently carrying a huge burden of environmental restrictions, affirmative action, redistribution of wealth to the so-called oppressed classes, and a myriad of other postmodern policies and programs. The last ten years of economic prosperity which carried this load may be coming to an end with the maturing of the technology and Internet industries. If so, we'll very likely enter into a period when the economy will have to shrug off inefficiency and unaffordable programs. If this happens, the following questions will have

to be answered:
1. Can the rural hunting and guiding industry in B.C. survive the endless assaults like the grizzly hunting moratorium?
2. Can existing B.C. environmental policies be continued that have brought the forest industry to its knees and chased mining interests from the province?
3. Can ecotourism actually replace the industries that are being reduced or eliminated in B.C.?
4. Can the Canadian ranching industry sustain the ever-increasing loss of animals due to the over-protection of predators?
5. Can Canadian taxpayers afford the half-billion dollar (and possibly much higher) cost of the gun registry that will provide no tangible benefits?
6. Can Californians really have cheap energy and hyper-environmental restrictions on building new power plants at the same time, without incurring massive state debt?
7. Can the global economy support the redistribution of wealth from the have to the have-not countries that postmodernists want to eventually achieve?

The questions could go on forever.

The most successful propaganda campaign in recent history has been the preservationist movement's ability to convince most people that environmental extremism doesn't cost anything.   There is presently a ridiculous denial taking place in many political jurisdictions, particularly California and British Columbia, that we can continue to arbitrarily place an endless burden on the free-enterprise system without any consequences.

The Postmodern cultural/political paradigm has created terrible disharmony in our culture between ethnic groups and special interest groups. It has invented a huge body of politically correct mythology, and in order to maintain a constituency of support, it has categorized vast numbers of our citizenry into victim groups with preferential treatment and handouts.   Worst of all, it has convinced European races to accept a heavy burden of guilt for all past wrongs. In addition, it has recently spawned the preservationist movement which extends the tenants of Marxist socialism to man's relationship with nature. And finally, the people who are most opposed to postmodernism are the very same ones who must, by government decree, foot the bill for its ever-increasing costs.

Those who are against present trends must continually improve their ability to convince the general public that they're losing a large amount of annual income and freedom due to an increasingly dubious political ideology, and they must do this without discarding their own intellectual honesty. This can be done only if the defenders of reality educate themselves thoroughly regarding issues where mythology is used to continually damage our society.

However, if our economy is able to continue the high level of wealth creation of the 1990s, postmodernism will accelerate, and if the Democrats in the U.S. should once again control the presidency and the majority in Congress at the same time, we're in for a wild ride toward the 'Marcusean dreamland'. But the disciples of Herbert Marcuse's ideology clearly understand that the final stages of postmodernism cannot be implemented unless European males are disarmed. This isn't a delusional theory about hidden conspiracy concocted by paranoid right-wingers, it's an obvious plain-to-see agenda that is part of the postmodern political doctrine containing long-term goals and spiritual purpose.

The federal government of Canada has become a surrogate for the United Nations, and it's no secret that both are working towards a plan to disarm all world citizens. And, of course, it would be only the law-abiding populace that is foolish enough to give up their guns. Criminals, terrorists, rogue states, and certain ethnic groups will never be disarmed, but they don't need to be disarmed for postmodernism to prevail.

Final thought:

My main purpose here has been to define the underlying philosophies that threaten the livelihoods and lifestyles of rural people and city dwellers who share the same value system. I have also provided some ideas for combatting the postmodernist assault. But it's against my nature to design a vast battle plan for action. I leave it to others to determine when and where appropriate action is needed.

In the long run, the only power that will stop the downhill slide of postmodernism with its amazing load of cultural guilt is the development of a common-sense philosophy that provides evenhanded rights and opportunity for all citizens without the Marcusean condemnation and taxation of the European races. We must no longer accept the politically correct myth that being proud of European ancestry automatically makes a person racist, and that members of minority groups cannot be racist—it just isn't true.

In the short run, there is an important strategy that could quite possibly turn a large number of people against our present course no matter what happens with the economy or in politics, and that would be to clearly demonstrate where we're headed.

What future conditions will our children and grandchildren live under? I will endeavor to answer that question in my next book.